IMAGES
of America

MIDDLETOWN TOWNSHIP
VOLUME III

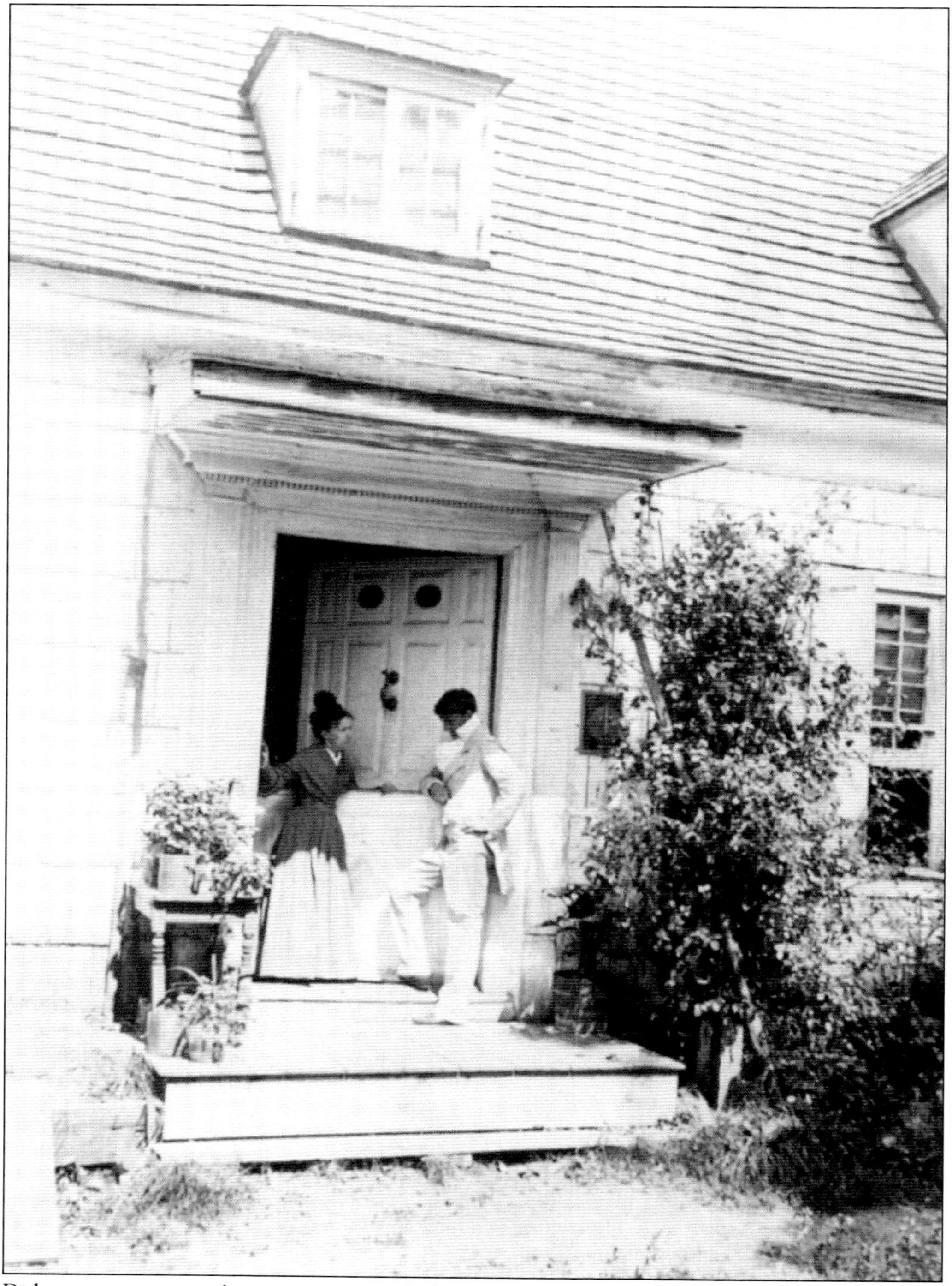

Did you suspect something was amiss with the Volume II cover and that, perhaps, you had seen it previously? Yes, the door opened on the "wrong" side because the image was, using artistic license, reversed. The picture was published in Mandeville's *The Story of Middletown*; the couple was unidentified then, as now.

IMAGES
of America

MIDDLETOWN TOWNSHIP
VOLUME III

Randall Gabrielan

ARCADIA
PUBLISHING

ISBN 978-0-7385-6456-2

Published by Arcadia Publishing
Charleston, South Carolina

Printed in the United States of America

Library of Congress Catalog Card Number: 2008940638

For all general information contact Arcadia Publishing at:
Telephone 843-853-2070
Fax 843-853-0044
E-mail sales@arcadiapublishing.com
For customer service and orders:
Toll-Free 1-888-313-2665

Visit us on the Internet at www.arcadiapublishing.com

COVER PHOTOGRAPH: See page 91.

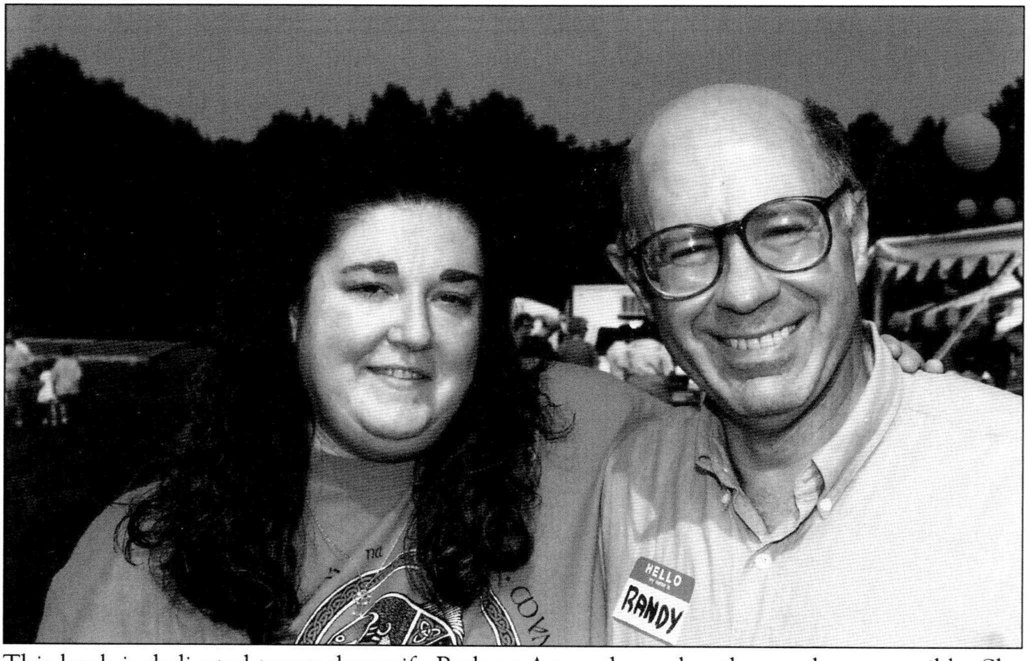

This book is dedicated to my dear wife Barbara Ann, who makes these volumes possible. She was photographed at the 1996 St. Catharine's picnic by Peter Fullen. The author appears due more to a lack of choice than vanity. However, he received a ruling (without asking) from a retired superior court judge deeming his visage worthy of preservation, too.

Contents

Acknowledgments

The author extends his deep, heartfelt gratitude for the support of a great number of picture contributors. You, my lenders, are the key ingredient to the book and are truly its co-producers.

Special thanks go to Jane Bartlett (and Linda Wellner for the introduction) for providing an album demonstrating there are spectacular archives in addition to the Edward Taylor collection, and to her daughter, Jane Bartlett, for the oldest and arguably the most outstanding image in the book (p. 50). My ongoing gratitude to Robert and Mary Johnson for access to Edward Taylor's collection, one so rich that after its enormous contributions to Volume II, it provided another seventeen images for this book.

I would like to give a special word of thanks for the long-term support from the following collectors whose holdings are available and so helpful: Kathleen McGrath, John Rhody, Robert Schoeffling, and Michael Steinhorn.

An extra acknowledgment and word of thanks goes to Beth Ann Sobieszczyk, who helped turn a family album of snapshots into a historical document related to one of the township's outstanding properties, Brookdale Farm, and to Amanda Mae Smack Edwards for sharing pictures of her relatives, which had been reserved for her family history. I hope your work soon sees the light of day and the folks in this book reappear as "old friends."

Photography Unlimited by Dorn's was literally uncovering its rich store of negatives as this work progressed, making the area's best archive even better and widening its scope as more towns are given depth in their publicly available vintage collection.

I want to extend a special word to two public collections that have demonstrated their commitment to public history by providing liberal access to their collections: the Monmouth County Historical Association and Rutgers University Libraries.

Thanks and appreciation go to all supporters, including the Atlantic Highlands Historical Society, Edwin Banfield, Lois Bodtmann, Olga Boeckel, Paul "Pete" Brady, Joseph Carney, the Honorable Lawrence A. Carton Jr., Michael and Mary Cassone, Gerald Ceres, *The Courier*, Martha Daverio and the Lincroft Inn, Mary Angela Doherty*, Joseph Eid, Robert Eigenrauch, Anne Ellis, James Fleming, Lynn Friis, Kay Groves, June Truex Hoffmire, Lester Horner, Paul C. Hunter, Thelma Jelliffe*, Bernard Kellenyi, Mary Ann Kiernan, John Lentz ("It's Lentz for Dents," great aerials and a fine cover), Scott Longfield, Elizabeth Roberts McCullough, Timothy J. McMahon, Susanna H. Maguire, the Middletown Landmarks Commission, the Middletown Township Historical Society, the Monmouth County Parks System, Thomas and Ruthanne Morford, the Newark Public Library, the Old First Church and the Reverend Carolyn Breese, P. & K. Aerial Photography, John Pillsbury*, Louanne Pillsbury, Richard Rathemacher, Shrewsbury Towne Chapter, Daughters of the American Revolution, Christine Simoneau, Grace Tetley, Charles Toop*, John Van Nortwick, Peter Van Nortwick, Sandi von Pier, Glenn Vogel, Alma Wuesthoff, and Robert Zerr.

*Deceased, who contributed material to the author prior to his Arcadia projects.

Introduction

A few words on this book's organization, the author's view of the series and Middletown Township historical organizations, and an errata make up this introduction.

The organization by geography was embraced by the readership of Volume II, as it addressed the local interest tendency in the township. The division among sections can be arbitrary, as not every neighborhood is marked by definitive boundaries. One building was even placed in a different chapter in Volumes II and III. One small section, Middletown Village, merits a separate chapter in this book. It is the oldest area, one maintaining the form of its seventeenth-century organization, and it is the subject of some of the township's richest pictorial archives.

The riverfront links connected waterways that are often seen separately, including the Shrewsbury River (prominent in Volume II, but conspicuously absent from this work), Claypit Creek, the Navesink River, and the Shadow Lake-Swimming River stems of the Navesink. The Bayshore and Rural Middletown are the two largest chapters, since these areas comprise most of the township. Each neighborhood is represented, although some sparsely, and there is a flow from place to place in both books.

Each volume stands on its own. Frequent references herein to the earlier works reflect one opportunity presented by an ongoing series, the exhibition of different images of the same place and an ability to make cross-references as new material becomes available. Linking images from different sources is a favorite practice of the author. The series, when it ends, should make a great CD-ROM. However, there is no reason to stop as long as the publisher, public, and author are willing to continue.

The process of compiling a series of books is a linked, continuous operation. Some pictures herein were considered for Volume II, while others are on hand for a prospective Volume IV. The author seeks the public's assistance with the loan of pictures for copying and publication and would appreciate your contacting him at 71 Fish Hawk Drive, Middletown New Jersey, (908) 671-2645.

Middletown's History Organizations

Middletown, a large and diverse township, has several organizations preserving their local history, which provide the advantage of a variety of outlets but has the potential drawback of lacking a strong, central voice. Each is worthy of support; a few words of background follow. The Monmouth County Historical Association, founded in Middletown Township in 1898 and headquartered at 70 Court Street, Freehold New Jersey 07728, has the distinction of owning the region's first restored house museum, Marlpit Hall. It has been illustrated in each of the three volumes (see p. 28) but has been closed the past three years while receiving restoration in a manner that will assure its long-term future.

The Township of Middletown owns three properties that are home to historic organizations. The Whitlock-Scabrook-Wilson residence (see p. 88), long-known as the Spy House and alternately as the Shoal Harbor Marine Museum, was the first acquired. Located at the foot of Wilson Avenue at Port Monmouth Road, the facility had been interpreted as a folk museum of bayshore people. One hopes its recent reorganization will assure it a meaningful long-term future. Poicy Park, Oak Hill Road, adjacent to the New York and Long Branch Railroad, is primarily a nature organization, but its restored Joseph Murray House is a center of history activities. The story of its rescue was told over pp. 56–57 in Volume II, with p. 59 of this book focusing on its programs.

The author has directed his historical efforts through the Middletown Township Historical Society, P.O. Box 434, Middletown New Jersey 07748, which has maintained a museum in the MacLeod-Rice House at Croydon Hall (Vol. I, p. 16) since 1985. Although its scope and constituency embrace the entire township, it needs wider participation and support to maximize use of its fine facility. The Society meets the fourth Monday of the month, except December, at the museum, with the August meeting usually held off-site.

The Middletown Landmarks Commission has a vital but often misunderstood role in preserving the township's built environment. This municipal regulatory body studies, classifies, and offers for historic designation individual properties and districts. The township's historic stature has a positive value, which the Commission protects. Not only do the Commission's efforts merit broad support, but development around historically significant property should begin at the planning stage. Developers are too inclined to destroy or discard colonial-era structures which could "mar" their new housing, too often mediocre and designed with a pale, weak smattering of eighteenth-century decorative elements. If builders wish to sell historic Middletown, force them to build around the historic setting, even if a lot or two is lost. Preventing the moving of the Grover House (Vol. II, p. 76) would have been a fine start.

Errata

Following are corrections of the two previous volumes.

Volume I

p. 17 top–The image of the farm at Poricy Park was unintentionally reversed.

p. 23 bottom–Ann Hendrickson Morford pointed out the teacher is her aunt Miss Mary Hendrickson. Elizabeth Roberts McCullough doubts the boy pointed out as her father is actually Howard Roberts.

p. 28 top–The Leonardo Beach Beacon and Chapel Hill Lighthouse are range lights for the Sandy Hook Channel.

p. 43 top–The image of the previous Coopers Bridge is likely early twentieth century. Note the trolley bridge at left.

p. 108 bottom–The view is west

Volume II

p. 31 bottom–The house is number 116 Kings Highway.

p. 115 bottom–The caption was intended for 501 Locust Point Road illustrated in this volume on the top of p. 120.

One

Middletown Village

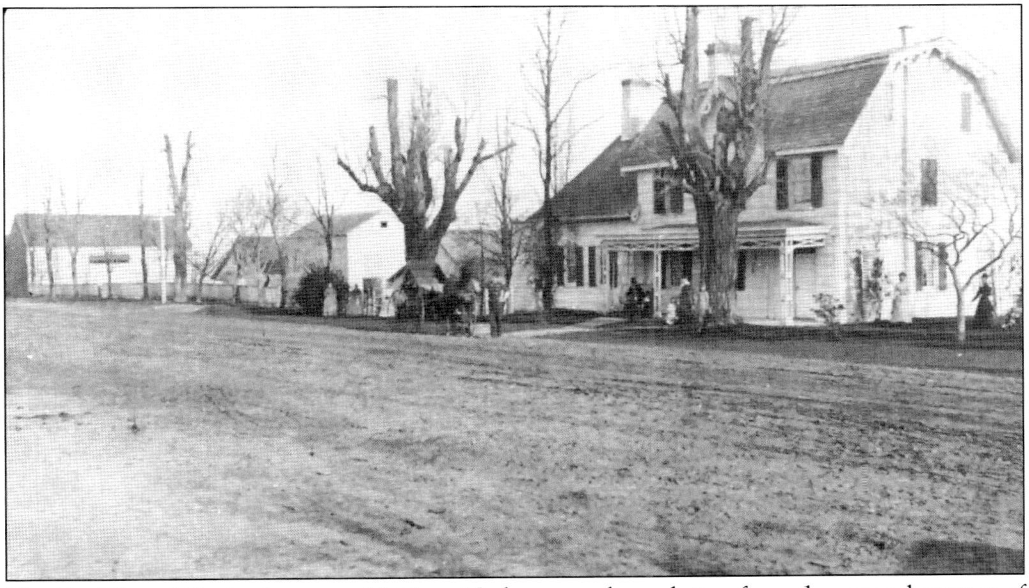

The Dr. Edward Taylor house at 82 Kings Highway, perhaps dating from the second quarter of the eighteenth century, is extensively illustrated herein. This *c.* 1880s image is extraordinary for its inclusion of the outbuildings east of the dwelling. The structures, clearly outlined on the 1889 village plan in the *Wolverton Atlas* (Vol. II, p. 23), no longer stand; in later years, Hartshorne Place was cut a few yards east of the house, and the telephone exchange—later a library and now a private residence at 78 Kings Highway (Vol. I, p. 12)—was built on that new street's other corner in 1931.

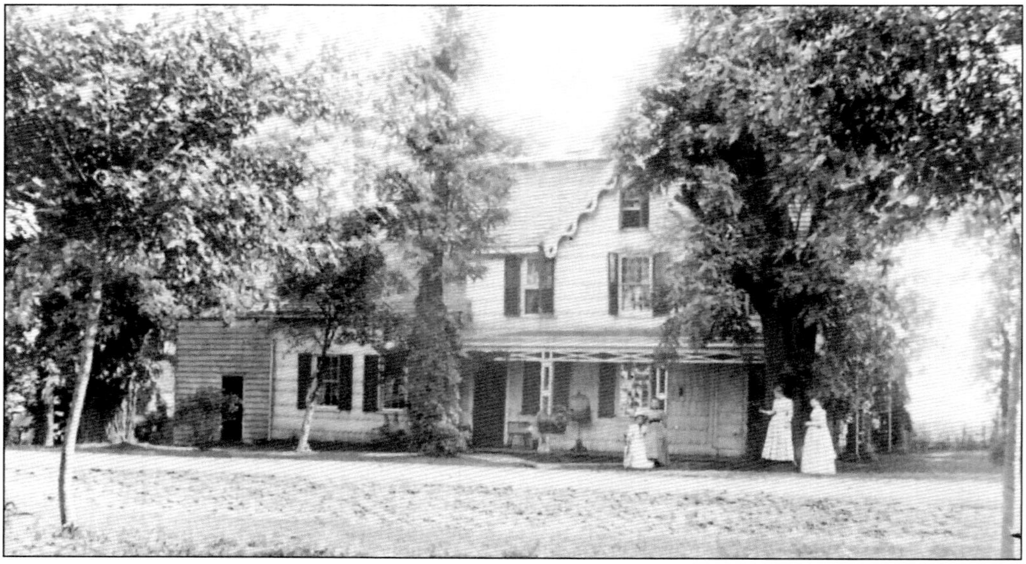

The basic appearance today of the Dr. Taylor house is similar to that depicted in this *c.* 1890s image, but changes include the removal of the full porch and replacement at right by a small canopied entrance porch, the addition of a second story to the wing at left (which may be an 1891 addition), and the replacement of the clapboard addition to the wing by a garage. The center gable and vergeboard are mid-nineteenth century additions, giving the house an undeserved Gothic Revival first impression.

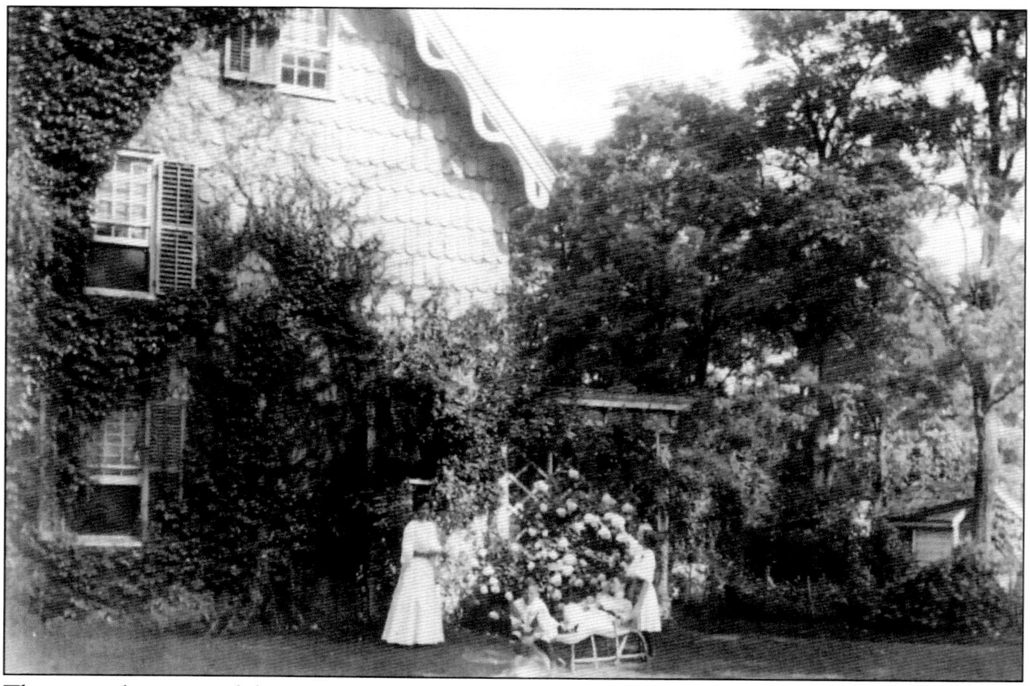

The west elevation of the Dr. Taylor house is the backdrop for Adele Taylor French (left) and her son, Rem (kneeling). The round butt shingles, popularly known as fish scale shingles, are one of the house's appealing architectural features.

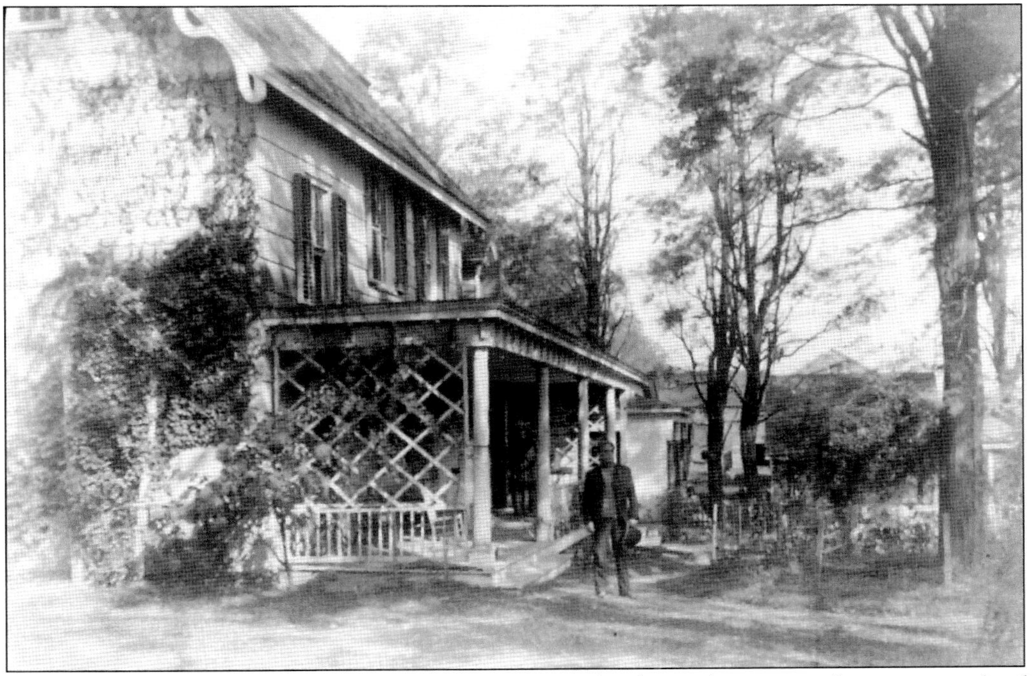

Edward Taylor, born c. 1878, brother of Adele, poses by the no-longer-standing rear porch of the Dr. Taylor house. A son of Henry C. Taylor, Edward was raised in this house and moved to California three years before dying there in 1929 from injuries received in an automobile accident. The wing in the rear was removed at an unspecified date.

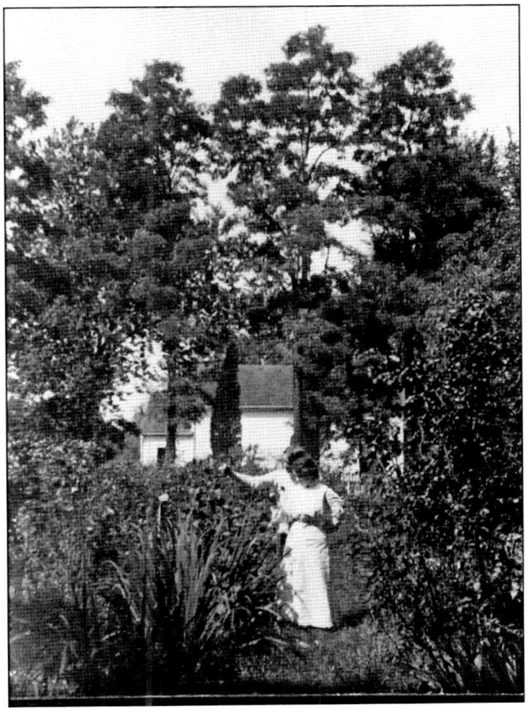

Two unidentified women, perhaps Taylors, stand in the garden of 82 Kings Highway. Stanley Silow recalled how Rachel kept her place neat in the 1930s: "She employed a gang of us kids to do all sorts of jobs. We weeded, feeded, cut the grass with hand mowers, painted the exterior, and even cleaned inside. She paid us 10¢ per hour, but we received a raise to 20¢ as we became older. She had an annual Halloween party for us and gave the high-schoolers graduation presents."

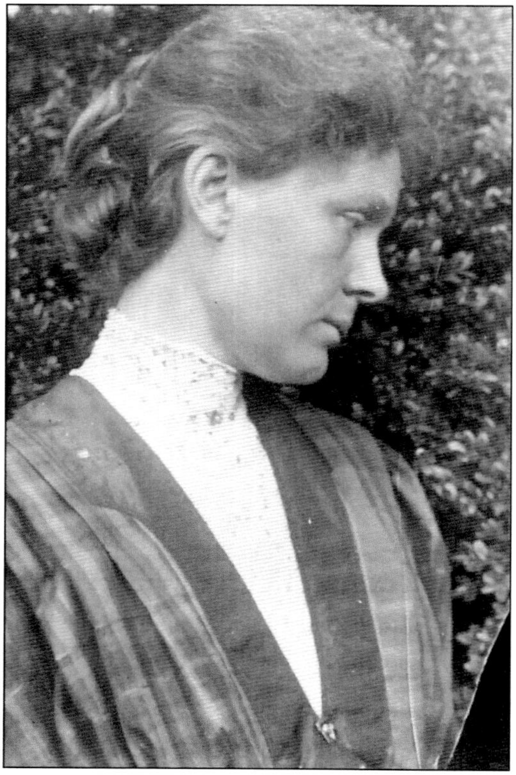

Rachel C. Taylor was born c. 1869, the daughter of Henry C. and Emaline. She never married and inherited the family home at 82 Kings Highway. This image dates to around the 1890s.

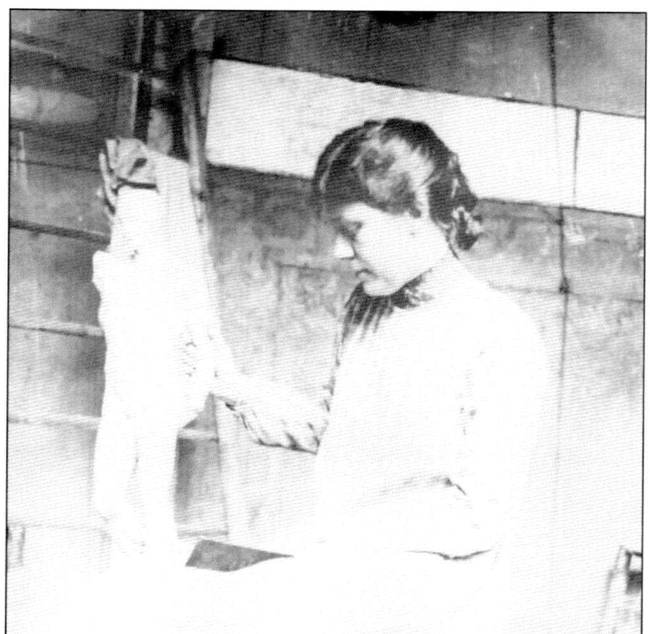

Rachel Taylor, known as Rae, painted and sculpted. She traveled to the West in winters of her later years to paint. The location of any surviving work is unknown. Stanley Silow asked aloud shortly before publication, "I wonder where her portrait of my brother Ed is."

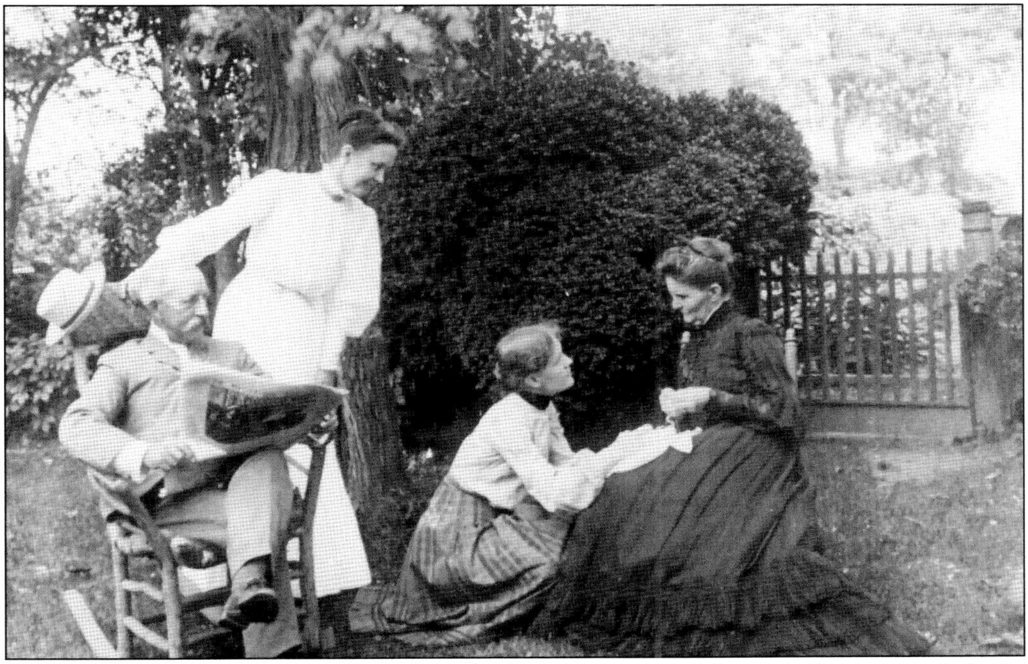

Henry C. Taylor, born 1845 in the Dr. Taylor house, is seen with his wife Emaline (right), the couple's elder daughter, Katharine (standing), and Rachel (kneeling), c. 1890s.

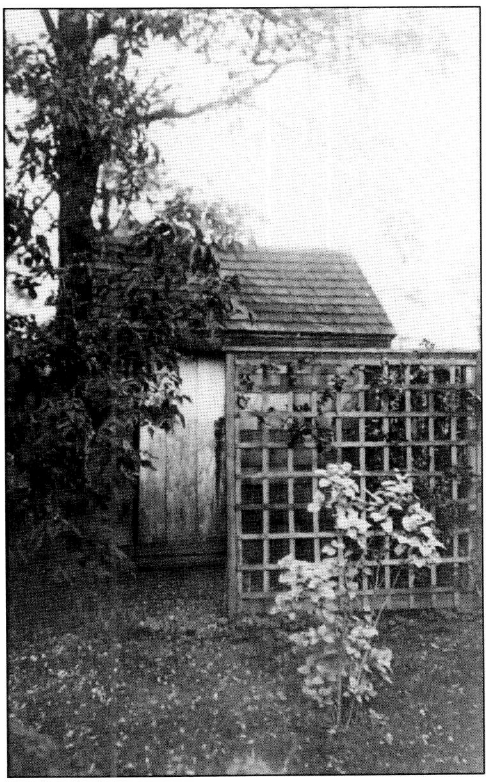

The frame necessary, or "outhouse" in plain talk, still stands at 82 Kings Highway. This commodious building seated five: three adults and two children.

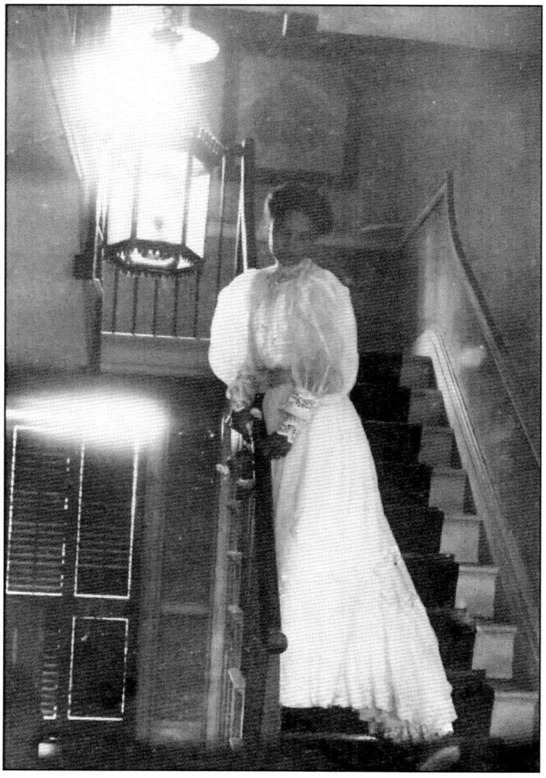

Adele Gillingham Taylor French Hendrickson, the bearer of the longest name to have appeared in the author's eight books for Arcadia, stands at the main stairs at 82 Kings Highway. The stairs are unchanged, although the chandelier is no longer there.

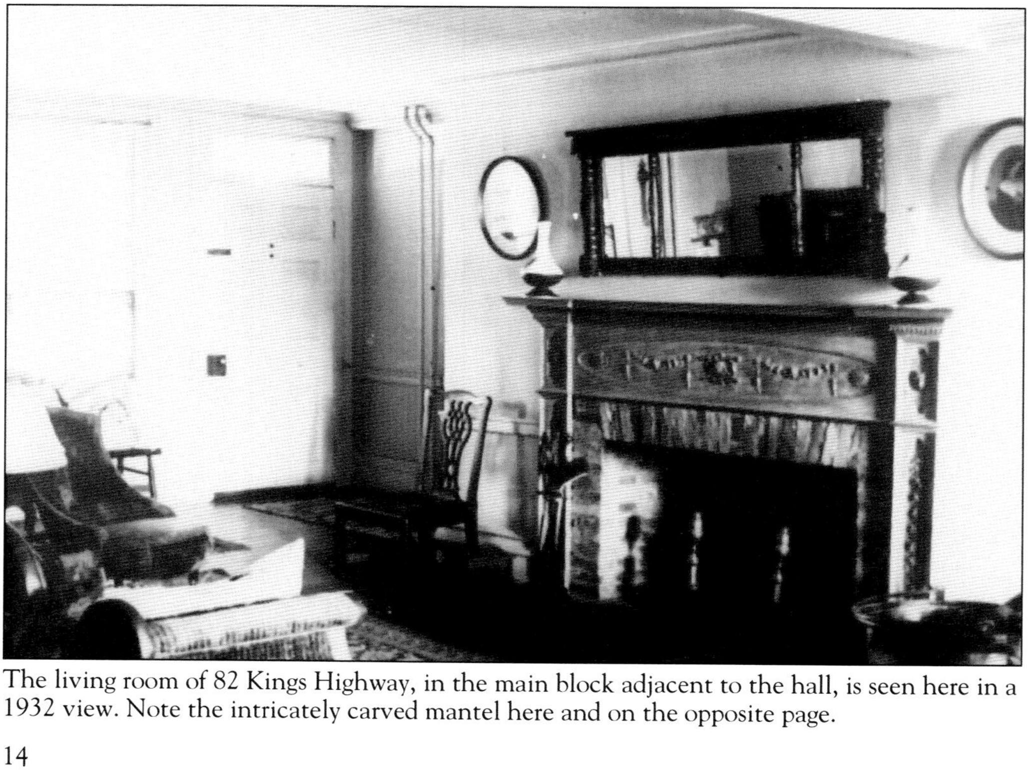

The living room of 82 Kings Highway, in the main block adjacent to the hall, is seen here in a 1932 view. Note the intricately carved mantel here and on the opposite page.

The Taylor at the split-leaf front door at 82 Kings Highway is not positively identified, but the person is probably Katharine.

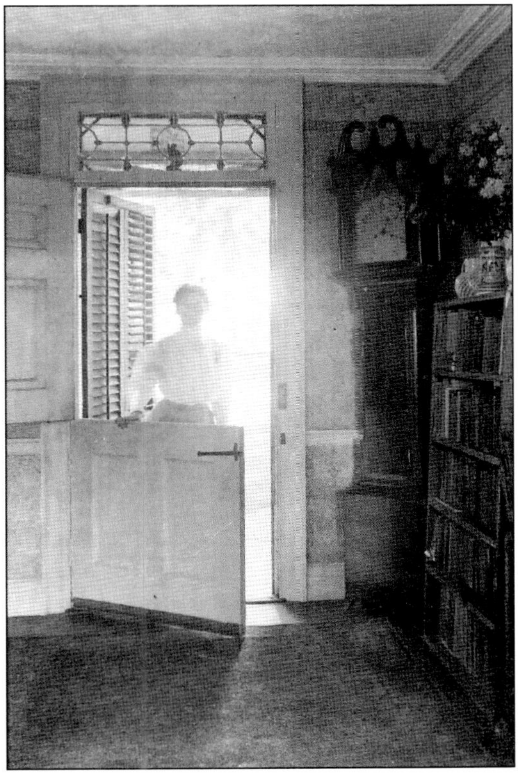

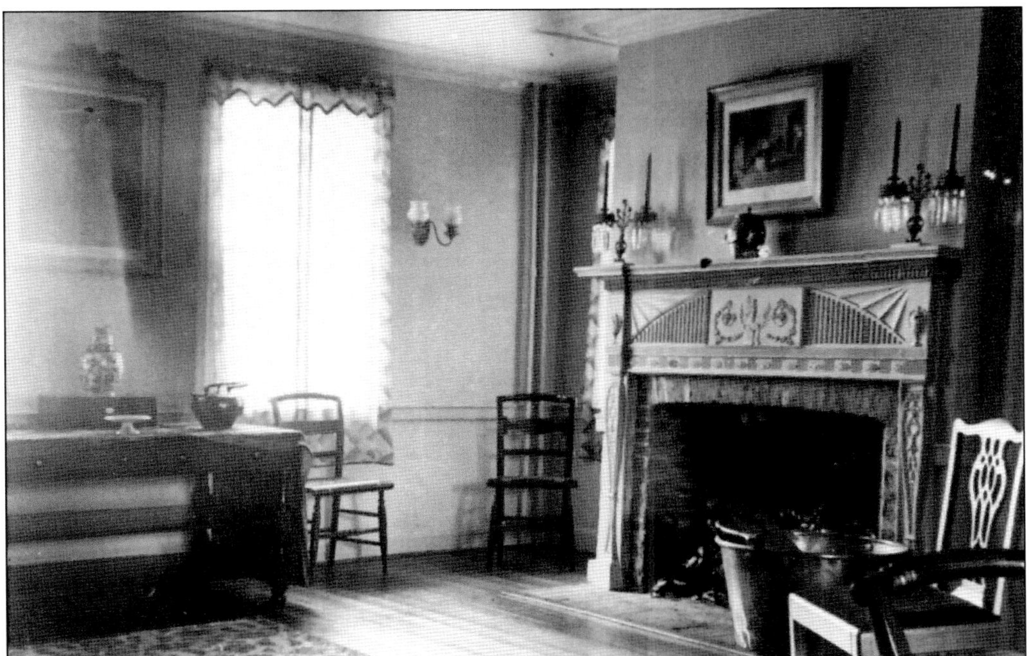

The dining room in the east wing of 82 Kings Highway was once the front parlor. The wide fireplace has been partially enclosed since this 1932 image.

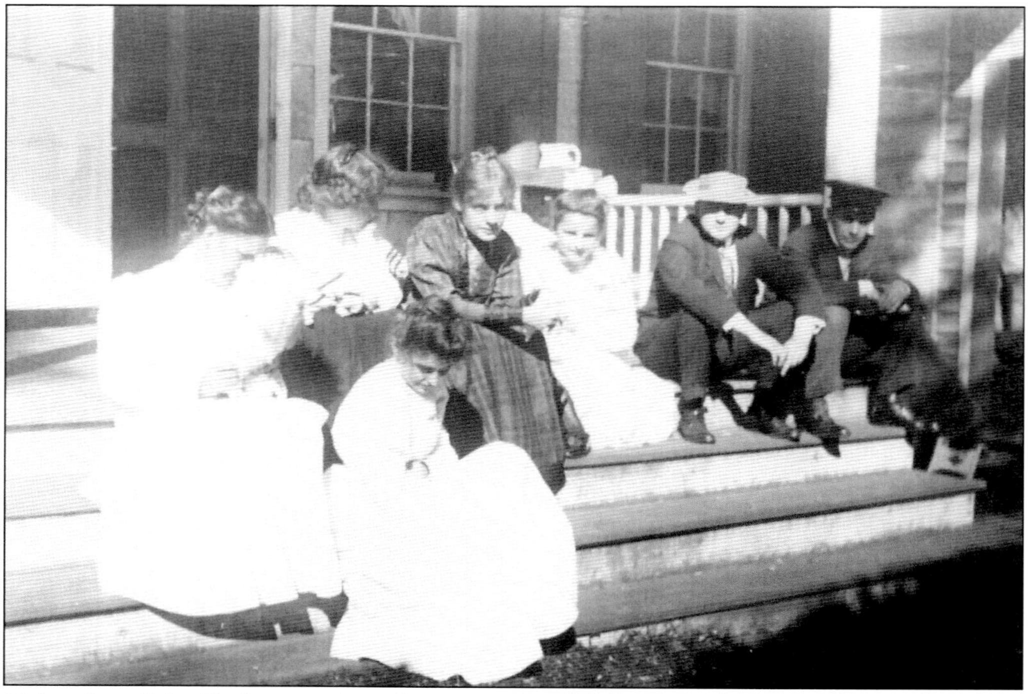

Only a few of the Taylor crowd on the rear porch of 82 Kings Highway are identifiable in this c. 1890s photograph. The beauty of Rachel Taylor, in the dark dress, is brought out in an intently serious pose. Adele Taylor French Hendrickson is at left, while next to her is Fern (with head turned).

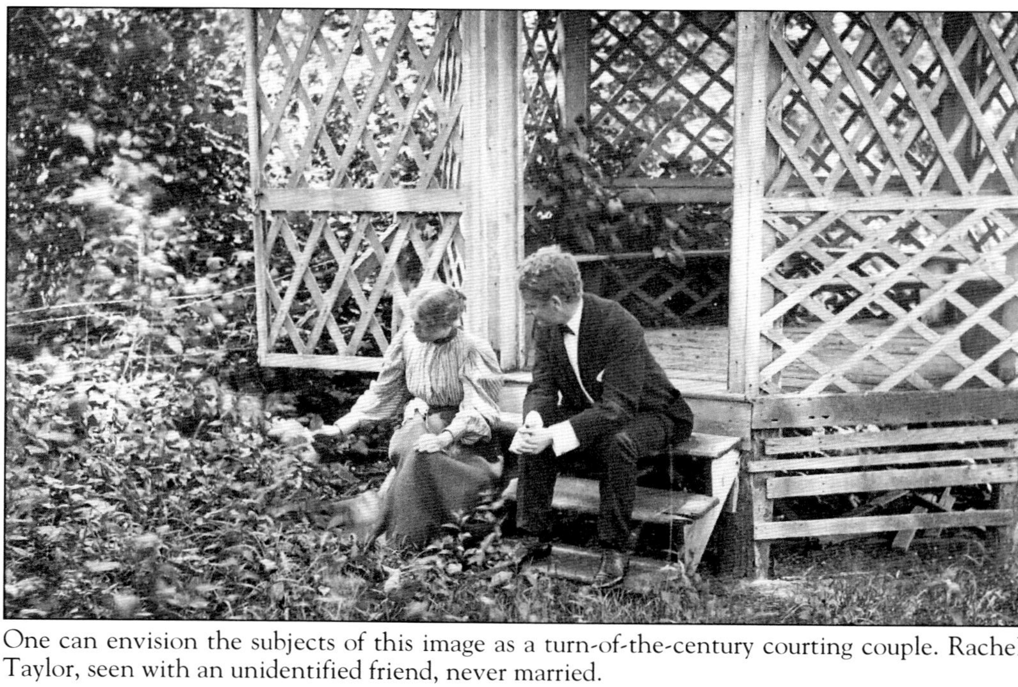

One can envision the subjects of this image as a turn-of-the-century courting couple. Rachel Taylor, seen with an unidentified friend, never married.

The thirty-seven-year-old Charles J. Hendrickson still looks adventurous only a few years after building and flying his own airplane. He and wife Adele strike a pensive pose in 1916.

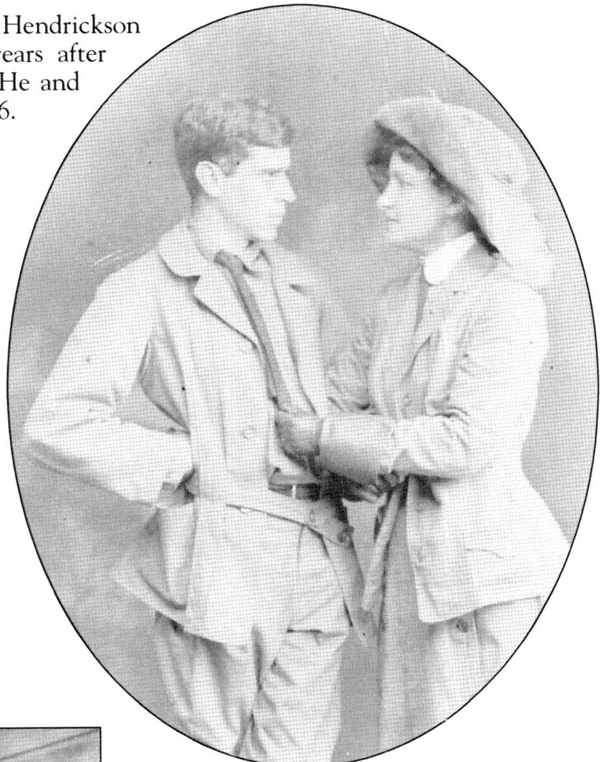

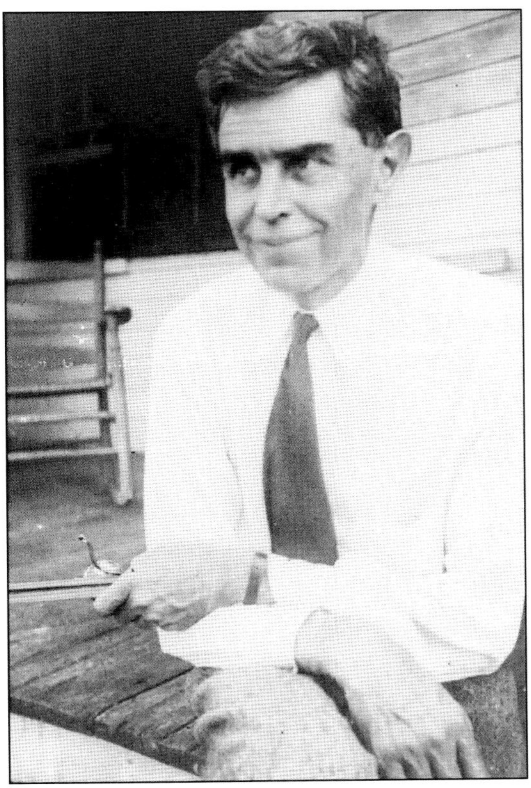

Charles J. Hendrickson, born 1879, son of Charles I. Hendrickson, was an engineer for Bell Laboratories and invented a machine for calculating the law of probability. He is seen here c. 1920s in a characteristic pose with his slide rule. This portrait is a favorite of Charles' daughter, Jane Bartlett, who so generously lent it, along with numerous other images, to the production of this volume. Charles died in 1948.

WARNING!

TO

BICYCLERS

An Ordinance prohibiting the riding of Bicycles upon the public sidewalks in the Township of Middletown.

1. Be it ordained by the Township Committee of the Township of Middletown, that from and after the passage of this ordinance, any person or persons riding, coasting, pushing or propelling any vehicle, bicycle or other conveyance of like nature, (Baby Carriages excepted) upon any public sidewalk in this Township, he, she or they shall forfeit to the said Township of Middletown the sum of ($5.00) five dollars.

2. And be it further ordained that this ordinance shall take effect immediately.

Passed and approved June 12, 1900.
Belford, N. J.

Bicyclists were a major force in the 1890s campaign for better roads. Apparently some wanted the sidewalks, too. Although no news account of this new ordinance was found, one can infer the background, particularly when viewing the character at the top on the opposite page.

Yes, this is the type of miscreant that required the bicycle ordinance outlined at left. The stem of sidewalk, if we wish to dignify this rough ground by calling it a "sidewalk," appears to be the north side of Kings Highway, west of the Reformed Church to Marlpit Place.

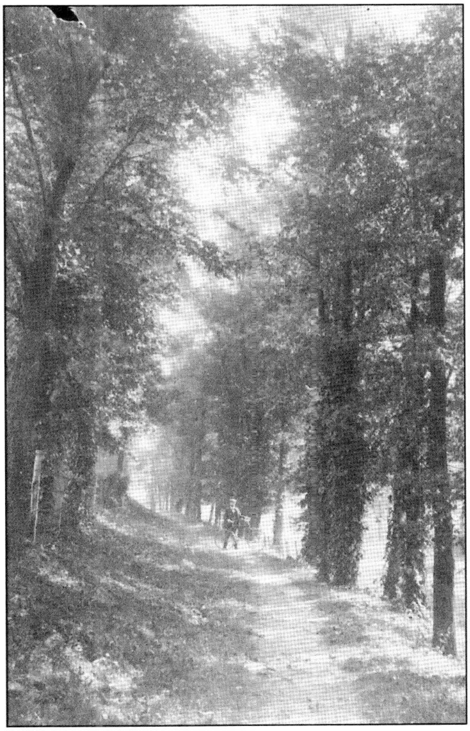

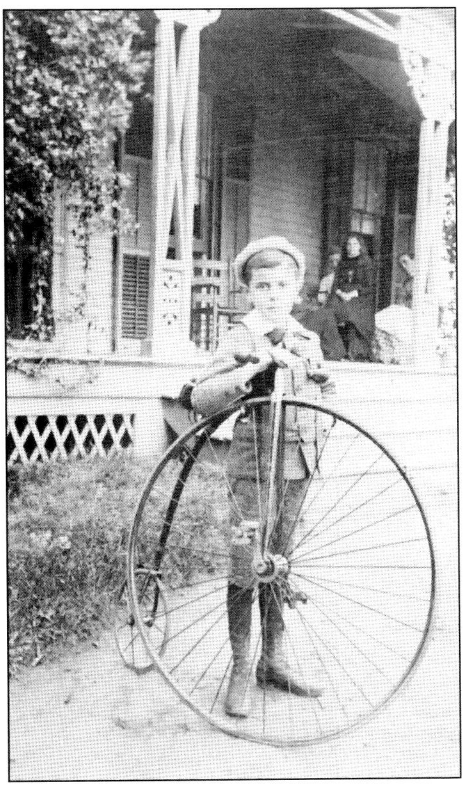

The youthful Charles J. Hendrickson is rightfully in the rear of 82 Kings Highway, as the front hardly has room for a sidewalk. The author does not even want to imagine mounting this bicycle; he understands the high shoes but thinks he would need a helmet, too. Hendrickson graduated to motorcycles and even built his own airplane.

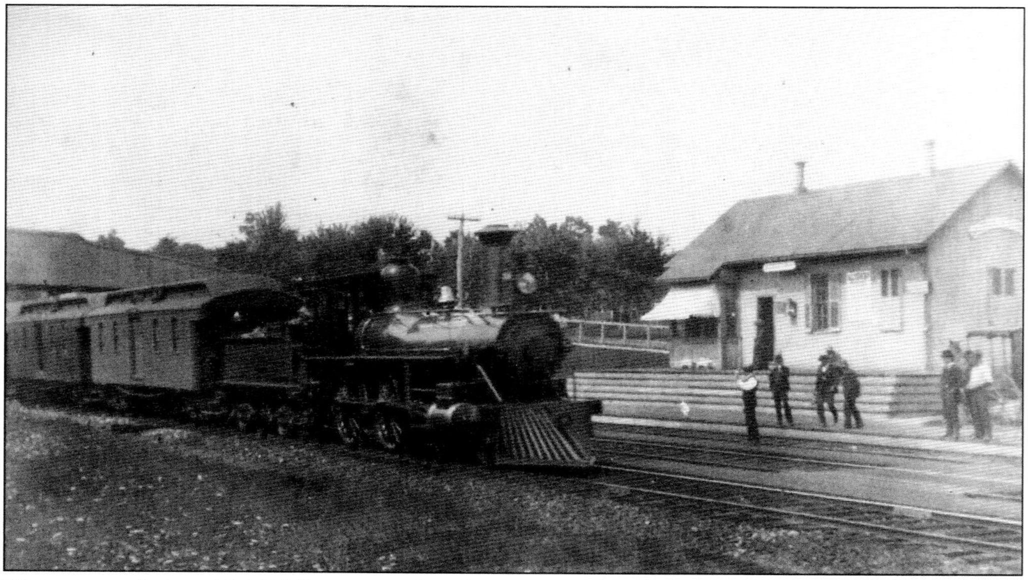

This view of the old Middletown railroad station is dated September 2, 1886, eleven years after the New York and Long Branch Railroad opened. Note the former bridge to the Conover property (Vol. I, p. 54). The station is one of the line's originals but is no longer used for railroad purposes. It has received needed stabilization and restoration care over the past few years. (Collection of Ed Banfield.)

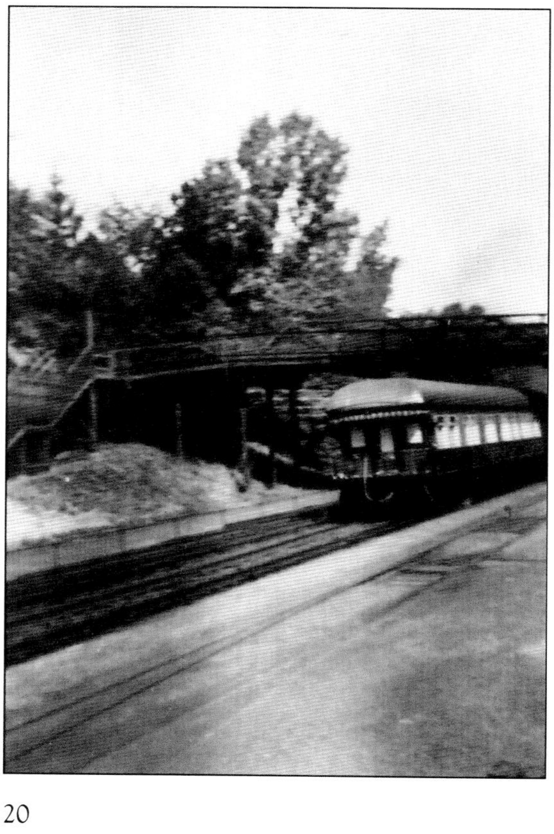

The Conover Bridge is seen in 1939 with a passing train that reportedly carried Great Britain's King George VI and Queen Elizabeth. The royal couple arrived at Red Bank, the next station, at 7:00 am. Security was likely a factor in the decision to route their trip to New York via rail and ship, but it apparently did not bar the photographer from taking a position close to the train.

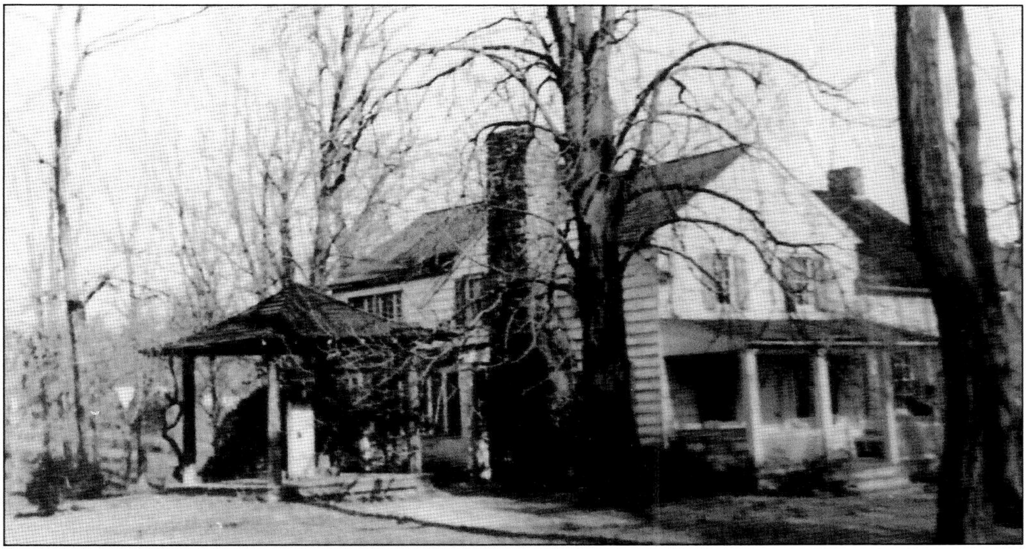

This appears to be a bridge from Kings Highway to the house south of it at number 120; it was perhaps a predecessor to the bridge closed as unsafe in 1986 and replaced with a covered bridge in 1988. The railroad's construction and maintenance of the bridge stems from an agreement made at the time of the line's acquisition, as the rails cut off the existing house from its principal street connection. (Collection of the Monmouth County Historical Association.)

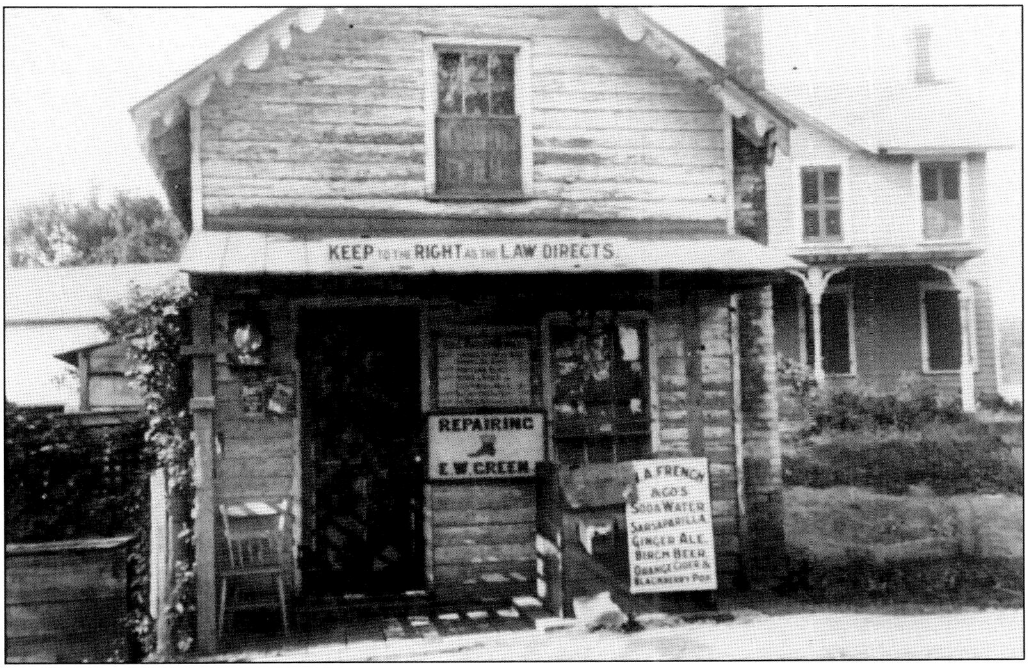

This image is labeled in two public collections as the toll house at the present five corners end of Kings Highway, known to have been moved to the S-curve at Middletown Railroad Parking Lot No. 2 and remodeled as a private residence. However, the house at 2147 Middletown-Lincroft Road (Vol. I, p. 63) is hard to match with this image. Look at French's beverages. What was orange cider, anyway? (Special Collections and Archives, Rutgers University Libraries.)

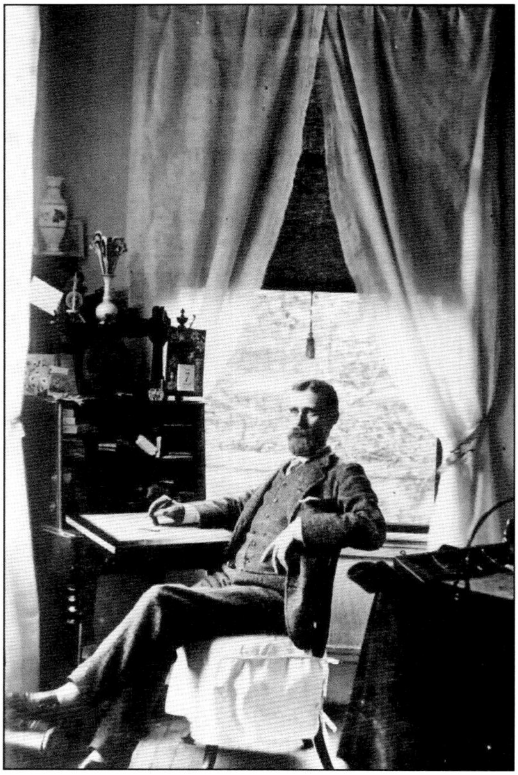

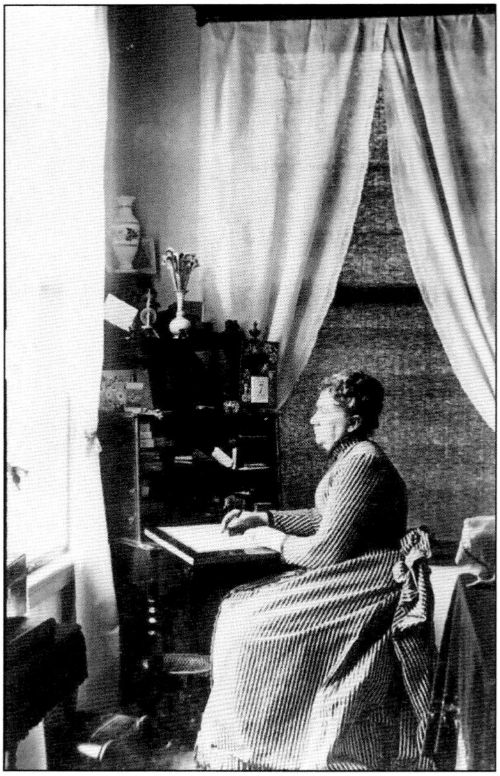

Edward and Margaret Taylor were photographed at a desk at Orchard Home (127 Kings Highway) on June 7, 1886. His is obviously a portrait, but she could pass as "The Letter Writer."

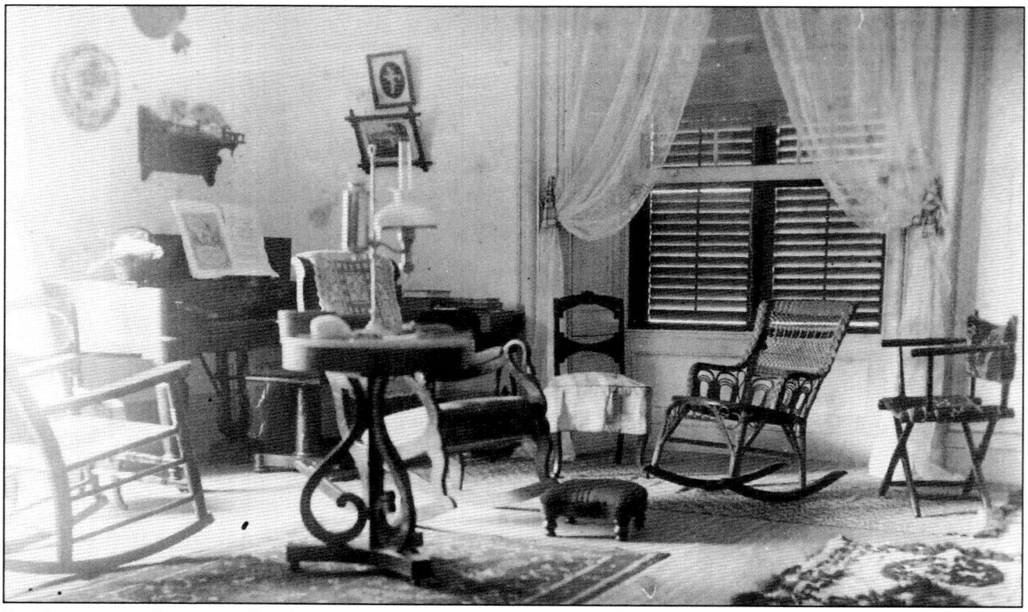

In this 1886 photograph, the back parlor in Orchard Home, also known as the library, remains a comfortable place away from the house's activity for quiet sitting.

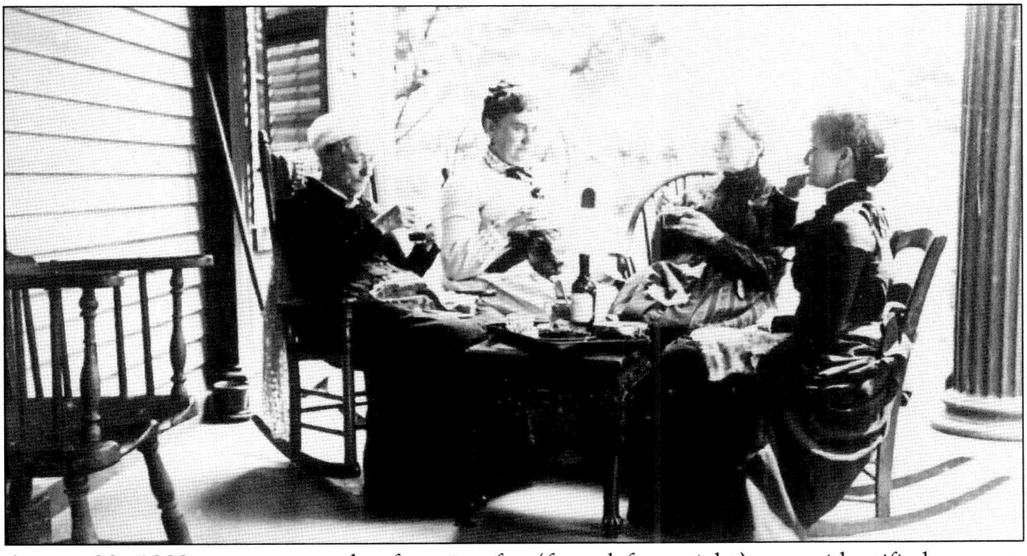

August 20, 1889, was a great day for wine for (from left to right) an unidentified woman, Margaret Taylor, and the two Mary Holmes Taylors on the porch of Orchard Home.

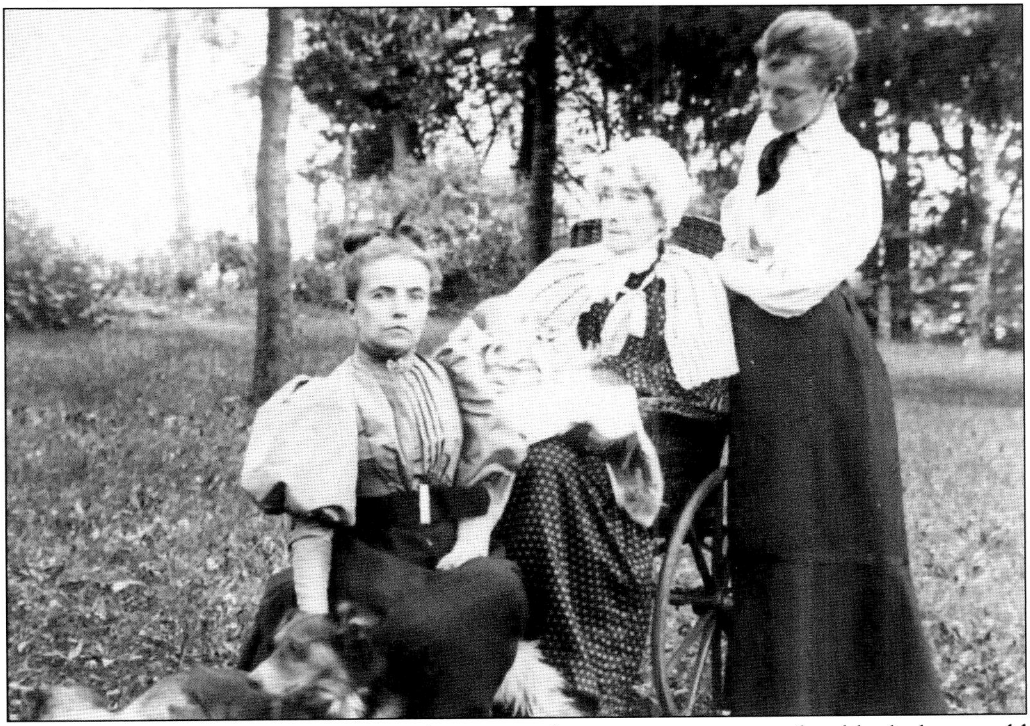

The younger Mary Holmes Taylor in the 1890s is beginning to assume a hard look that would result in the visage illustrated on the top of page 27. Life must have had its difficulties; Taylor, apparently alone later, had to maintain a large house with perhaps static or declining revenues. The house, Orchard Home, was the largest and grandest in the township when it was built c. 1850, but it did not have indoor plumbing when Mary died in 1930. The attendant to the elder Taylor is not identified in this October 7, 1894 photograph.

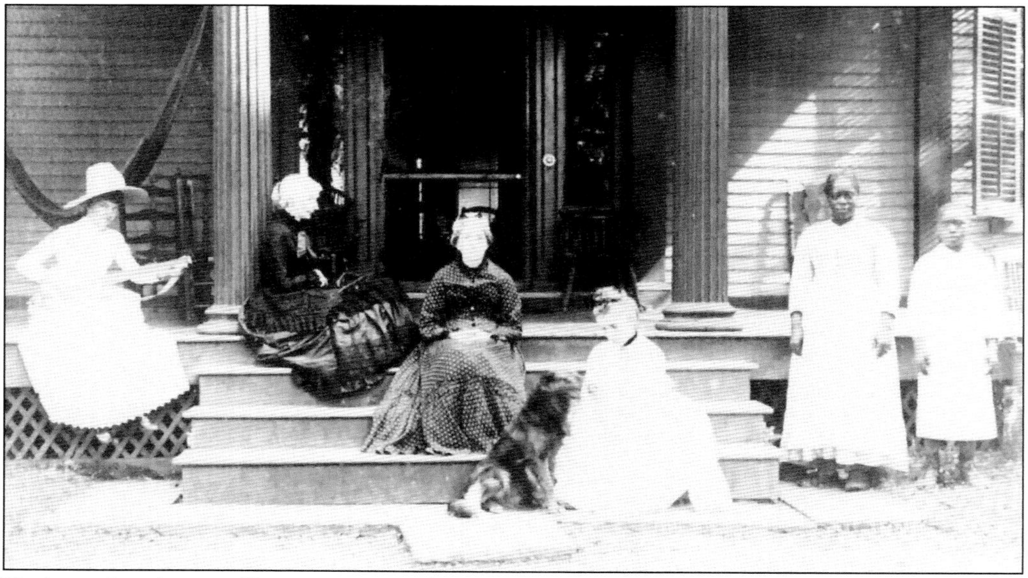

Taylors often have a Hopperesque quality of appearing solitary, even when they are grouped together. The younger and elder Mary Holmes Taylor are on the first and second steps respectively, with two domestics at right. The banjo player barely manages a faint smile, as if testing a rule on reserve. She and the other woman on the porch in this August 13, 1887 Edward Taylor photograph are unidentified.

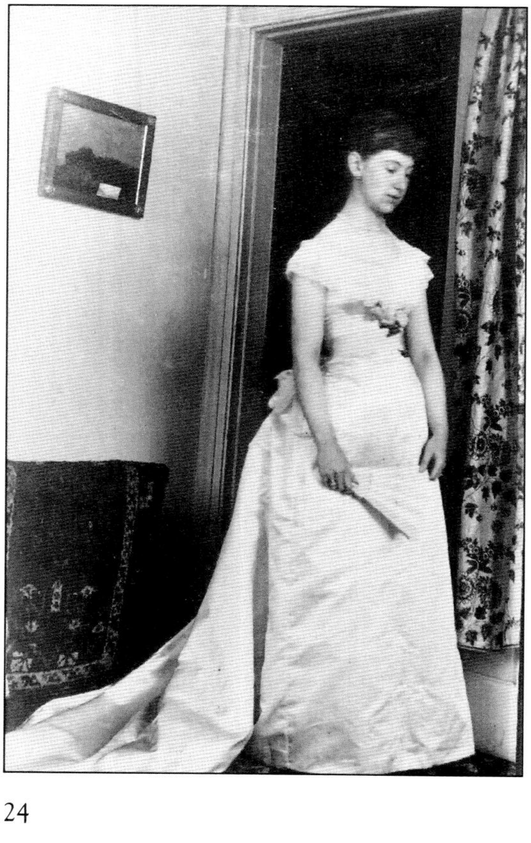

Our mystery woman from Vol. II, p. 22, is known only by her initials "M.A.D." She is still a suspected relative of Margaret Taylor, but her charm rather than her identity merit a second look. This Edward Taylor photograph was taken *c.* late 1880s.

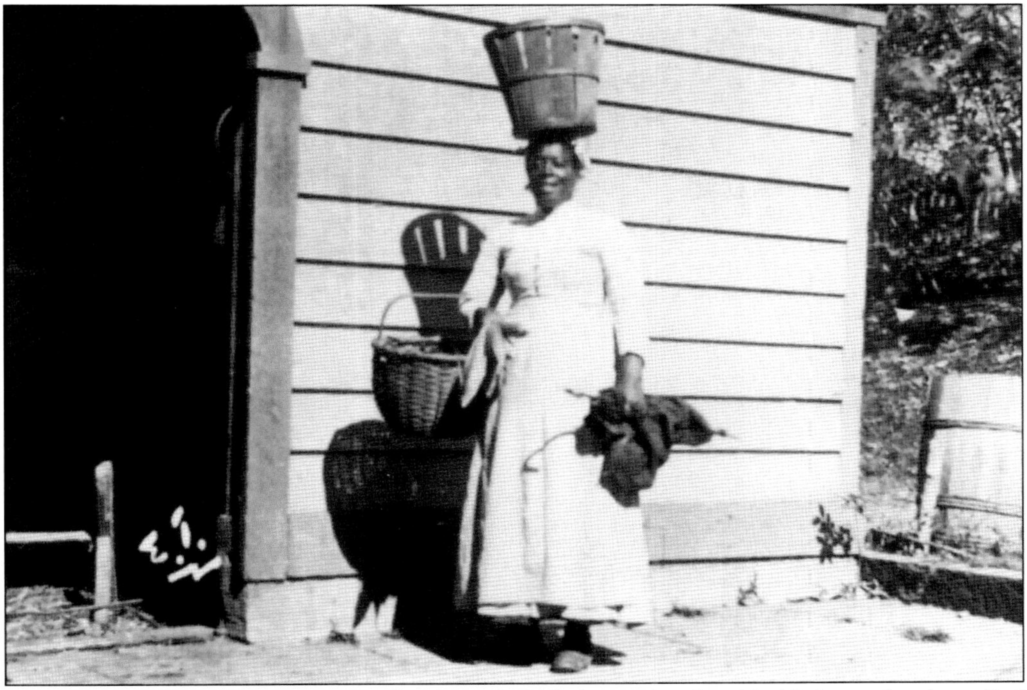

Edward Taylor photographed two of his household help on October 13, 1887, in what he called "war sketches." Isabelle was labeled "commander-in-chief."

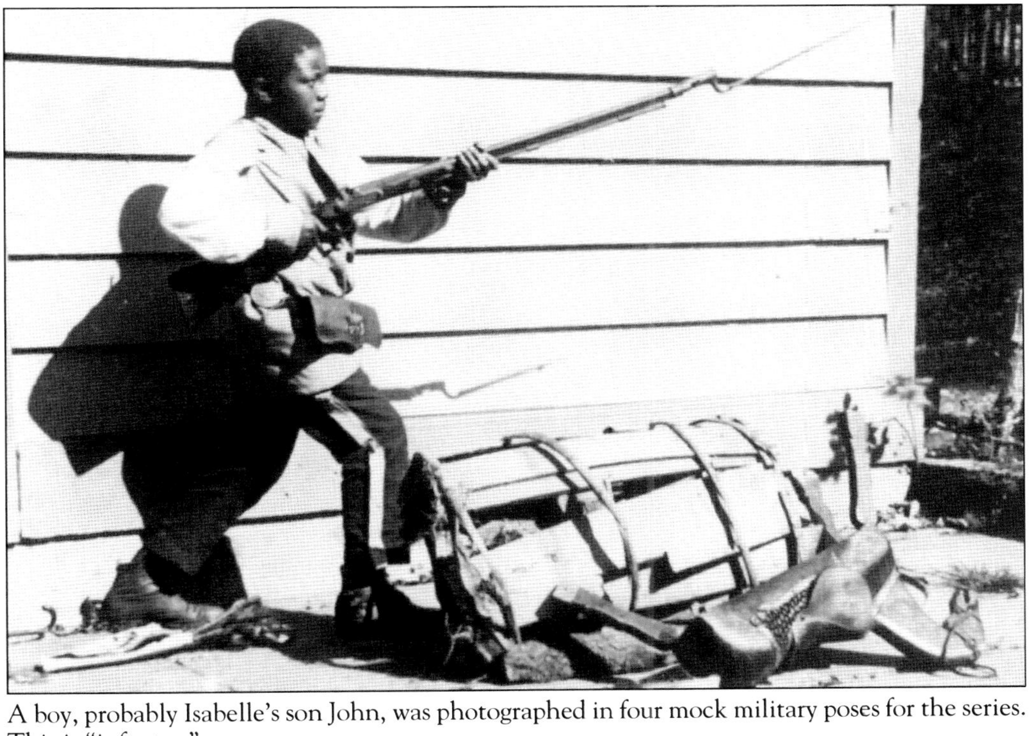

A boy, probably Isabelle's son John, was photographed in four mock military poses for the series. This is "infantry."

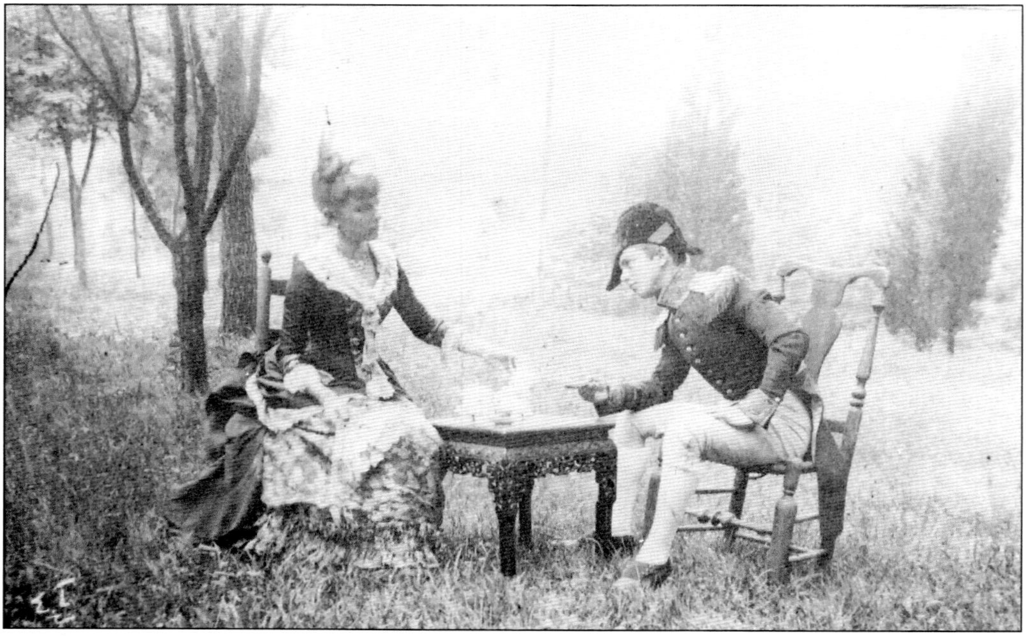

"Uncle Joe" assumes a pleading pose with "mother." Both figures are unidentified in this Edward Taylor series from August 1887. The series was probably photographed on the grounds of Orchard Home.

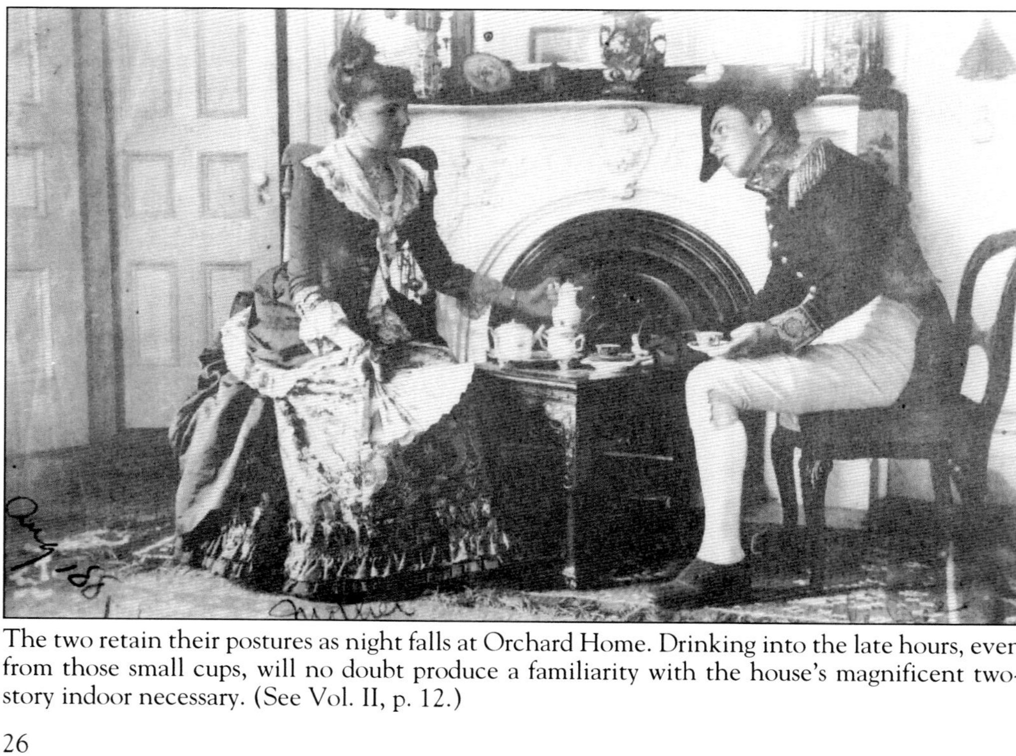

The two retain their postures as night falls at Orchard Home. Drinking into the late hours, even from those small cups, will no doubt produce a familiarity with the house's magnificent two-story indoor necessary. (See Vol. II, p. 12.)

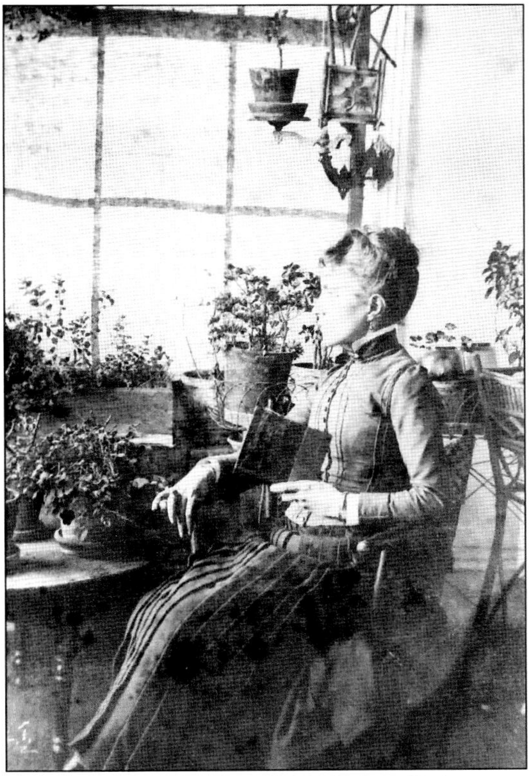

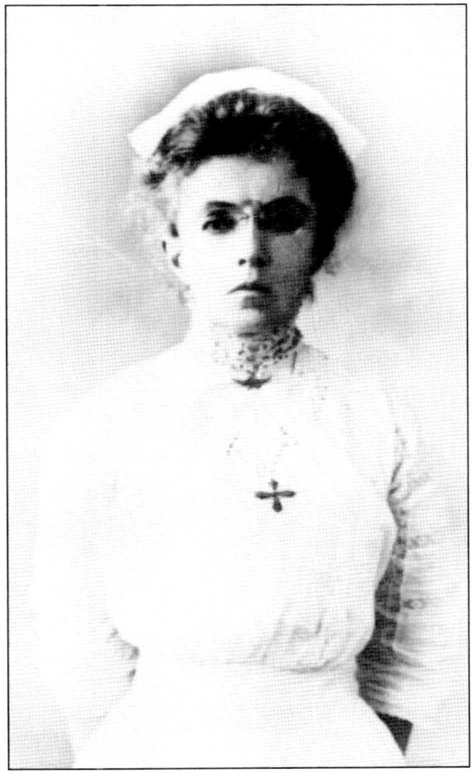

The most appealing pictures of Mary Holmes Taylor may be those in the mood series photographed by brother Edward on January 2, 1886. This is "Study." Little is known of Mary's life. Although she appears to be in a nurse's uniform here, she was a librarian c. 1920—a service rather than an occupational position.

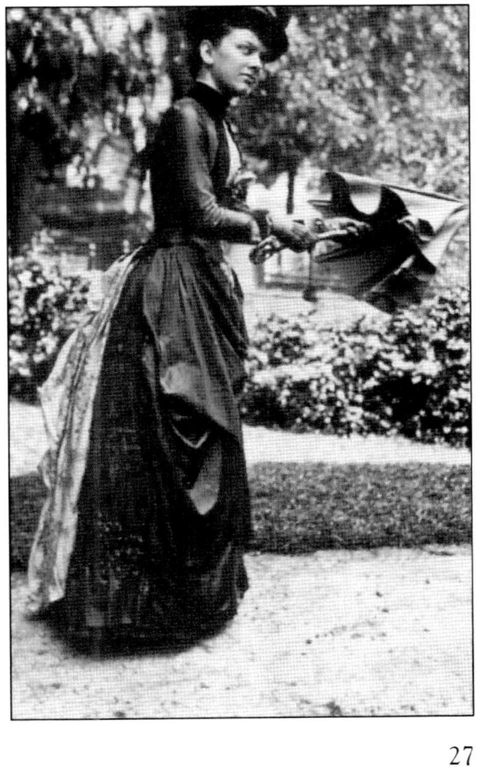

In an image titled, "Is It Going to Rain?" a member of Edward and Margaret's circle is captured with an umbrella c. 1890. The photograph's charm and feeling for a moment overcome the absence of the subject's identification.

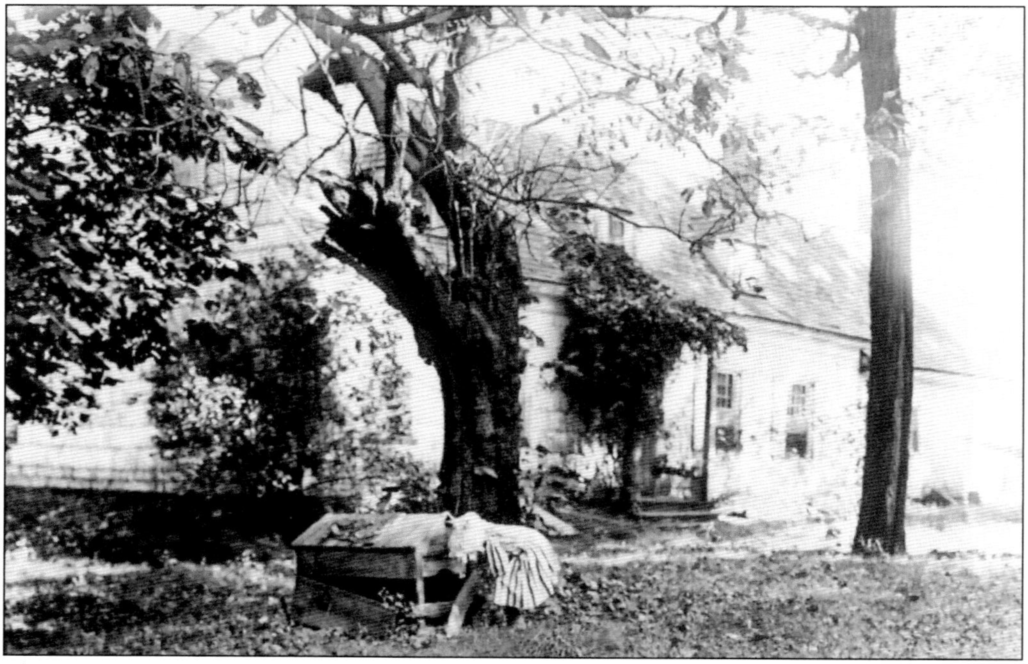

The ancient Taylor home now known as Marlpit Hall is traditionally thought to have been an eighteenth-century Georgian main block that was affixed to a smaller, late-seventeenth-century Dutch-style house built by James Grover. Ongoing research is questioning conventional wisdom, however. This image, taken *c.* late 1880s, was probably made by Edward Taylor, with the dress conveying playful suggestiveness.

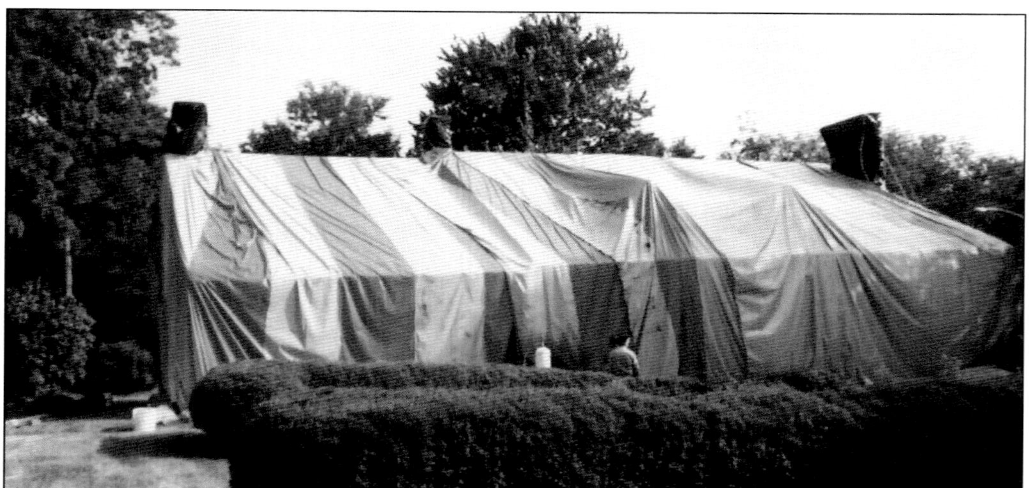

The artist Christo did not wrap Marlpit Hall in 1993, the resemblance of this image to one of his projects notwithstanding. Fumigation to eliminate powder-post beetles occasioned the sealing of the building. Initial restoration plans were expanded to include archeological examination and a historic structures report, resulting in a longer-than-anticipated closing of the house museum owned by the Monmouth County Historical Association.

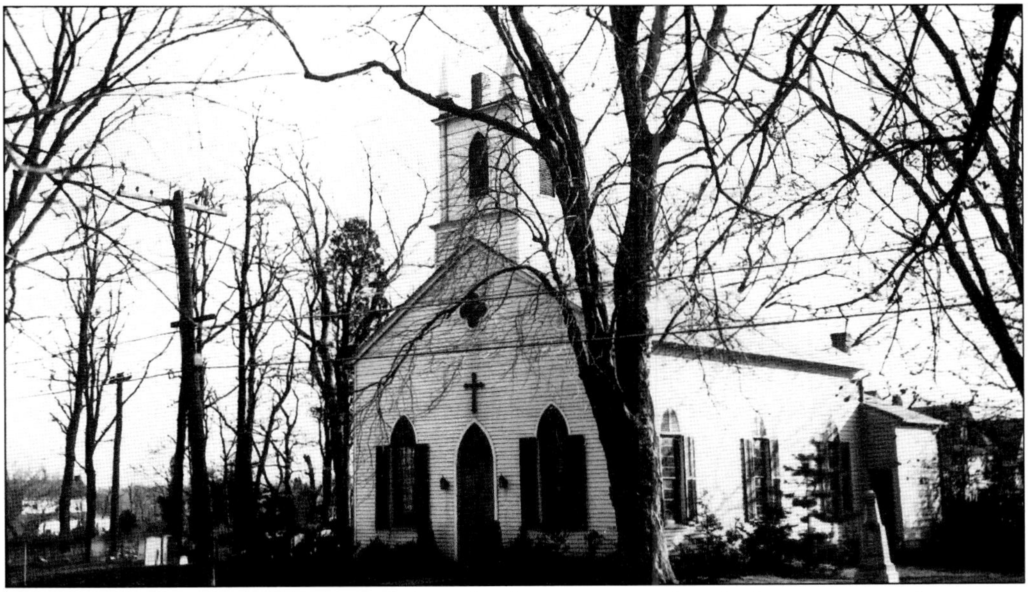

Anglican worship in Middletown is believed to have originated in the late seventeenth century, with Christ Church dating its founding to 1702. It was then a joint parish with Christ Church, Shrewsbury; the two churches separated in 1854. This edifice, seen in a *c.* 1940s photograph, was built in 1835, replacing an earlier, deteriorated building. The 1950s parish hall is now located to the west.

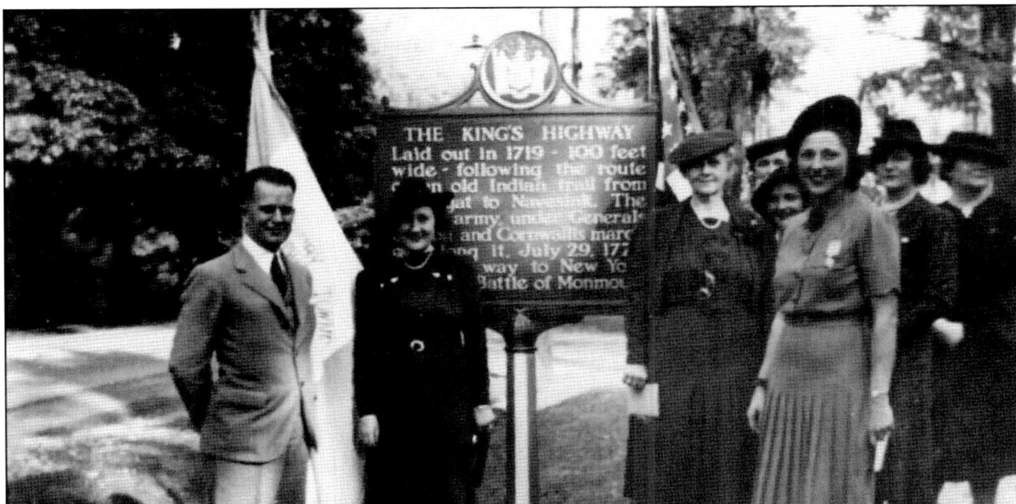

Shrewsbury Towne Chapter #78 of the Daughters of the American Revolution presented a road marker to commemorate historic Kings Highway adjacent to Christ Church on October 9, 1939. State official Thomas Marple is at left. The original photograph identifies others present, from left to right, as follows: Mrs. Dorman McFaddin (a former chapter historian who prepared a history of the highway), an unknown person (to the right of the sign), and Mrs. Joseph C. Irwin (chapter regent). Rachel Field Mount of Middletown, second vice regent of the chapter, unveiled the monument. It was moved to Highway 35 near the town hall at an unknown date, having been in its original position at least into the 1960s.

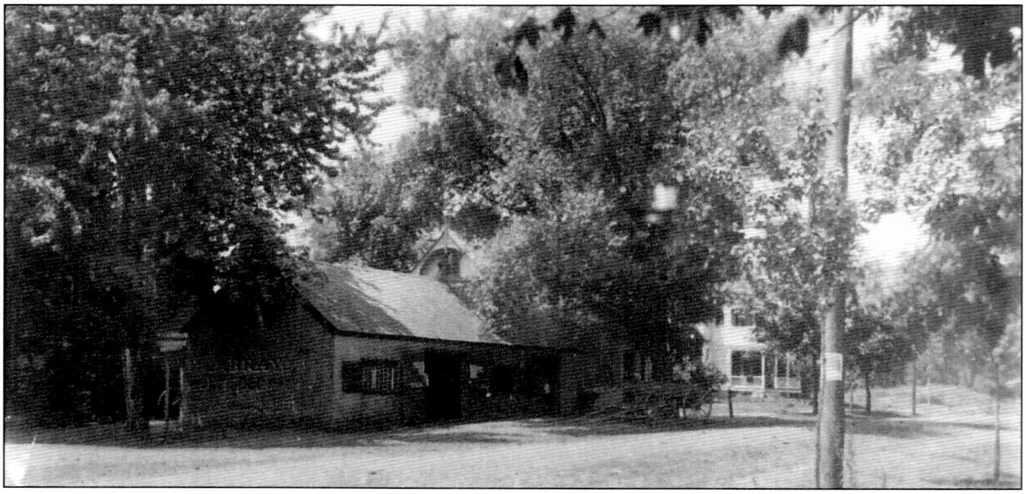

The c. 1825 stucco-clad, brick blacksmith shop on the southwest corner of Kings Highway and Conover Avenue, seen here in a June 1898 image, was long in the Casler family. John the village smithy is listed in a c. 1850 business directory; Daniel D. Bray was listed as a "horseshoer" from c. 1897–1901, indicating a reduced scope of business. Legend has it that William S. Truex drilled troops here in the c. 1860 period. The earliest telling of that story seen by the author was dated February 1925 in the *Newark Evening News*, although a contemporary account is still needed to establish the tale's credibility.

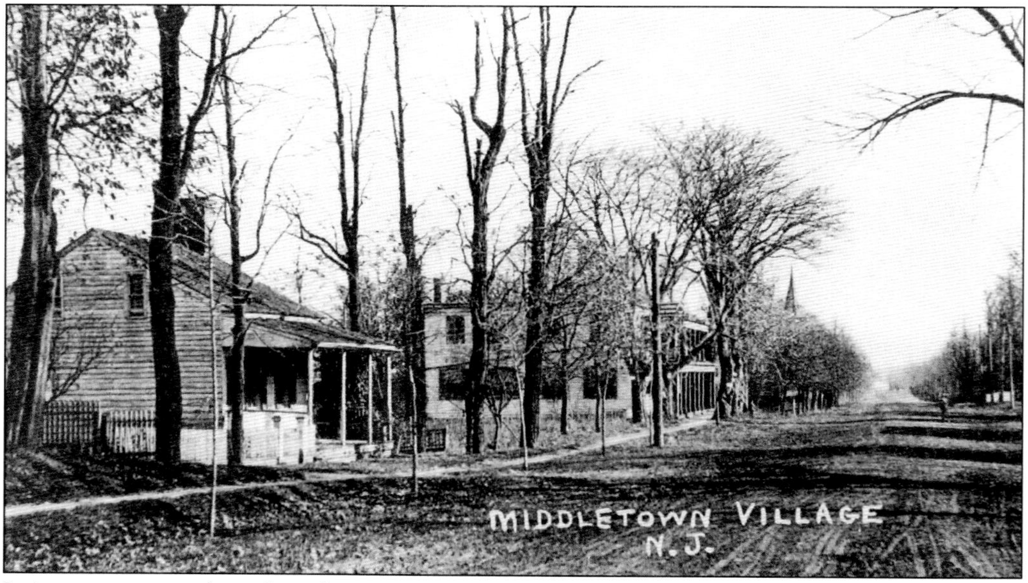

It is easy to speculate that this c. 1905 postcard depicts a view of the north side of Kings Highway from Marlpit Place. The First Baptist Church appears to be in the background, the since-removed American Hotel had a two-story porch, and 109 Kings Highway could be in the foreground. Problems exist with this identification, however. Although the roof line, chimney position, and attic windows of the latter location "fit," the building is no longer as close to the ground or street as it appears here. The authors suspects a new foundation was built; the owner Russ Till suspects not. If so, the much-changed porch would be explained. A definitive contemporary account of this scene is needed.

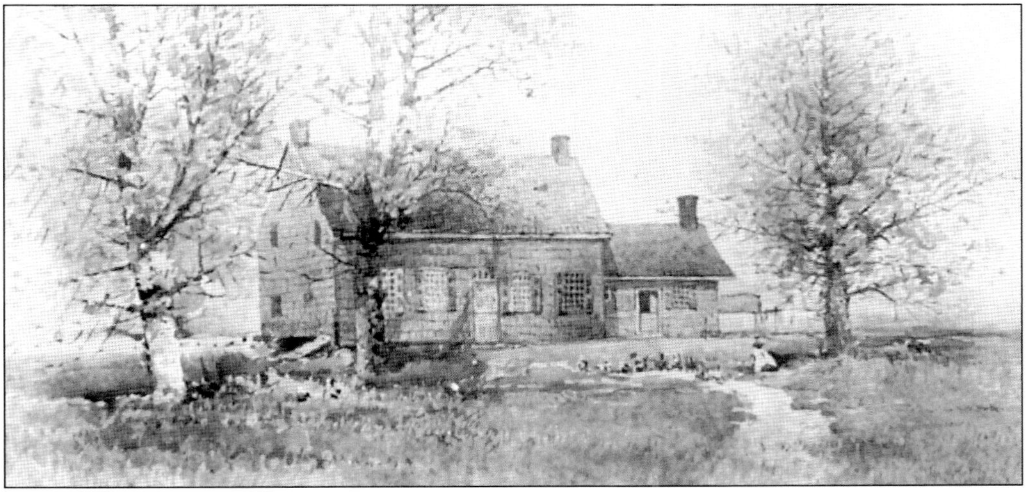

The Richard Hartshorne house at 61 Kings Highway, seen in a *c.* 1890s painting by R. Shaw, is reported to have late-seventeenth-century origins, but repeated repairs and remodeling may have obliterated the oldest section on the east, or right. Hartshorne, born in England in 1641, owned an extensive tract in the Highlands of Navesink, settling there *c.* 1670. He held various public positions and is regarded as the first lawyer in Monmouth County, although he lacked formal legal training. He retired to Middletown Village in 1703, died in 1722, and is buried in the family graveyard adjacent to this house. (Special Collections and Archives, Rutgers University Libraries.)

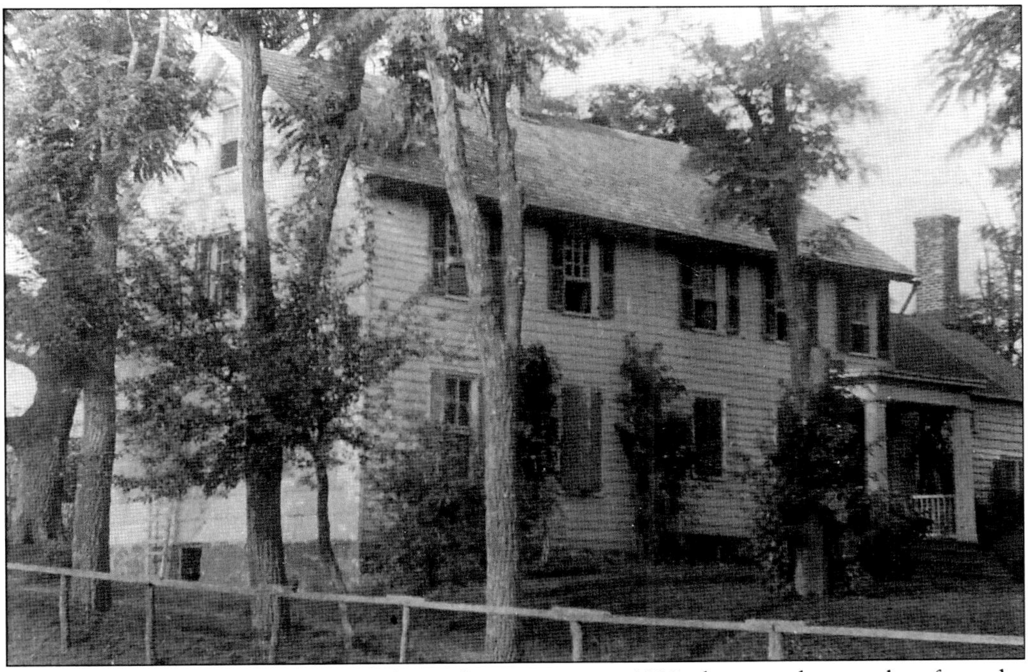

The earliest part of 2 Red Hill Road at right, seen in a *c.* 1900 photograph, may date from the late seventeenth century. The property is known as the Wilson house or the Bowne house for early- and late-nineteenth-century owners and also known as the Rising Sun Tavern. (Collection of the Monmouth County Historical Association.)

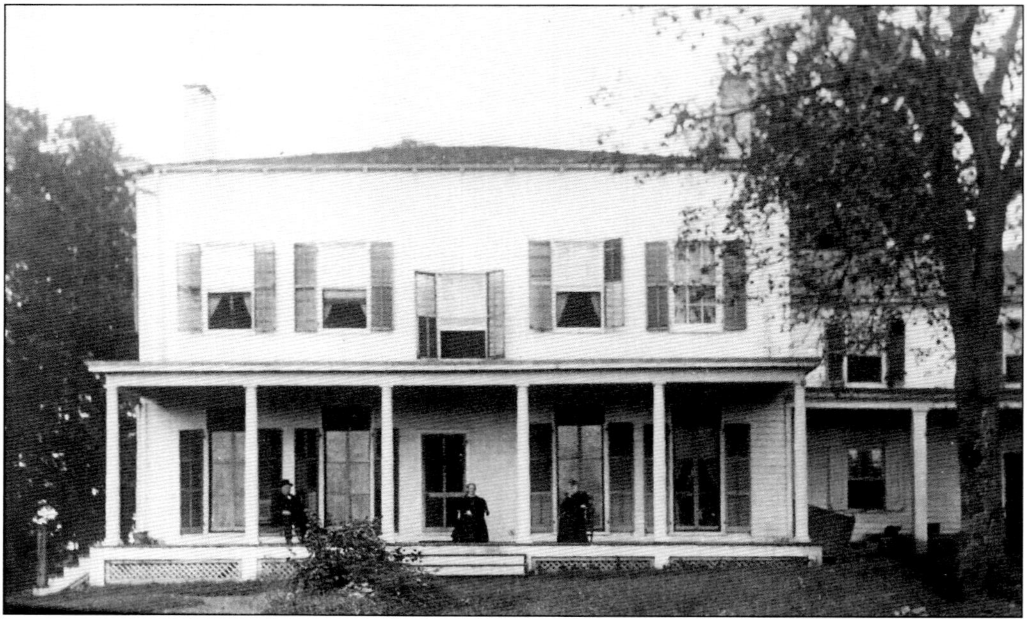

Locustwood, located at 28 The Trail, is the 1832 Greek Revival home of Charles I. Hendrickson. It once commanded a vast farm running well north of the village. The main block is unchanged today, except the porch, which now spans three bays. Now a two-bay extension is on the west, or left, while a one-bay extension is on the east. The absence of the fine door enframement from this *c.* 1890s picture is a puzzle.

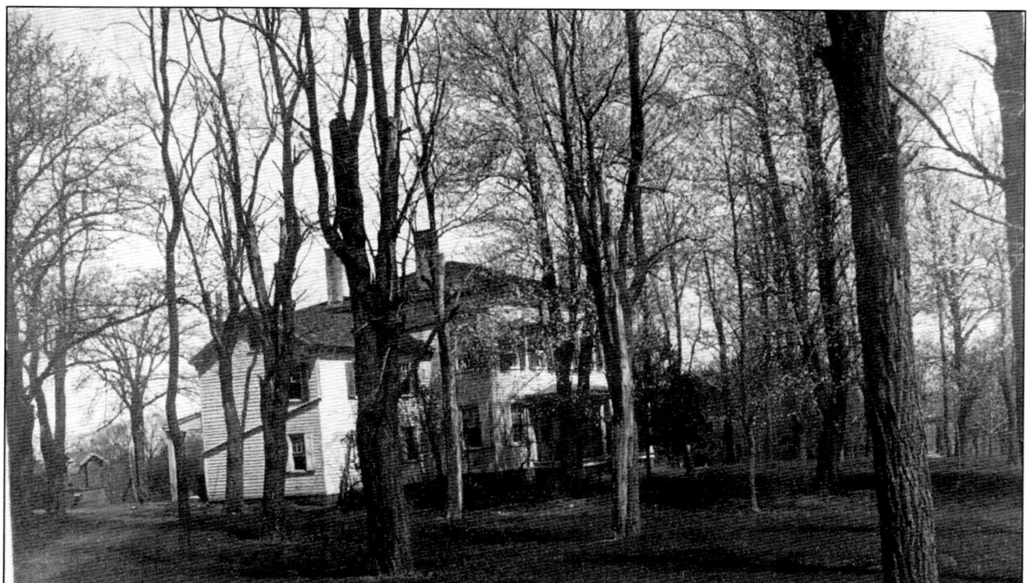

The rear of Locustwood is seen *c.* 1890s.

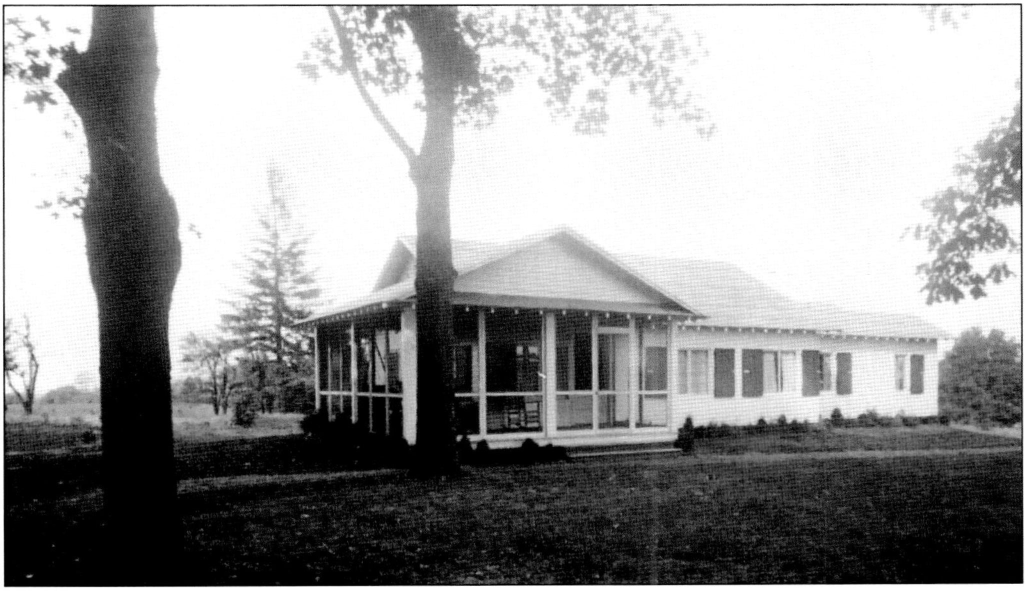

Ernest H. Taylor built this house east of Locustwood following the 1914 fire that killed his father-in-law, John S. Hendrickson. It was moved nearby in 1929 after Frederick G. Adams bought the property and built a new house for himself on the site of this one. The remodeled dwelling still stands at 21 The Trail.

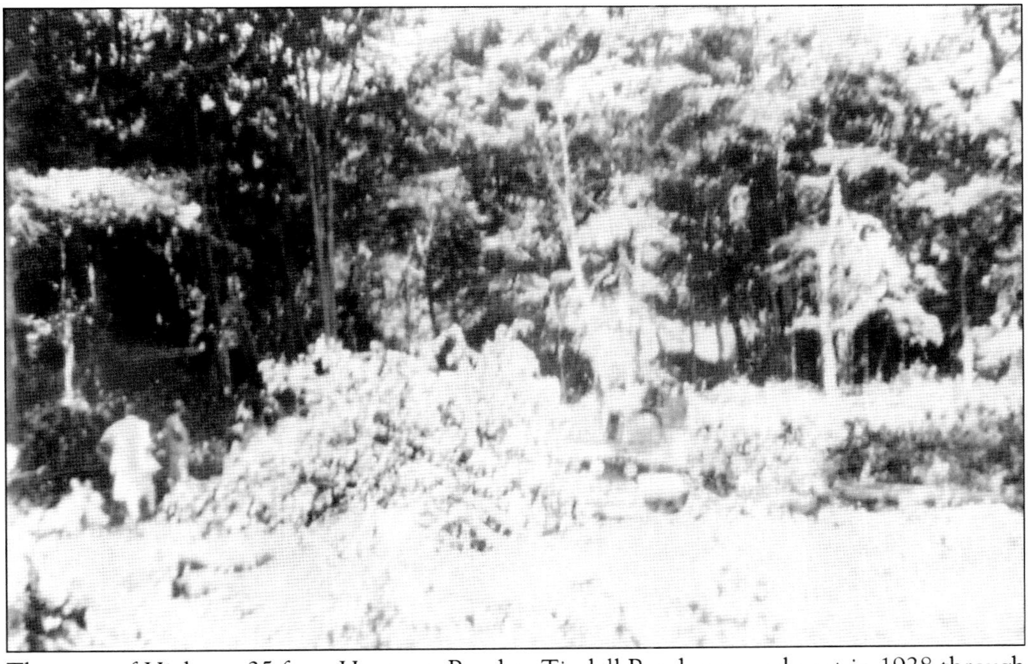

The stem of Highway 35 from Harmony Road to Tindall Road was newly cut in 1928 through hilly farmland. It was designed to relieve automobile traffic from historic Middletown Village. This image shows trees being cut in the rear of Locustwood. While the image lacks clarity, it conveys sharply the sense of destruction of one's home grounds. Increasing traffic now appears to be destroying the intent of the earlier highway planners.

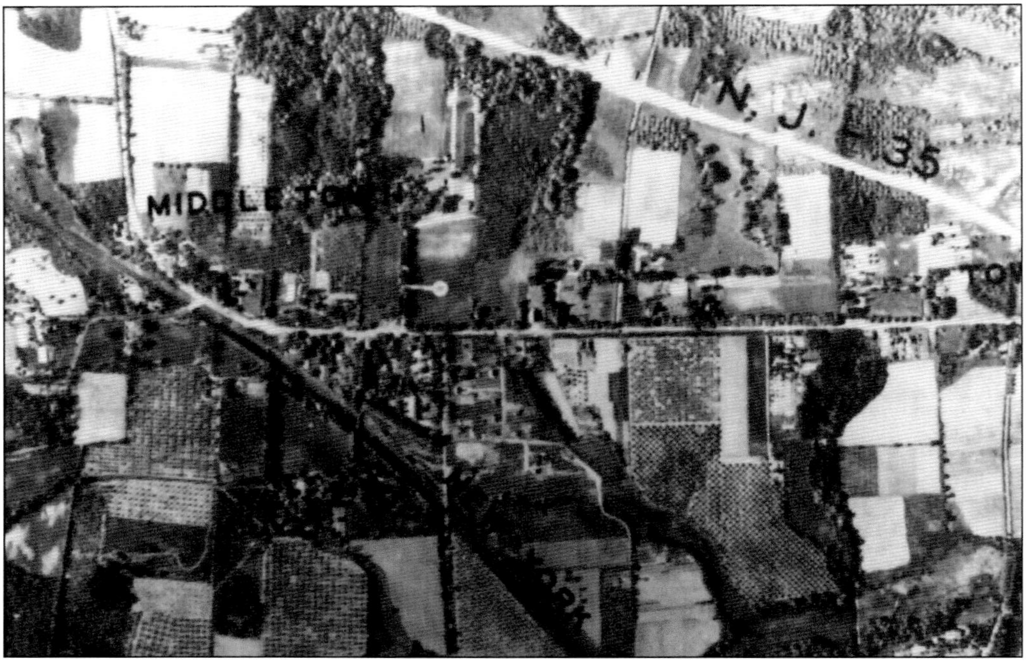

An aerial view, taken not long after construction of the 1928 Highway 35 cut-off, outlines clearly the new concrete road diagonally at top, along with Kings Highway, curving from top to right, which the new road relieved, and the New York and Long Branch Railroad, diagonally at left. Kings Highway was realigned in 1919 at the sharp curve at left. A few of its landmark buildings, notably the churches, can be discerned. The dotted sections are orchards; the square-shaped one right of center is shown below.

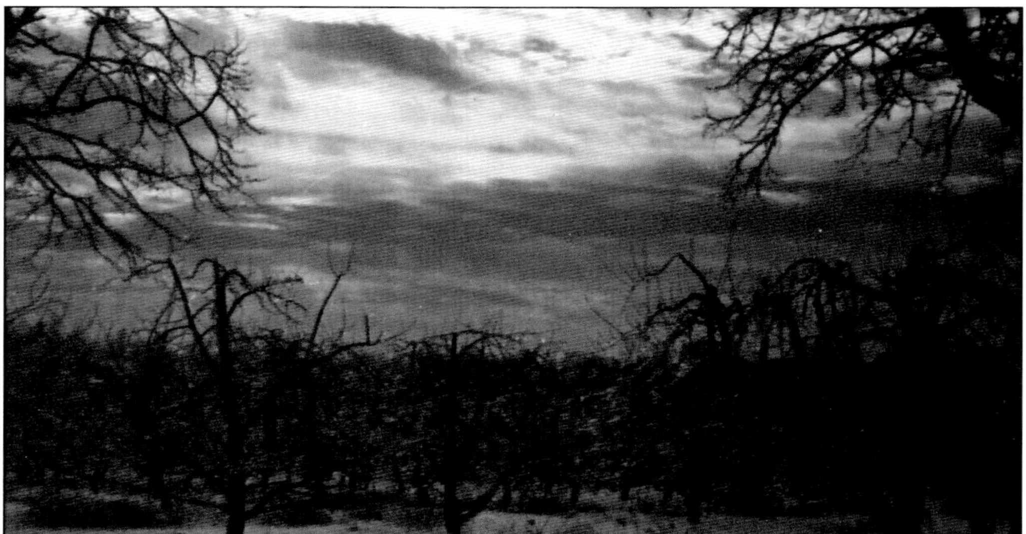

Hendrickson's cherry orchard was, until the mid-1970s, a historic district reminder of Middletown's agrarian past. It can be seen above on the south side of the road bisecting the center, roughly under the "N" over the diagonal road at top. The Brandywine Estates houses were built here *c.* 1980.

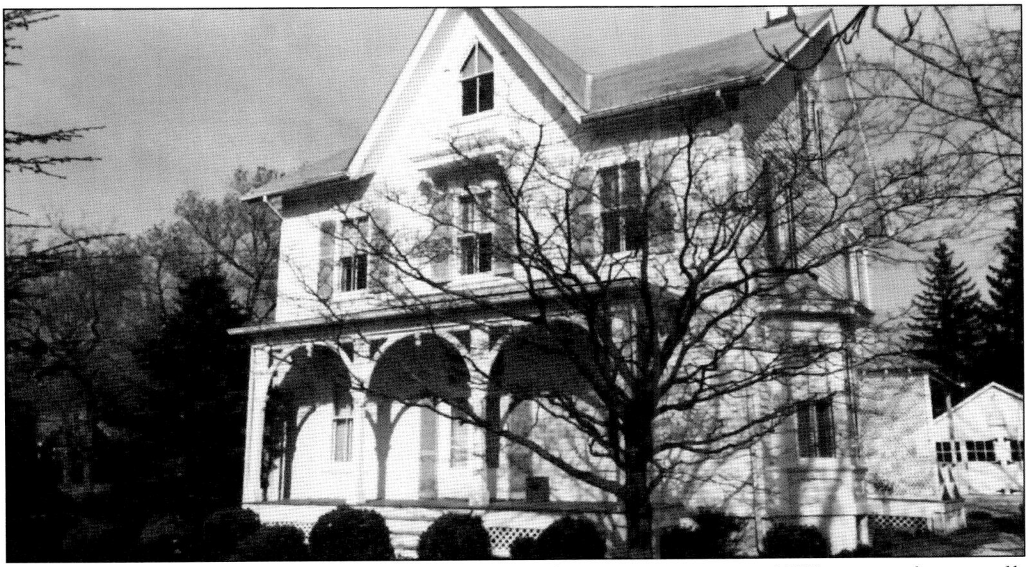

The historic First Baptist Church sold its substantial 1876 parsonage in 1955, opting for a small, easy-to-maintain new house. Margaret and Joseph Lopez found the four-master-bedroom house they had been seeking, seen here in a 1980s image, and began restoration of the then-faded Gothic Revival gem at 59 Kings Highway. A one- and one-half-story structure (either a small house or part of one) was moved from an unknown nearby locale and attached to the north, or rear of this house.

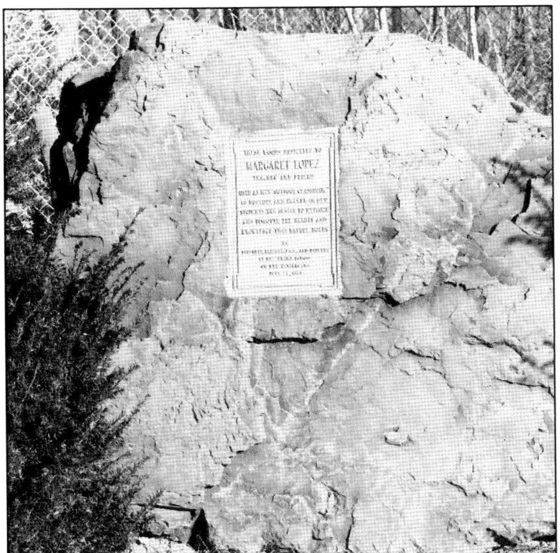

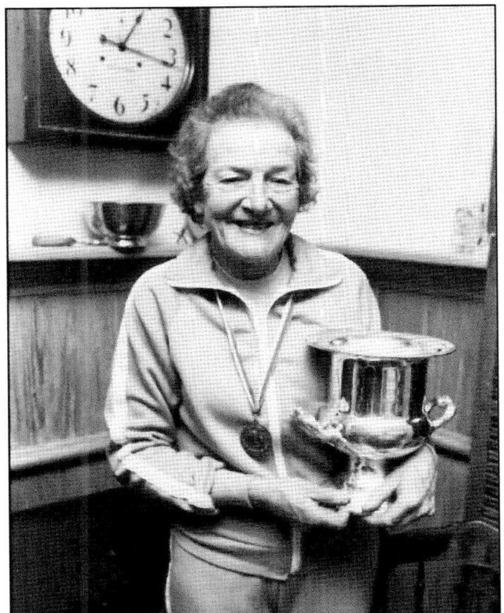

Margaret Lopez, after a long career as a fourth grade teacher at Nut Swamp School, began a second one as a long-distance runner and cyclist. She is seen accepting a silver trophy for winning Age Group 70–79 at the New York Marathon in 1982. A rock monument outside the school has a 1981 retirement plaque which reads: "These Woods Dedicated to Margaret Lopez, Teacher and Friend, Used as Her 'Outdoor Classroom' To Nurture and Awaken in Her Students The Desire To Explore and Discover The Beauty And Knowledge That Nature Holds." Mrs. Lopez published her autobiography in 1996, entitled *Hooray Margaret!*

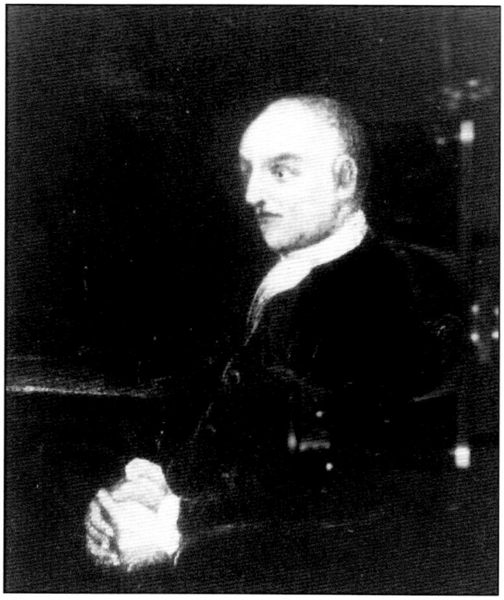

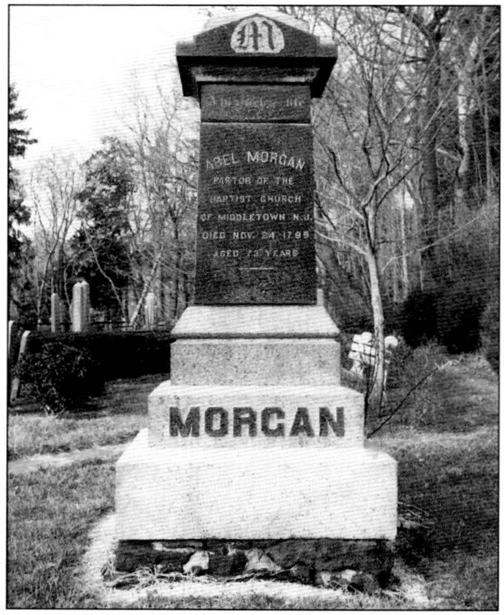

The Reverend Abel Morgan, born 1713 in Delaware, died in Middletown at age seventy-two in 1785, after serving fifty-one years as a minister, forty-seven of those at the Middletown Baptist Church. He was regarded as one of the most important of the early Baptist clergy. His original monument was destroyed by the steeple's falling in the wind in May 1890, and the monument was replaced by this one in September 1891.

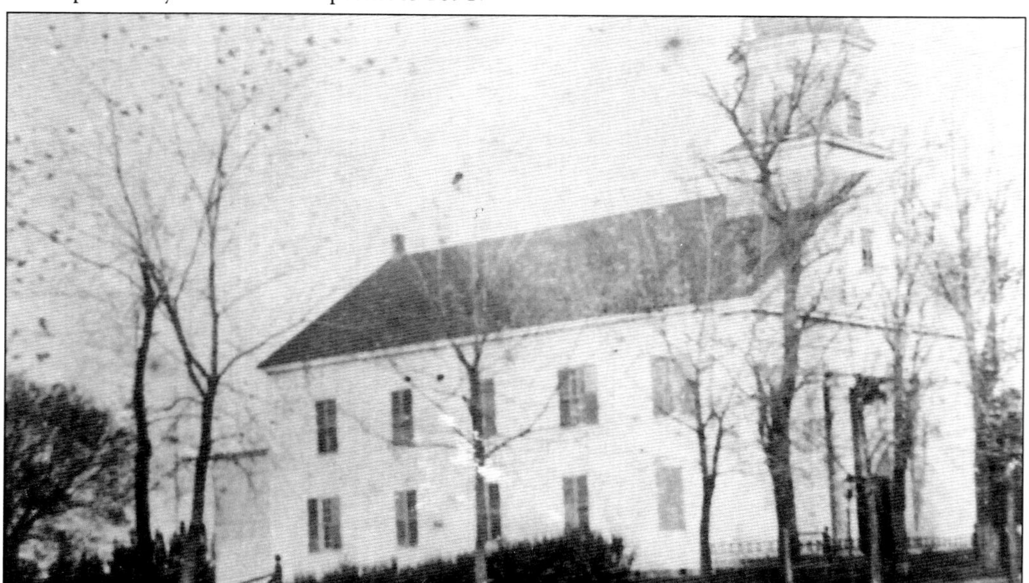

The Baptist church in New Jersey was founded in 1688 in Middletown. This edifice at 69 Kings Highway is the third on the site. The 1888 photograph on p. 58 of Volume I shows its original steeple, which was blown down in a storm in May 1890. This image post-dates the building's 1891 replacement costing $900 but pre-dates the *c.* 1894 placement of the Women's Christian Temperance Union building, moved from Church Street, adjacent on the west. (Collection of Old First Church.)

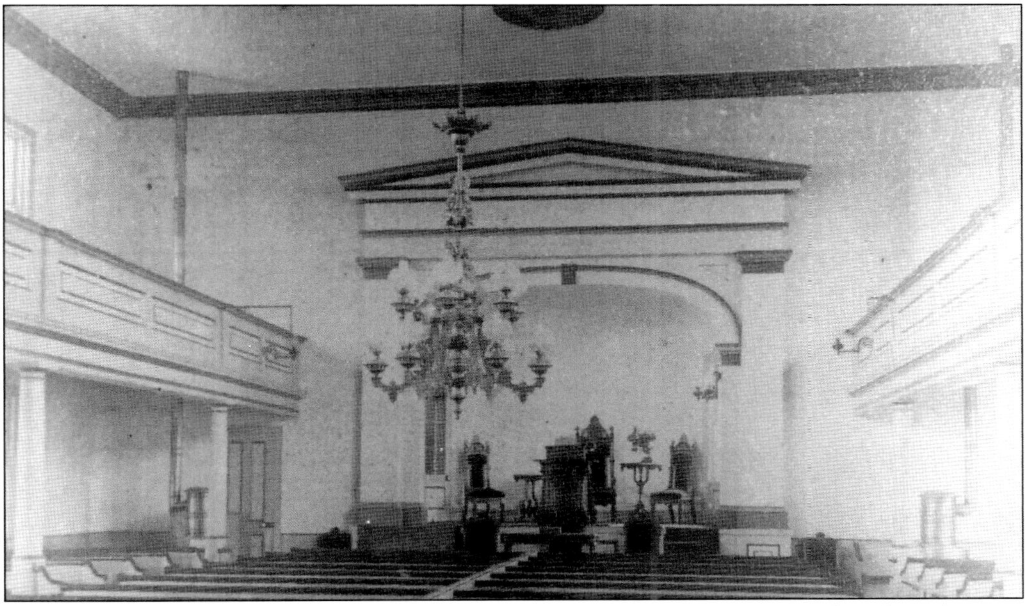

This c. 1910 photograph of the interior of the First Baptist Church by Edward Taylor predates changes beginning with a c. 1908 extensive interior remodeling. The side balconies were removed and the pews replaced. The entablature over the altar is now gone, with this space separated by a curtain. Modern electric lighting was installed in 1921, and the chandelier was replaced. (Collection of Old First Church.)

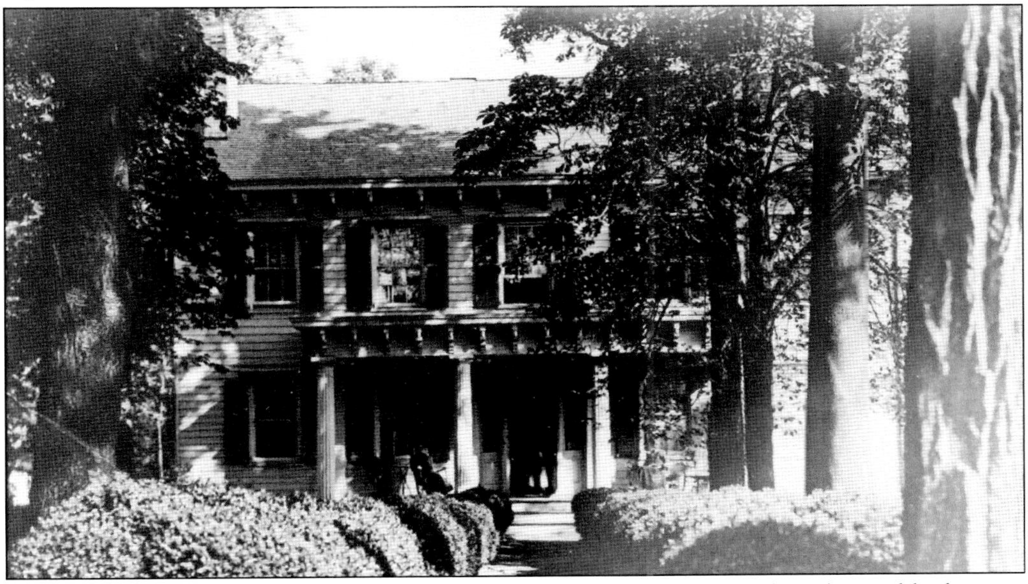

The Greek Revival Hendrickson-Morford house at 35 Kings Highway has changed little since this c. 1890 photograph was taken, but the tall trees and the boxwood hedges, present when the Morford estate sold the house in 1931, are gone. The western part, at left, is c. 1830, while on the east is a c. 1850s Thomas Morford addition. The house's most charming lore is the reported 1778 sharing of lunch under a tree by Lord Cornwallis and Sir Henry Clinton following the British withdrawal from the Battle of Monmouth.

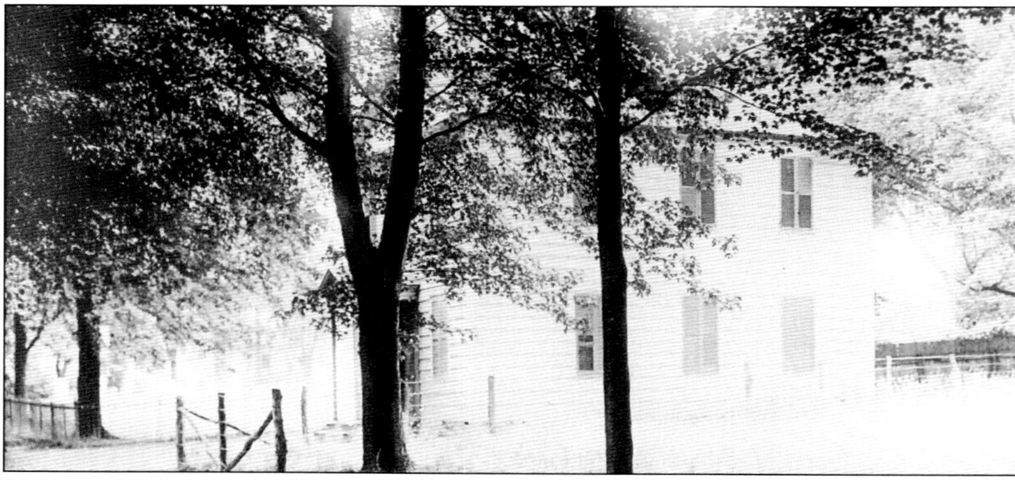

The Franklin Academy at 53 Kings Highway was built in 1836 and opened in 1837 as a private school. This image is likely from the early twentieth century. The two- and-one-half story, three-bay Greek Revival structure became a township school around mid-century and served until it was replaced by a modern brick structure *c.* 1906 (Vol. II, p. 48). The academy, the building still known for its early name, was the library of the Middletown public system from 1915 to 1942, but it began a period of decline while vacant for the next several years.

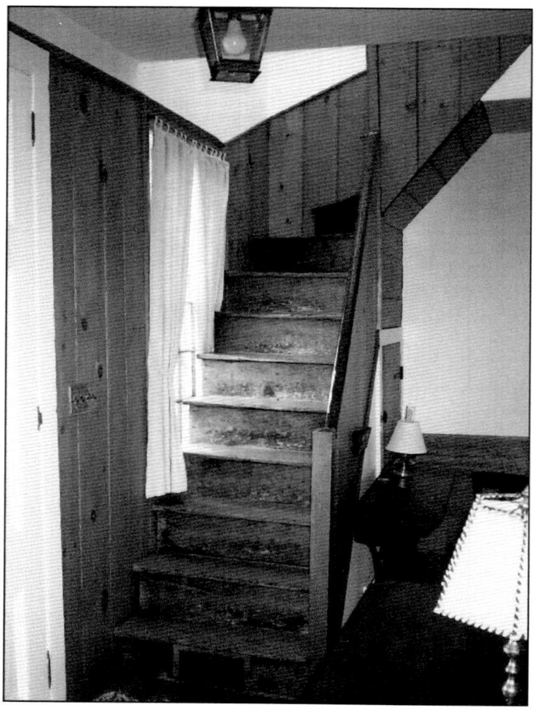

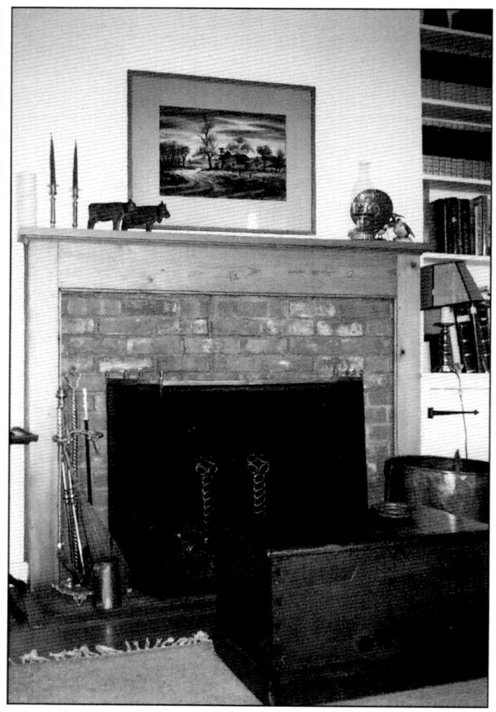

Thelma Jelliffe and Maltby Jelliffe, a fine arts graduate of Mt. Holyoke and long a local historian, bought the academy in 1950 and remodeled the building as a residence. An interior wall was likely removed, the door newly opening to the living room. The two-seat desk is original, and the stairs remain unchanged. The fireplace on the north living room wall was a remodeling addition.

Two

Rural Middletown

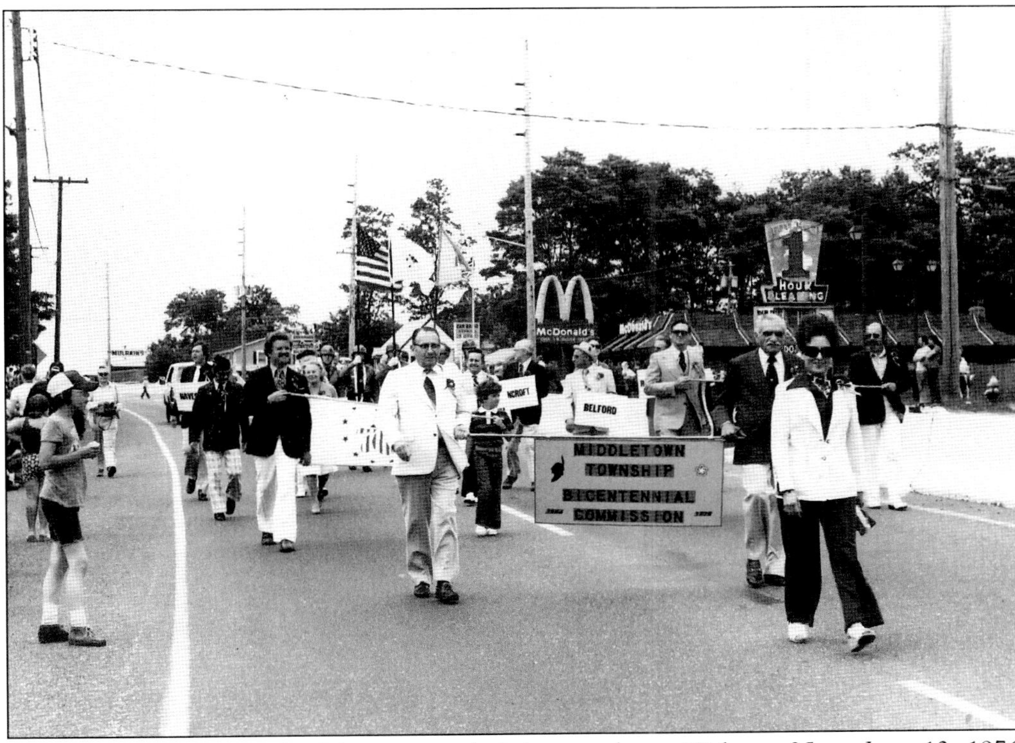

Middletown bicentennial celebrations included a parade on Highway 35 on June 13, 1976. Bicentennial Commission Chairperson Catherine Lentz, photographed by her husband Jack, leads. Holding the banner in front are Paul Lefever and Joe Tomaso. The banner at left is held by commission member Gary Kaplan and an unidentified boy, while Charles Walker and library director William LeKernec hold the banner at right.

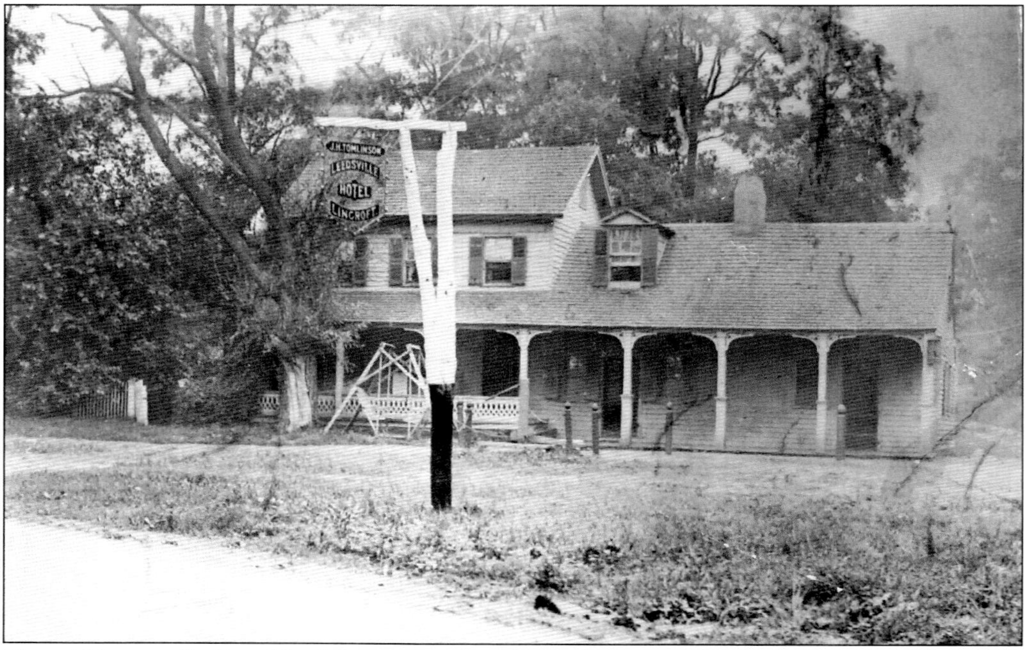

The old Leedsville Hotel had deteriorated in the mid-1920s under Otto Linburg's ownership, prior to its acquisition by Dante Daverio. The few physical changes since the late-nineteenth-century photograph on p. 30 of Volume I include removal of the well and a tree and a lowering of the chimney. Note Tomlinson's old sign, with current and former names of Lincroft, suggesting the hotel did not change its name when the locality did.

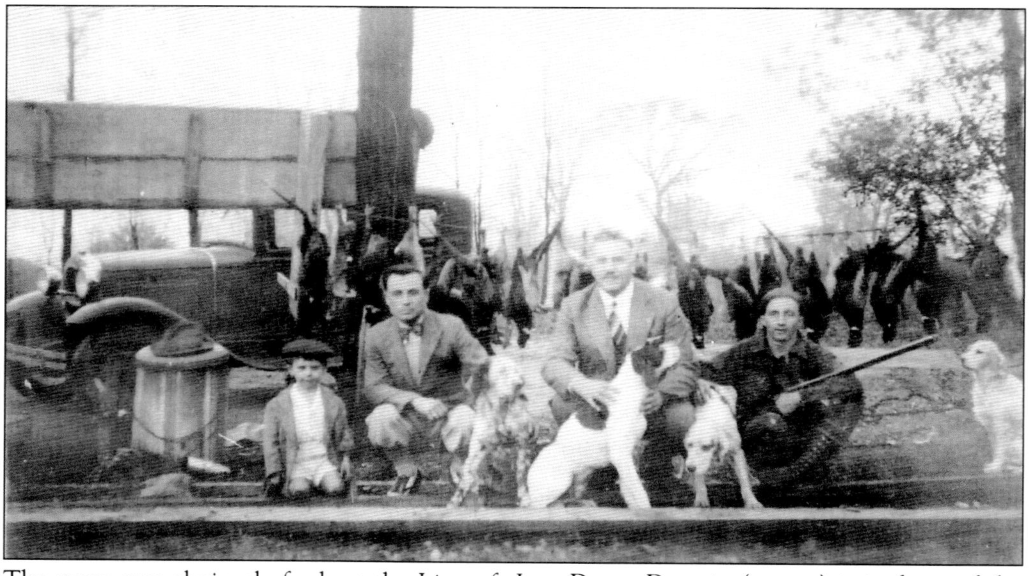

The game was obviously fresh at the Lincroft Inn. Dante Daverio (owner) is in front of the automobile with his son Bob (a later owner) at left, together with friends and dogs returning from a successful pheasant hunt, c. 1920s. See the original pictures at the Lincroft Inn. The copies were provided by Martha, who with husband Terry make up the third generation of Daverio ownership.

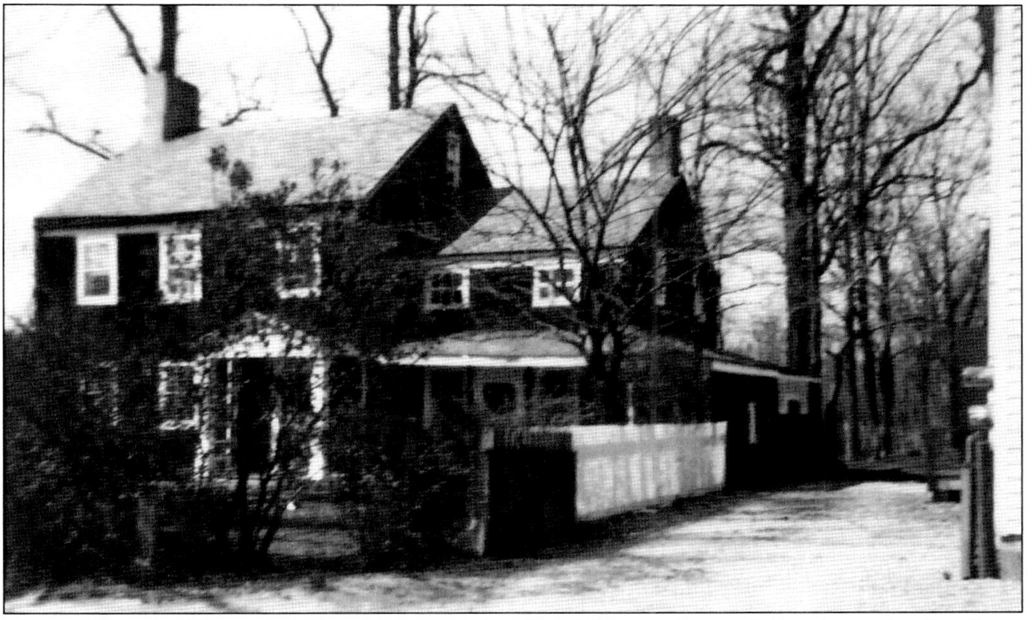

This unidentified house stood on the east side of Middletown-Lincroft Road, north of and not far from the Lincroft junction. As new houses are constructed off the road in 1997, there are few reminders that this street had been previously built up, since the earlier structures were apparently removed in the 1960s and 1970s.

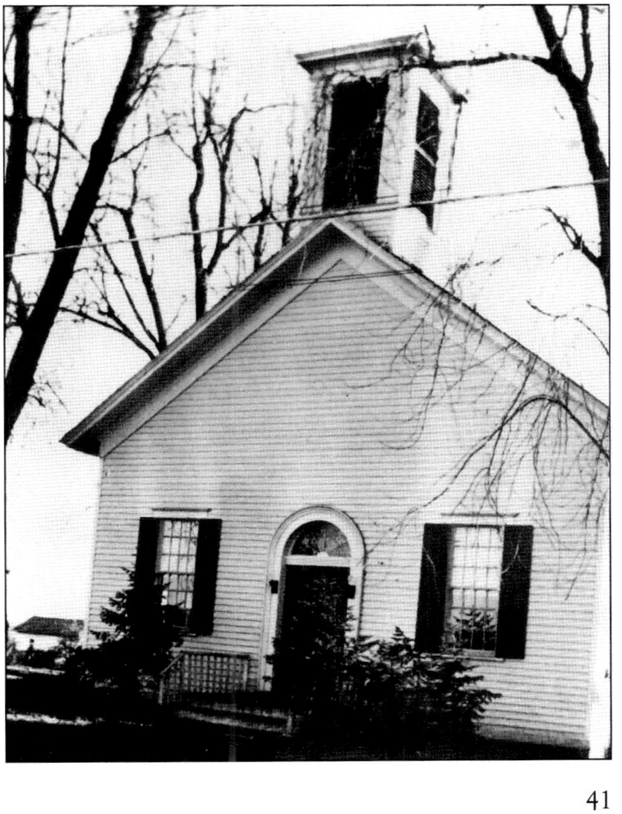

The Lincroft Community Chapel on the south side of Newman Springs Road, west of the firehouse, was dedicated February 17, 1869, as a unit of the First Baptist Church in Red Bank. The organization changed its affiliation to Presbyterian, with a service held there on January 31, 1960, chartering the Lincroft Presbyterian Church. The congregation moved to the northeast corner of West Front Street and Everett Road in 1966. The earlier church is now a restaurant.

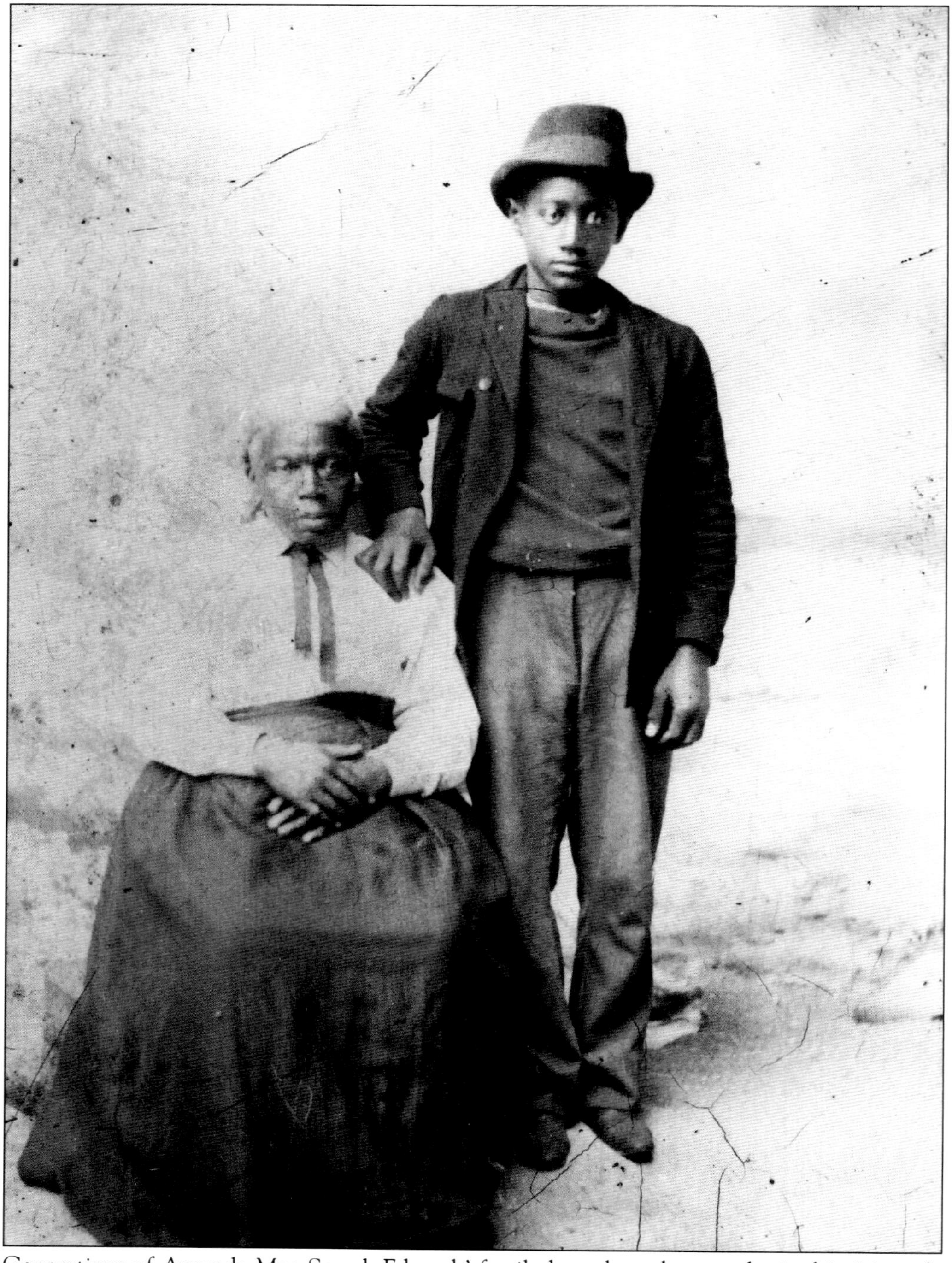

Generations of Amanda Mae Smack Edwards' family have been born and raised in Lincroft, the locale of one of the township's oldest African-American communities. Many are buried in Cedar View Cemetery, the final resting place of a number of Civil War soldiers. Hannah Reeves, born 1824 in Monmouth County, is seen *c.* 1890 with an unidentified young man. She enjoyed good health into her elder years, dying in 1918.

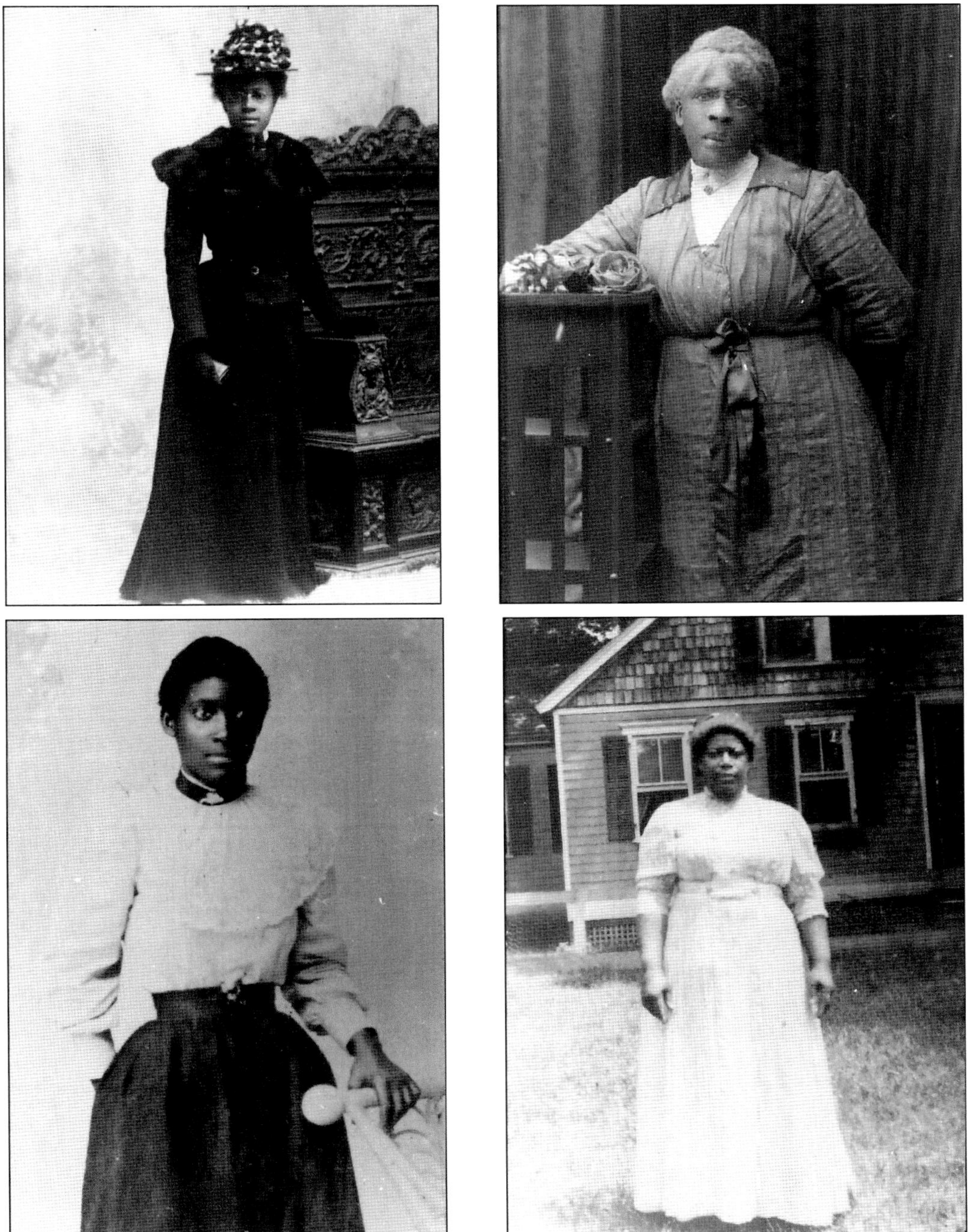

Four of Mae Edwards' ancestors portray dignity of character and show interesting costumes of their times. They are, clockwise from upper left (an uncertain identification) Lulu Mumford, Sarah Reeves (1878–1950, reflecting her prosperity), Jane Reeves Mumford (who lived in Navesink but is buried in Cedar View), and Amanda Reeves (1872–1918).

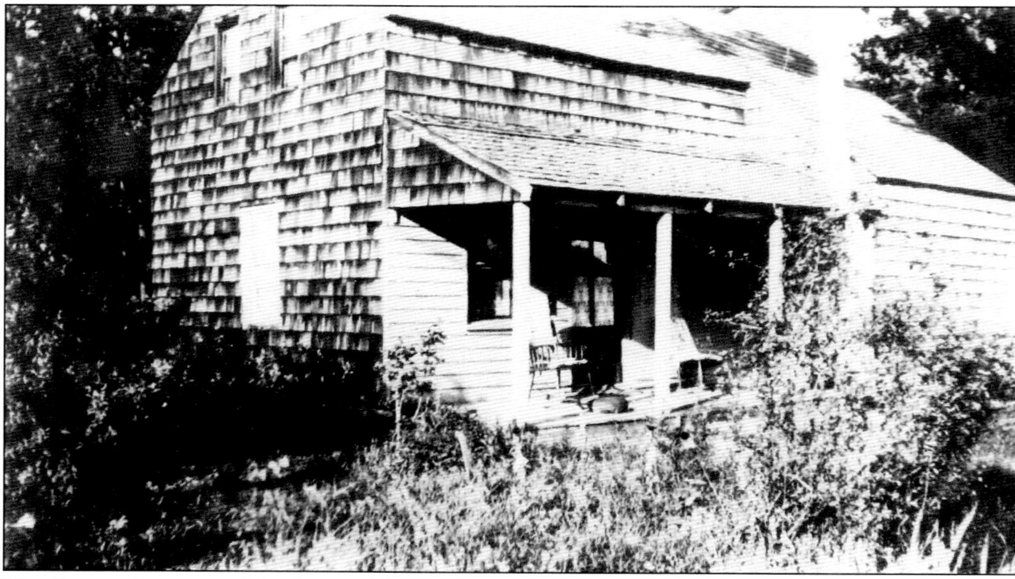

The Reeves homestead, built near Newman Springs Road around the present Christian Brothers Academy, was moved *c.* 1863 to the east side of Middletown-Lincroft Road, south of Fairways Park. Having been sold outside the family, the house, an unlikely prospect for expansion, was demolished *c.* 1972.

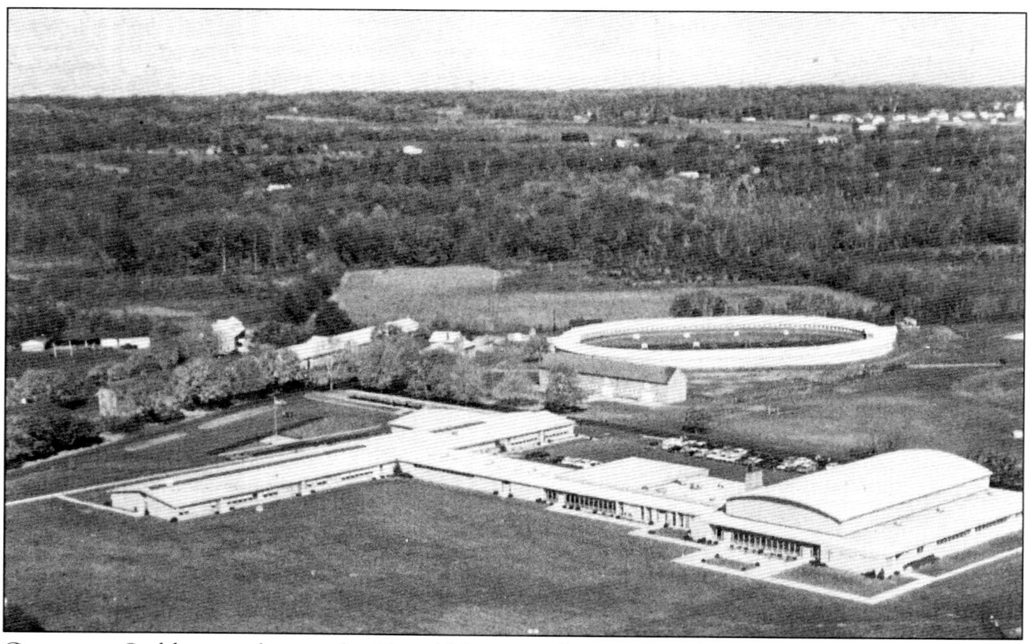

Greentree Stables on the north side of Newman Springs Road, once part of the nationally prominent Whitney racing operation, was sold in the late 1950s for the erection of the Christian Brothers Academy. Many farm buildings were remodeled and new ones were designed as sympathetic additions, all under the direction of architect Bernard Kellenyi. This image is *c.* 1970s.

Jerry Vaughn was known as "The Cow Man" at Brookdale Farm c. 1920s. Brookdale was organized in the 1880s as a racehorse farm by David D. Withers, a nationally prominent horseman who assembled 800 acres around Newman Springs Road.

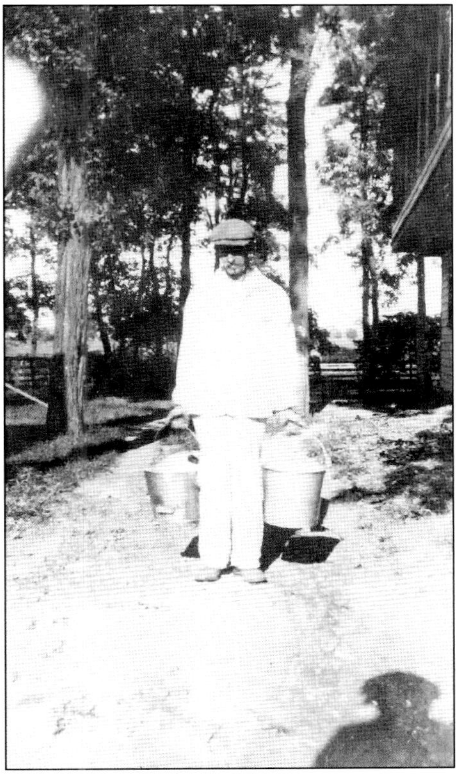

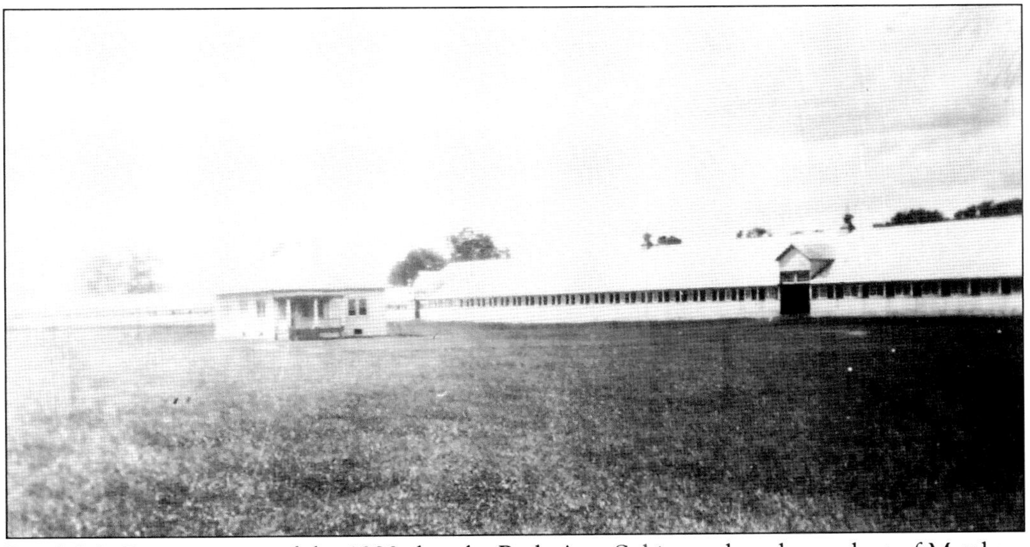

Brookdale Farm pictures of the 1920s lent by Beth Ann Sobieszczyk, a descendant of Matthew Mullin Sr. and Matthew Mullin Jr. (both of whom were superintendents of the farm), reflect Brookdale as it was then. This barn, not now part of Brookdale, may have been part of Greentree Stables. It is not unlike one on the bottom of page 44.

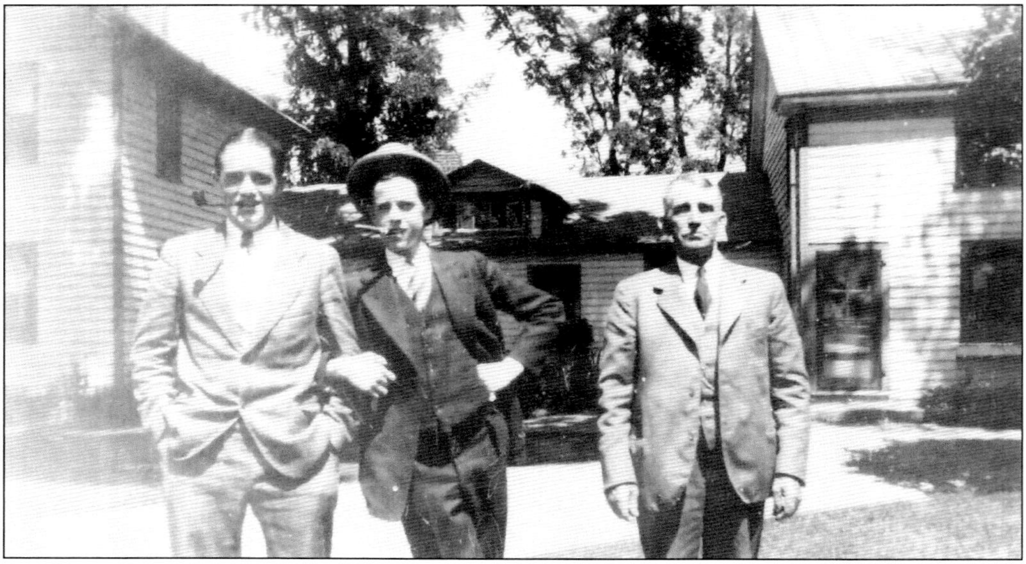

Matthew L. Mullin, son of the man of the same name at right, is arm-in-arm with an unidentified friend at Brookdale in the 1920s. The elder Mullin was born in Ireland c. 1863. He was Brookdale's superintendent for thirty-five years, retiring in 1943; the position was later held by his son. The younger Mullin was a World War II veteran, a graduate of Rider College, and a member of the Lincroft First Aid Squad. The Mullins died in 1950 and 1995 respectively.

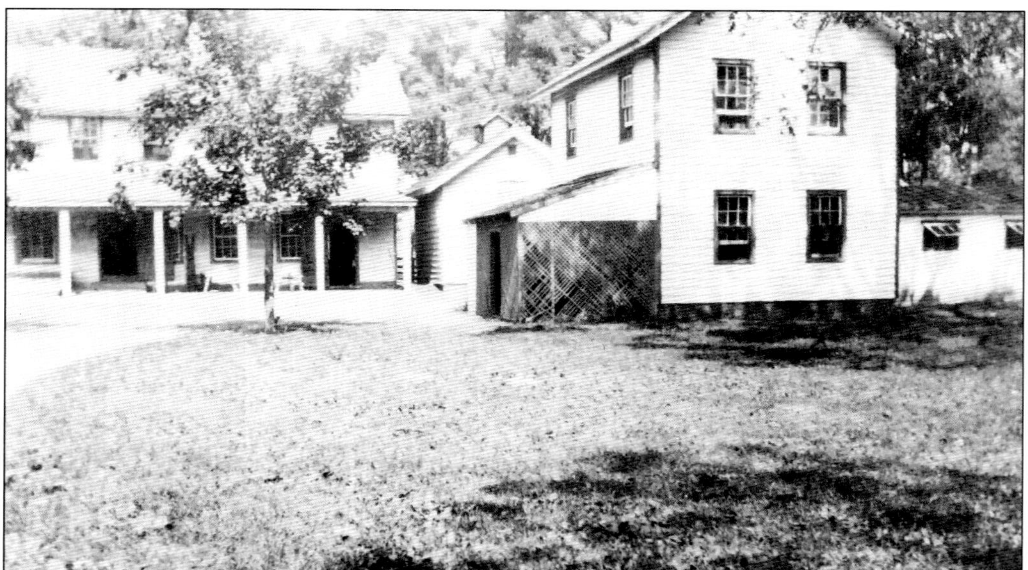

The men's quarters may have been part of the Marlu section. The building was demolished by the Monmouth County Park System in the early 1990s.

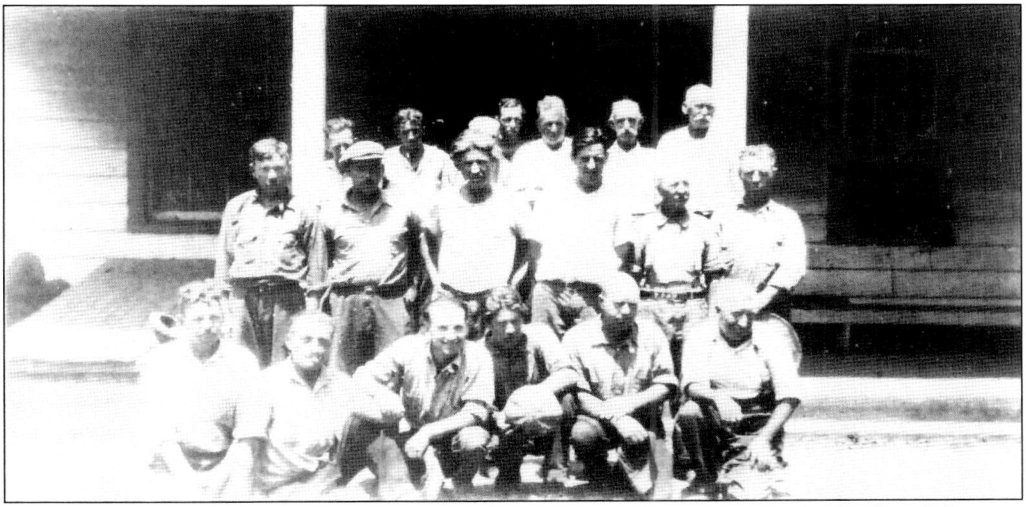

A Brookdale Farm crew is shown here c. 1920s. William P. Thompson bought the farm following Withers' death in 1892. It was left to his son Louis Steenrod Thompson; his widow Geraldine Thompson willed much of Brookdale to Monmouth County for the establishment of a county park. Another segment was purchased by the county in 1967 from Lewis Thompson Jr. for the establishment of a county community college.

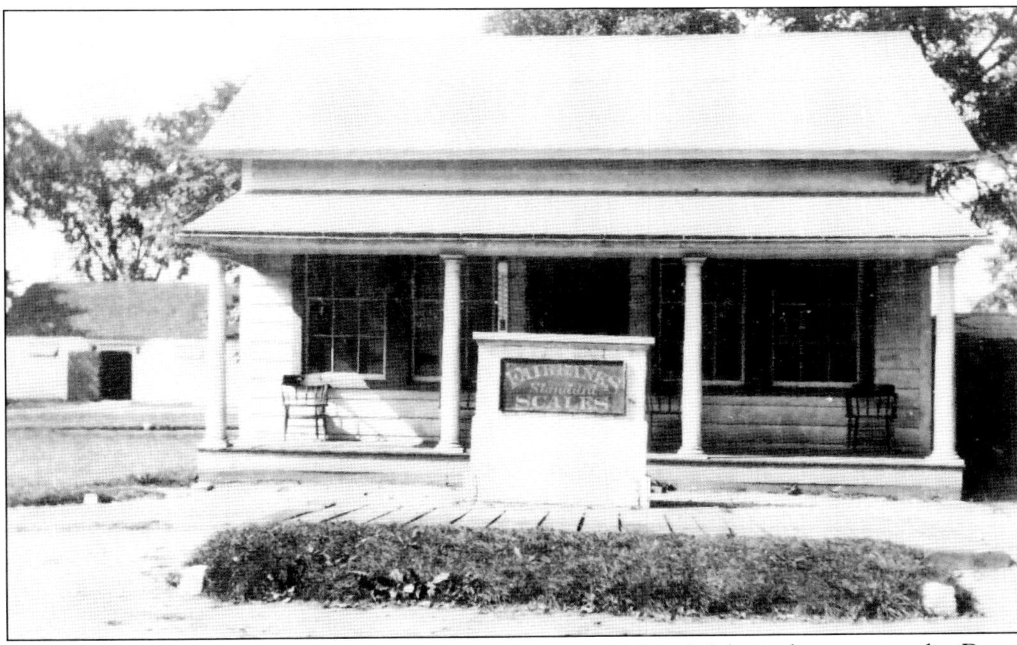

The former scale house is located at the western stem of Brookdale Park, opposite the David Withers Forty Horse Barn. It is known as the Farm Office and has been used for a variety of recreational activities.

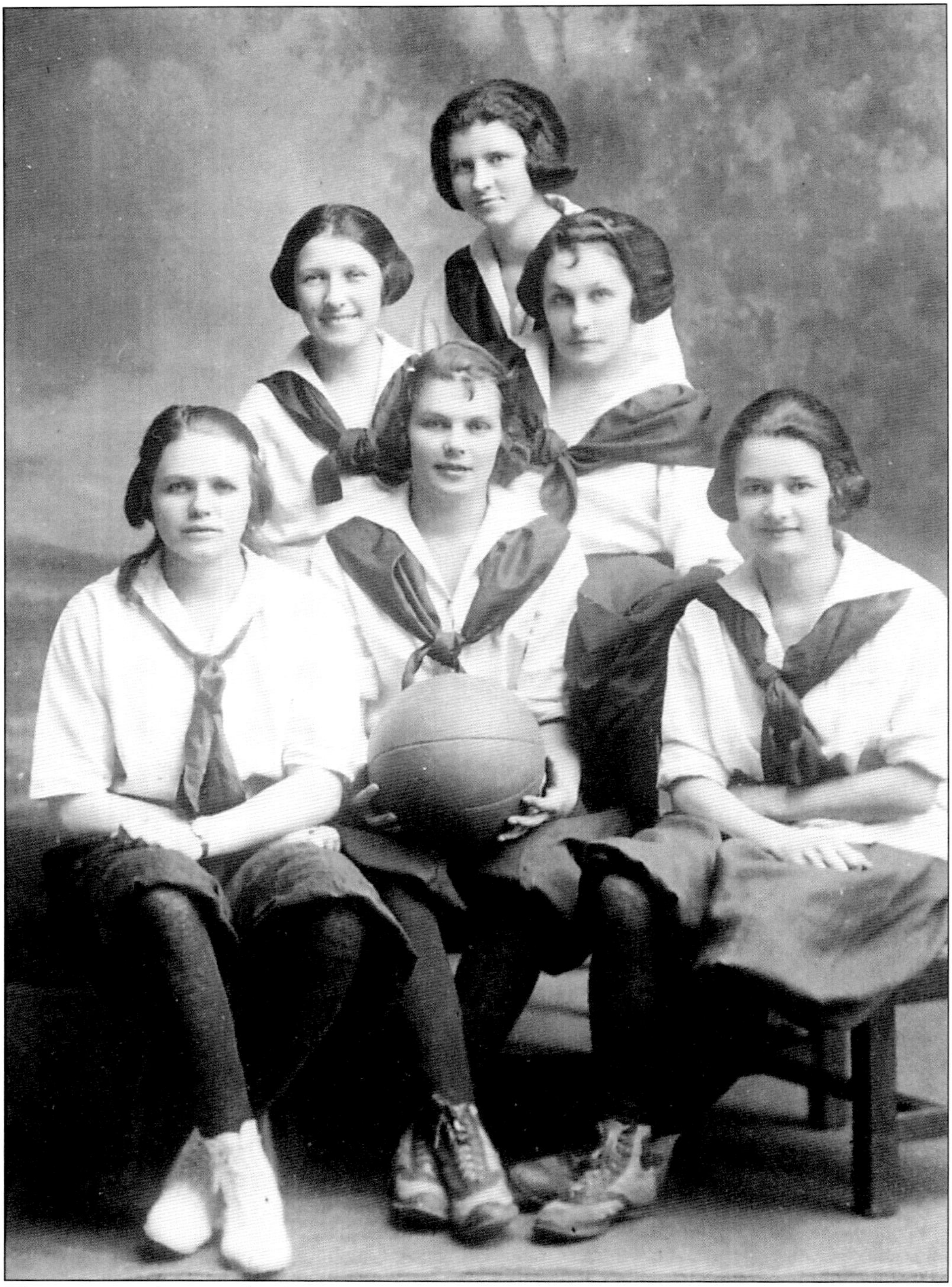

This c. 1920 photograph of a winsome group of unidentified basketball players came from a Lincroft collection, but, perhaps, they were a township high school squad. They are overdressed by today's standards, although one suspects that attire was not the origin of the girl's half-court game of the time. There were only six, so one hopes that more than one never fouled out.

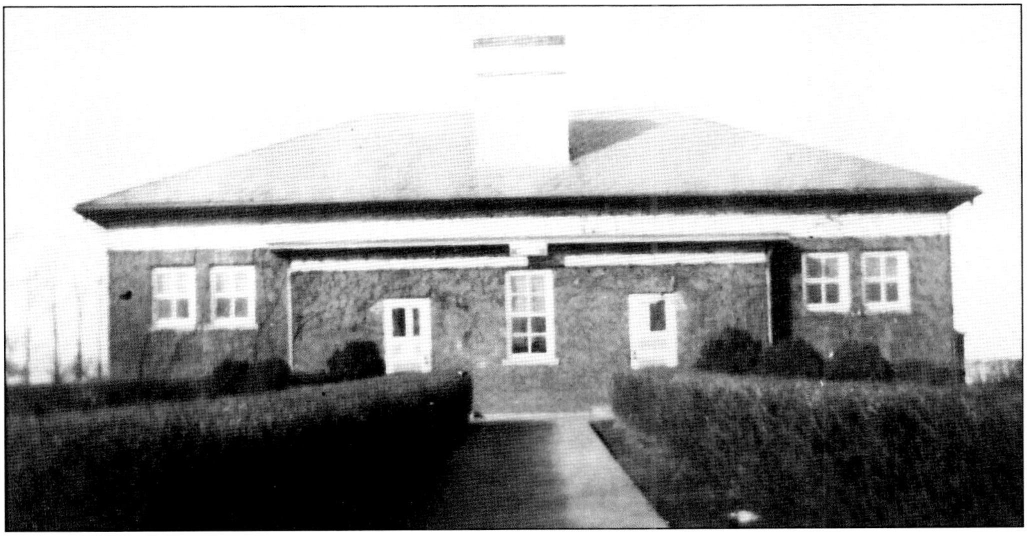

The former Lincroft Elementary School at 722 Newman Springs Road, seen here c. 1920s, was built in 1907 during a period of modernization for many township schools. It served as an annex for a number of years after the present Lincroft Elementary School was built in 1957. It is now the Lincroft Branch of the Middletown Public Library.

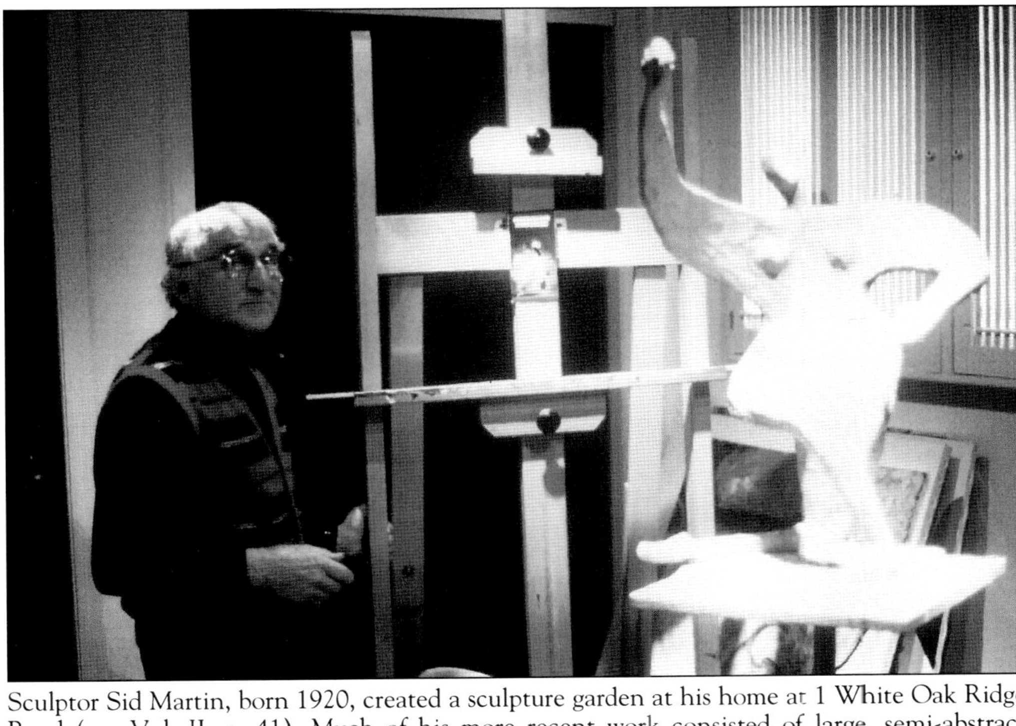

Sculptor Sid Martin, born 1920, created a sculpture garden at his home at 1 White Oak Ridge Road (see Vol. II, p. 41). Much of his more recent work consisted of large, semi-abstract fiberglass figures, often in action or contemplative poses. He is seen in his studio with a frequent design inspiration, a photograph on the easel, and a clay maquette of the type sent to a foundry for enlargement and casting. Sid's passing on April 26, 1996, left the art world poorer for his absence.

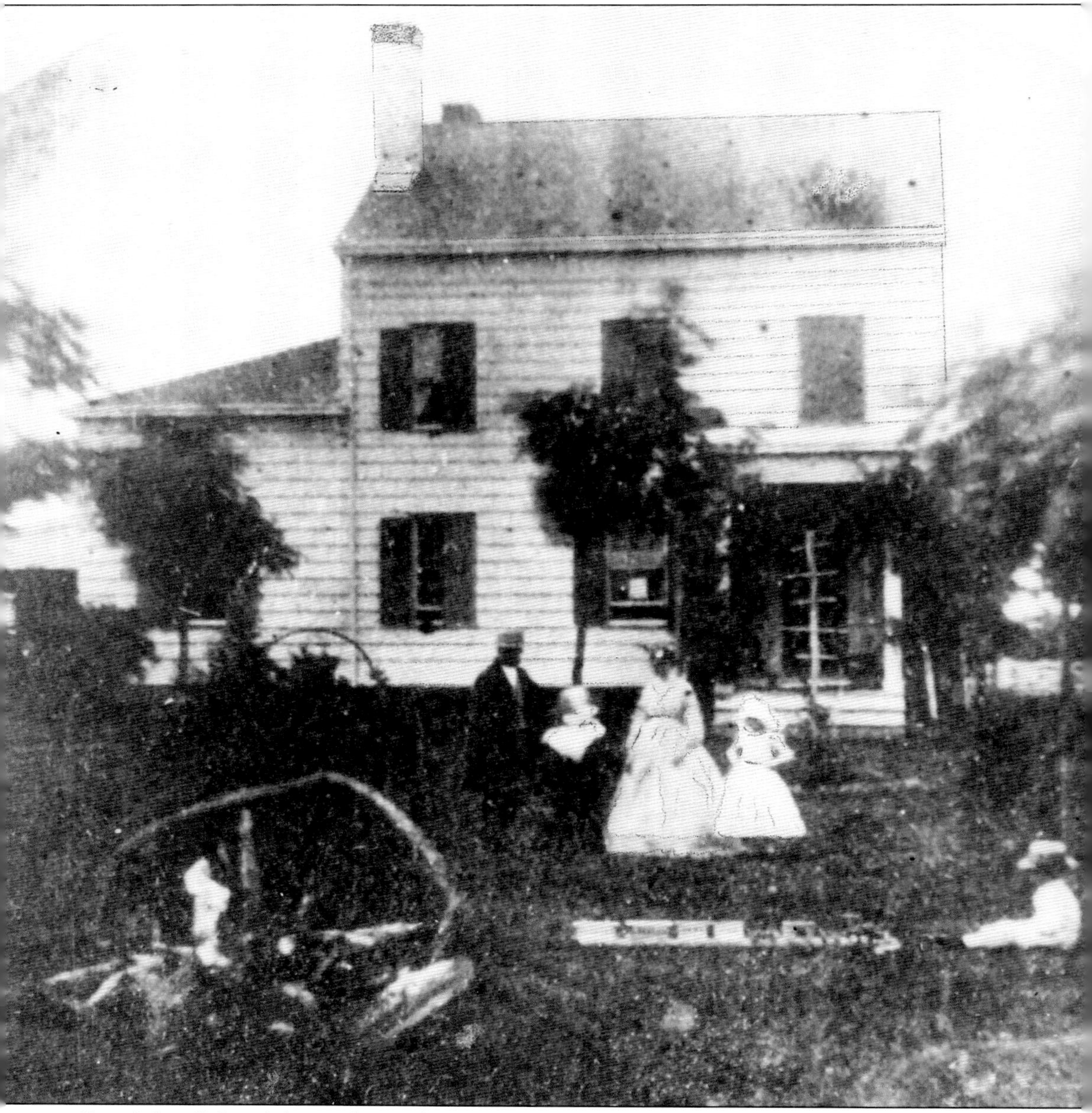

Ezra Asher Osborn's house, located on Red Hill Road east of Middletown's border with Holmdel, was probably built around the middle of the nineteenth century. An 1886 view with a wing added to the right is on p. 28 of Volume II. This image dates to c. 1861, as inferred from the Osborn's youngest child, Susan. Their elder daughter Mary is beside her mother Sarah, while son Frank is in the foreground. Osborn began his career in his father's harness-making shop, although he later abandoned the trade and became a notable land surveyor. He was politically active and died in 1895. The farm was bought in 1903 by Mrs. Norman Munro, widow of the publisher of the well-known *Munro's Magazine*, whose Long Branch house was destroyed by fire in 1902. (With special thanks to Katharine Bartlett.)

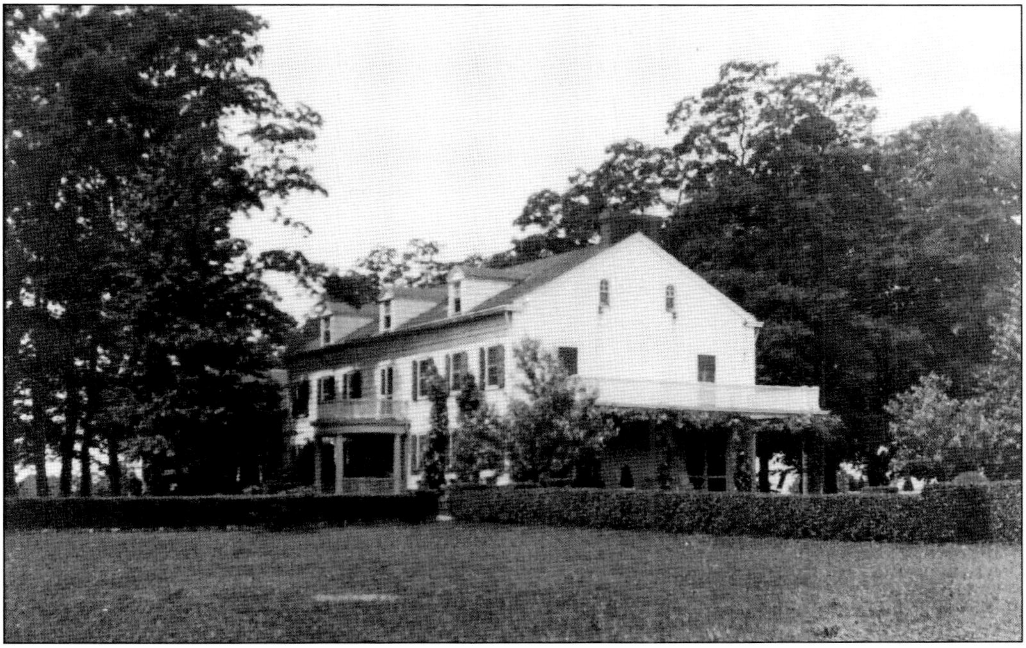

The Ezra Asher Osborn house was given an extensive Colonial Revival remodeling, probably during the Munro years, with this view likely c. 1920s. The place was bought by Edward D. Lentilhon in 1914, who long operated Deep Dale Farm, a name recalled in the Deepdale houses. The house, later owned by Matthew Gill, was destroyed by fire in March 1967 after Gill was denied permission to open a restaurant there.

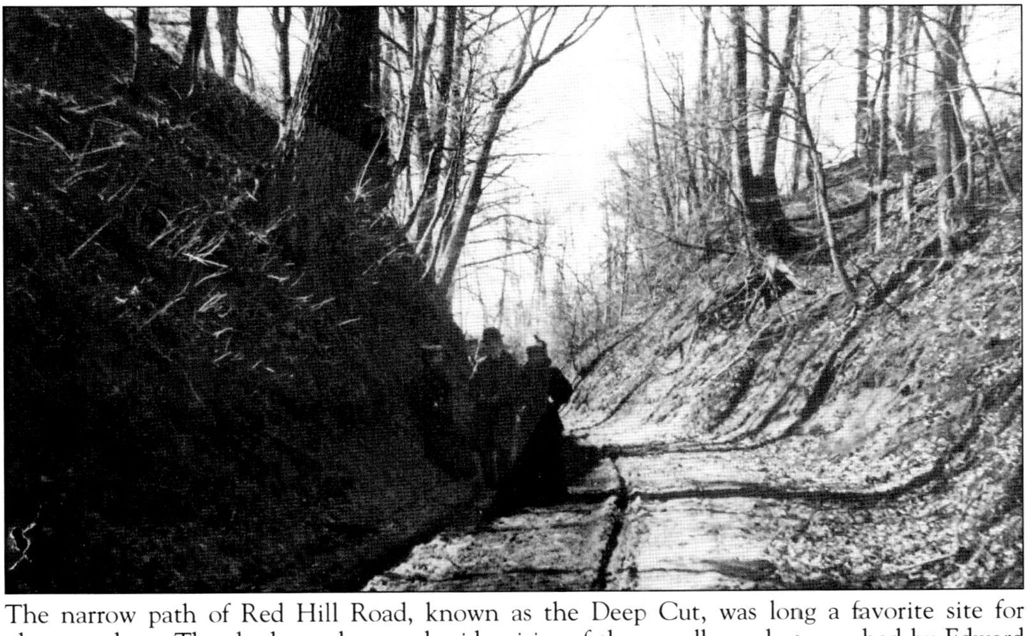

The narrow path of Red Hill Road, known as the Deep Cut, was long a favorite site for photographers. The shadows obscure the identities of these walkers photographed by Edward Taylor. One attempts to date photographs of the site by the width of the road, with this c. 1890s view reflecting conditions similar to those on p. 68 of Volume II.

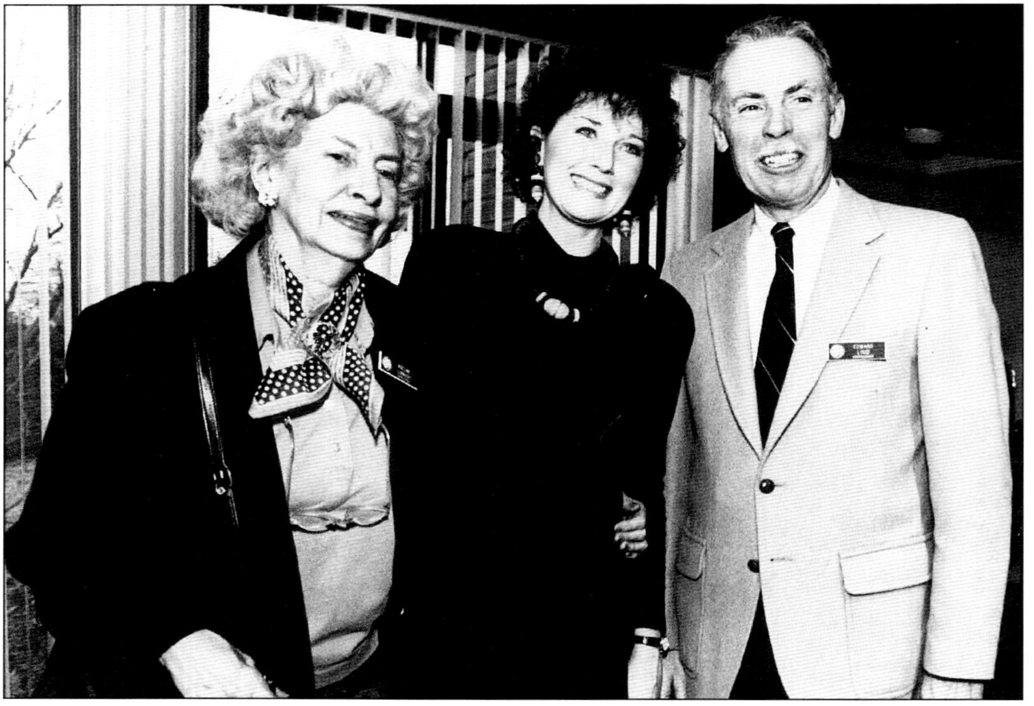

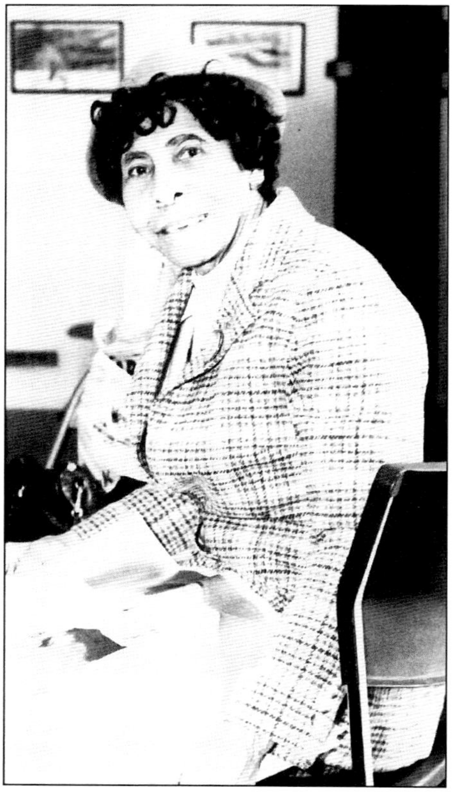

Jane Clark (center), a social psychology graduate of the University of Kentucky, is the community extension program director for the Monmouth County Park System. She has organized and run the system's annual African-American History Celebration at the Heath Wing of the Tatum Park Red Hill Activity Center since its 1984 inception. She is seen here flanked by Adeline Lubkert and Edward Loud, the present chairman and vice-chairman of the Monmouth County Board of Recreation Commissioners.

Bertha Clara Heath was born 1909 in Middletown at the family farm, the daughter of former slave Clinton P. Heath (Vol. I, p. 42) and his wife, Mary. After graduation from Leonardo High School, she became a nurse in New York, earning a B.S. from New York University in 1948 and a master's degree in public health from Columbia University in 1959. The original farm has been reduced over the years, with the homestead destroyed by fire. Bertha lives on Harmony Road, where she is establishing the Health Memorial Garden. She has long been dedicated to honoring her family; one of her generous gestures was a donation to help build the Heath Wing of the Tatum Park Red Hill Activity Center.

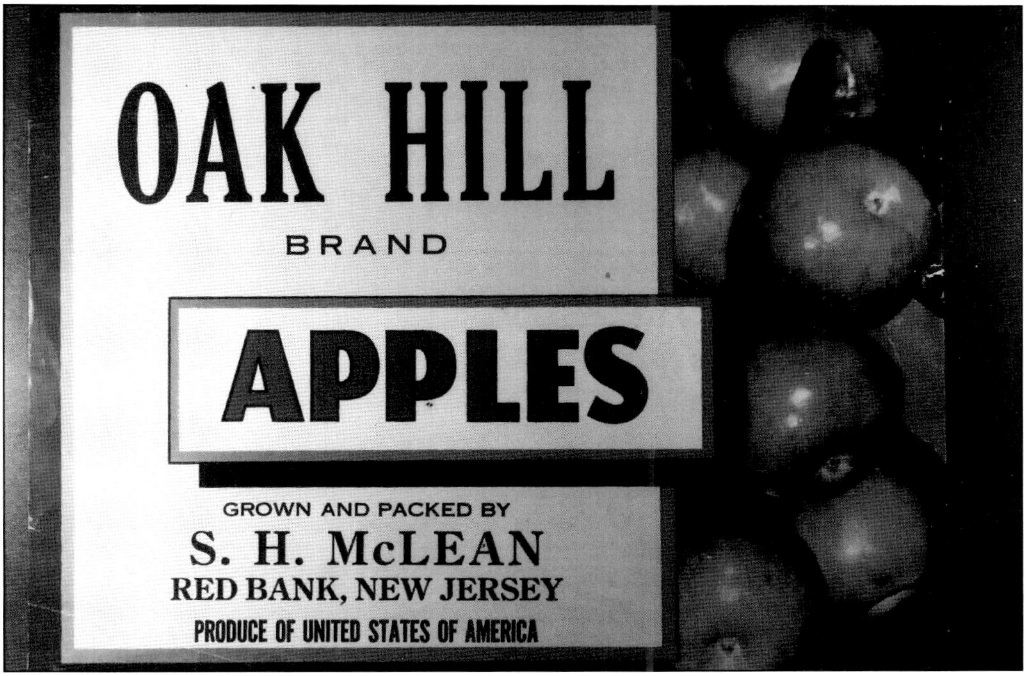

McLean's orchard fronted on Oak Hill Road and is seen on the overleaf. Its locale was entirely Middletown Township; the fruit crate label, perhaps c. 1940s, reflects a shipping and/or mail address. (Collection of Glenn Vogel.)

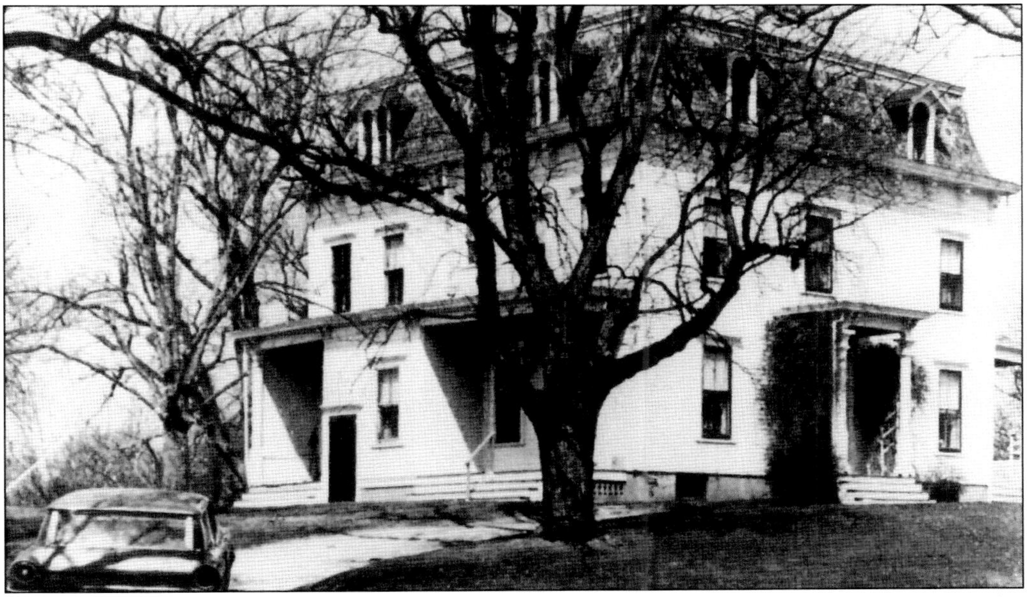

The rear of the Second Empire style McLean house on Oak Hill Road is seen in 1961 at the time of its greatest notoriety, when some scenes in Arthur Penn's *The Miracle Worker* were filmed there. The front is in Volume I on p. 37. It is dated stylistically as c. 1870s, when it replaced the old Stillwell house, then still retained on the premises. Both are visible on the overleaf, uncomfortably close to the fold.

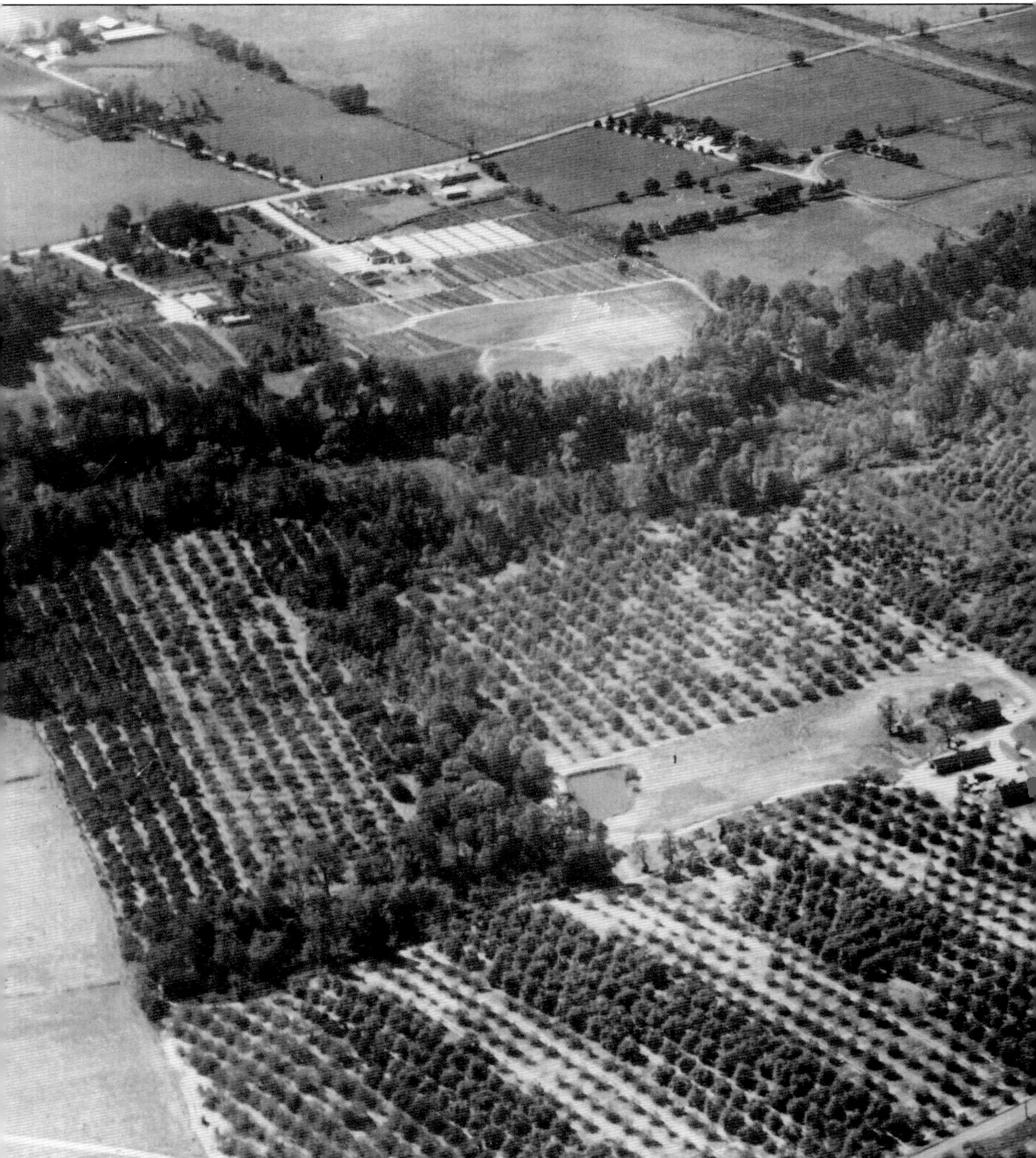

The McLean orchards, 126 acres on Oak Hill Road that comprised the remainder of Joseph Stillwell's (a McLean ancestor's) reported 500-acre tract, was sold in 1967 for the Colts Glen housing development, seen in its entirety in this 1960 aerial. Just out of view at the bottom of the picture, the New York and Long Branch tracks run, with Oak Hill Road running diagonal from the lower left corner to the fold. The McLean and Stillwell houses are in the center, near the fold. Normandy Road (the Navy Road) curves at right. An entrance to the Murray Farm

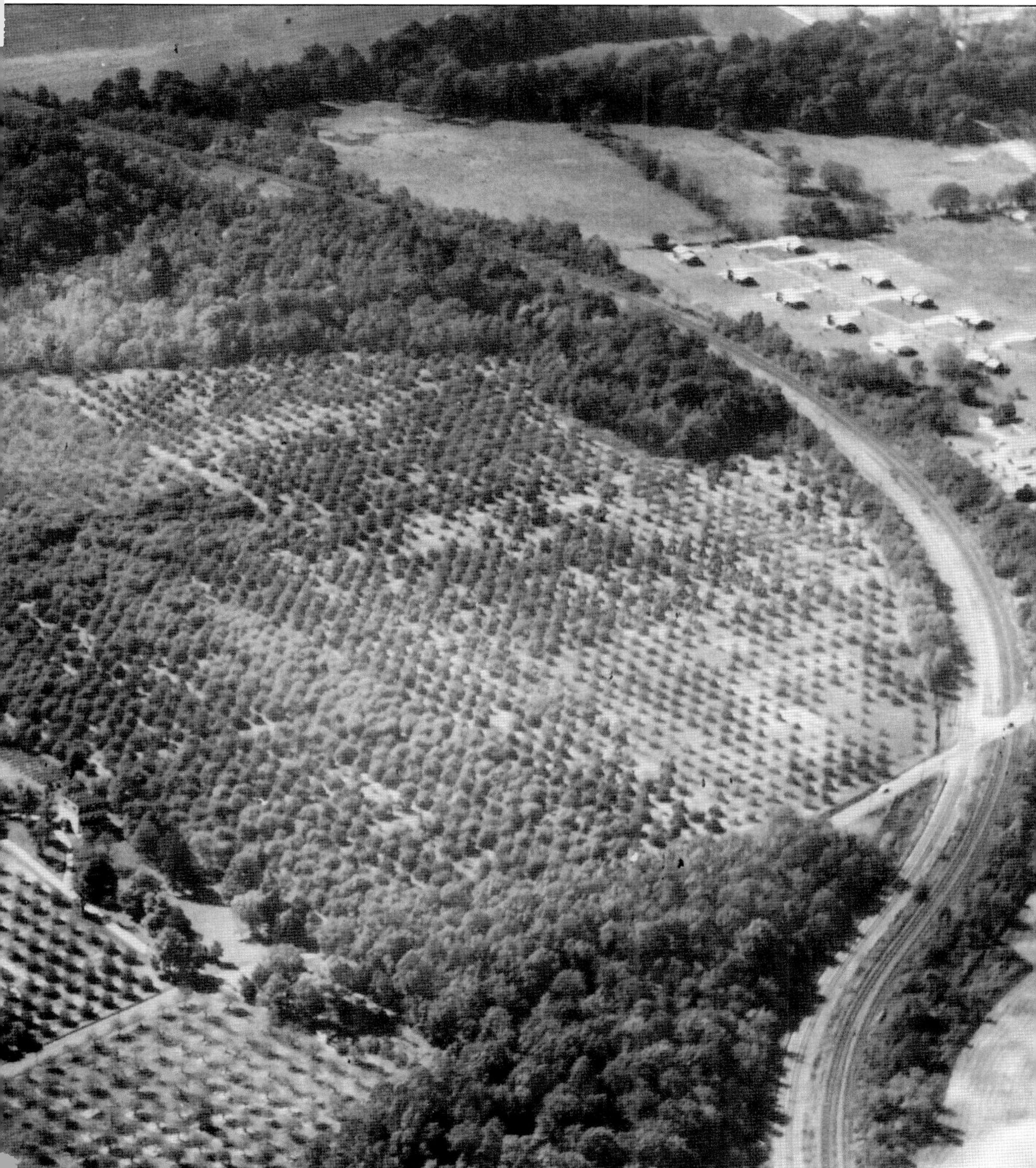

House at Poricy Park , since relocated, is in the lower left corner, near the enclosure for the railroad flag man, on the other side of the road. Nut Swamp Road is at top, leading at right to the Thomas S. Field house (Vol. II, p. 55) and the area of Nut Swamp and Thompson Schools. The location of the former driveway to the McLean house can be discerned today on the south side of Oak Hill Road by searching for the tree noticeably higher than those planted for the development.

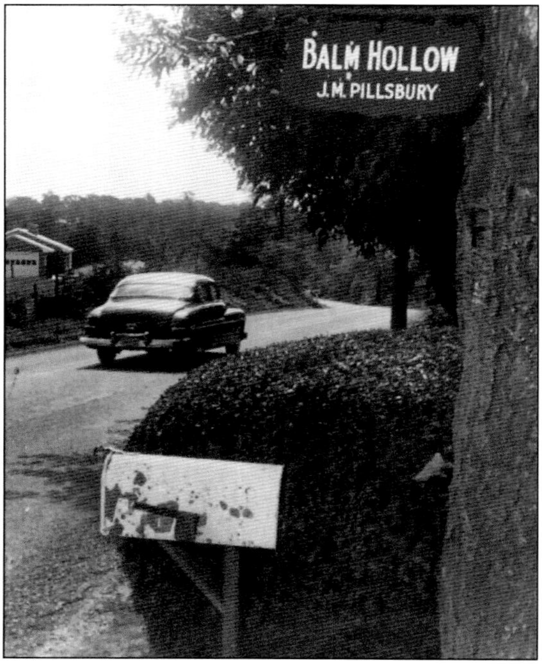

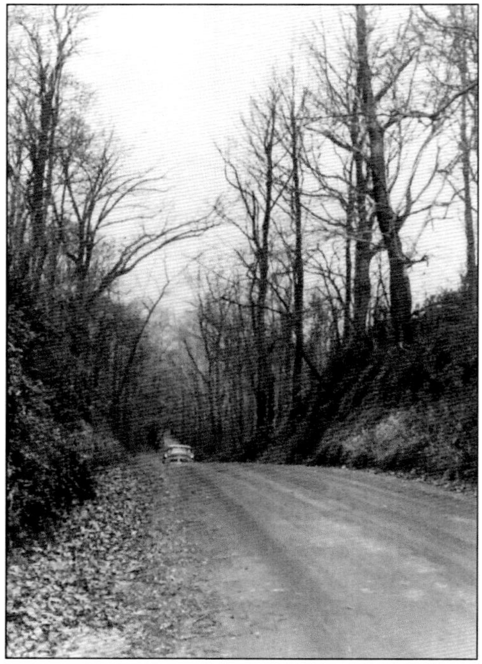

The folklorist priest, Henry C. Beck, visited Middletown *c.* 1953 seeking the legend of Bamm Hollow. One stop was the 2049 Middletown-Lincroft home of John M. Pillsbury, then so named with a variant spelling. The legends of a haunted section of woods could not be affirmed, but Beck's photographer, William Augustine, preserved images of a then-rural path that is now a well-traveled secondary highway, part of the county road system. The view at left is south, looking towards Iler Drive. The scene at right is not identified, but is probably close to Bamm Hollow Road. (Special Collections and Archives, Rutgers University Libraries.)

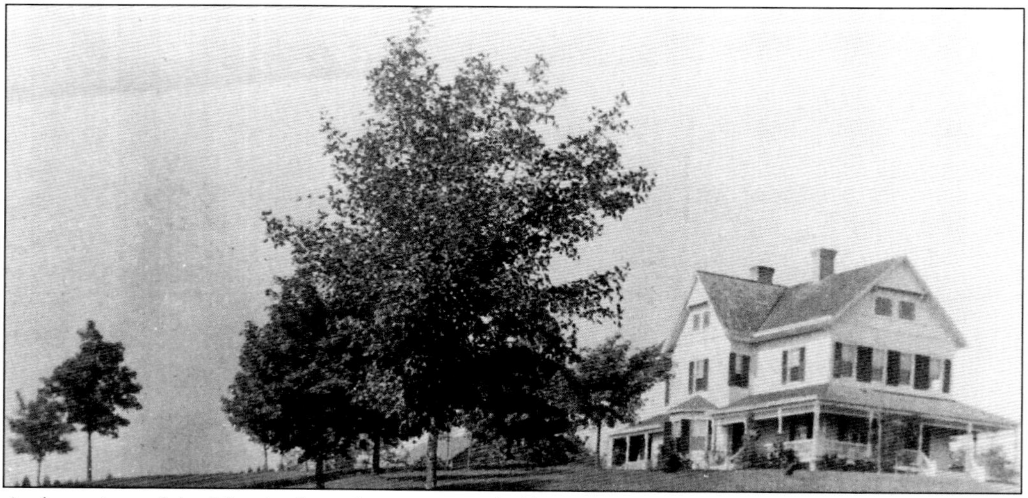

A close view of the Hendrickson house expanded by Robert Adamson in the 1920s is in Volume II on p. 51. The hilltop setting is one of the most appealing features of 2049 Middletown-Lincroft Road, one that inspired former owner Louanne Pillsbury to exclaim, "On a clear night I feel that I can reach out and nearly touch the stars." The recently refurbished house has long had a Colonial Revival appearance.

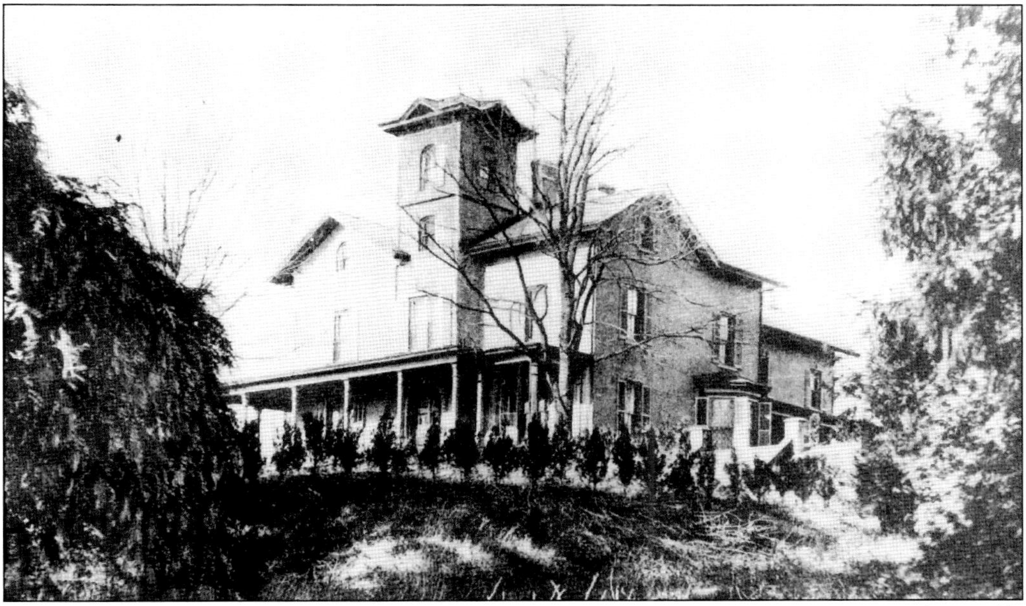

Elnathan T. Field bought a large farm *c.* 1860s and built one of the county's finest Italian Villa houses in 1878 at the northeast corner of Middletown-Lincroft and Oak Hill Roads. It is seen here in a 1920s postcard, while greenhouses of Field's Oak Hill Nursery can be seen in Volume II on p. 52. He also engaged in dairy farming and was an investor in a failed Florida coconut-growing project, which was tried on land that became Key Biscayne and Coconut Grove. The house stands at 600 Oak Hill Road, although new housing close to it has marred its once-fine site. (Collection of Michael Steinhorn.)

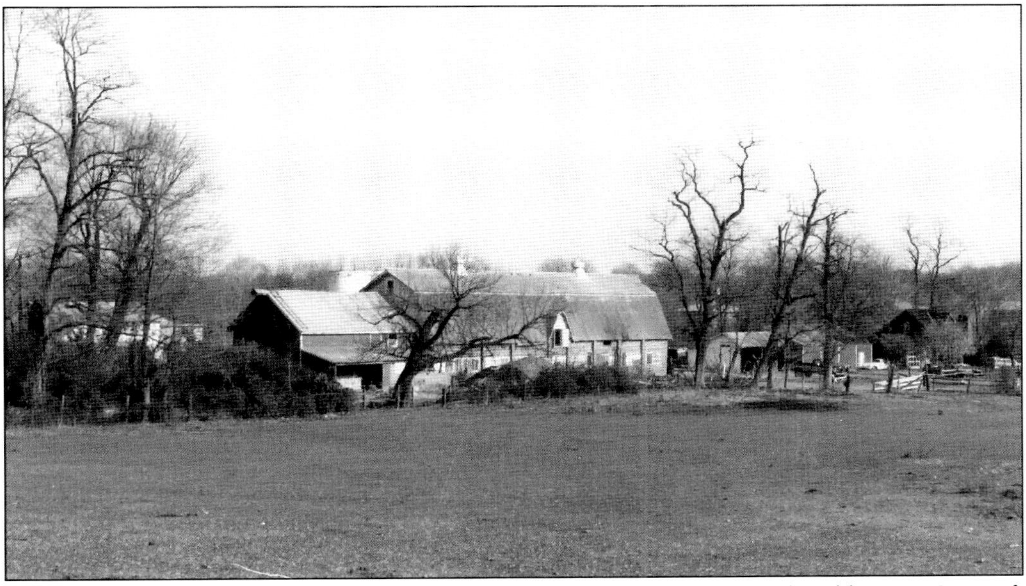

The Alexander B. Iler Sr. Farm, Rolling Knolls, located on the east side of Middletown-Lincroft Road and south of the railroad parking lot, was developed in the 1970s as housing with the tract retaining the name. Its barn, viewed here in 1984, stood until a *c.* 1990 expansion of the development.

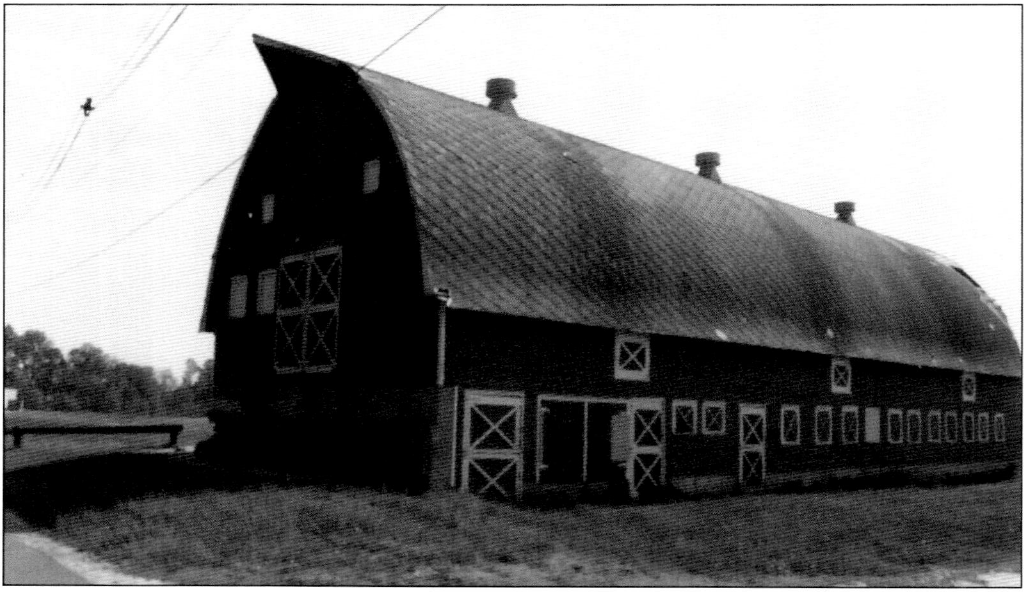

Charles Brasch's mid-nineteenth-century barn on Nut Swamp Road, near Middletown-Lincroft Road, was destroyed by fire on October 9, 1934. He built this one as a replacement in the following two months. It was designed by the Jamesway Company, measured 34 -by-96 feet, was built over a concrete foundation, and was reported to have modern facilities for cattle. It is seen in 1984, when used by the township for storage.

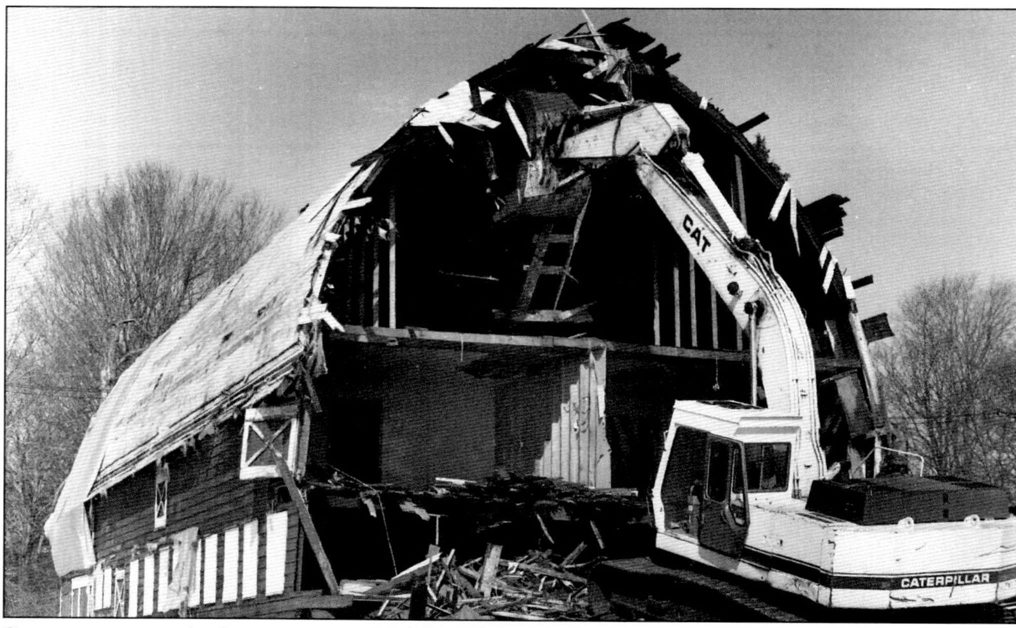

Support to save the barn was vocal, although local opposition over its proposed use as a youth center was louder. Rising costs to repair a sadly neglected building may have precluded its rescue. Scott Longfield photographed its demolition on March 9, 1994. At least two lessons should be learned: reuse should be planned while buildings are still salvageable, and an ounce of preventive maintenance is worth a pound of restorative care.

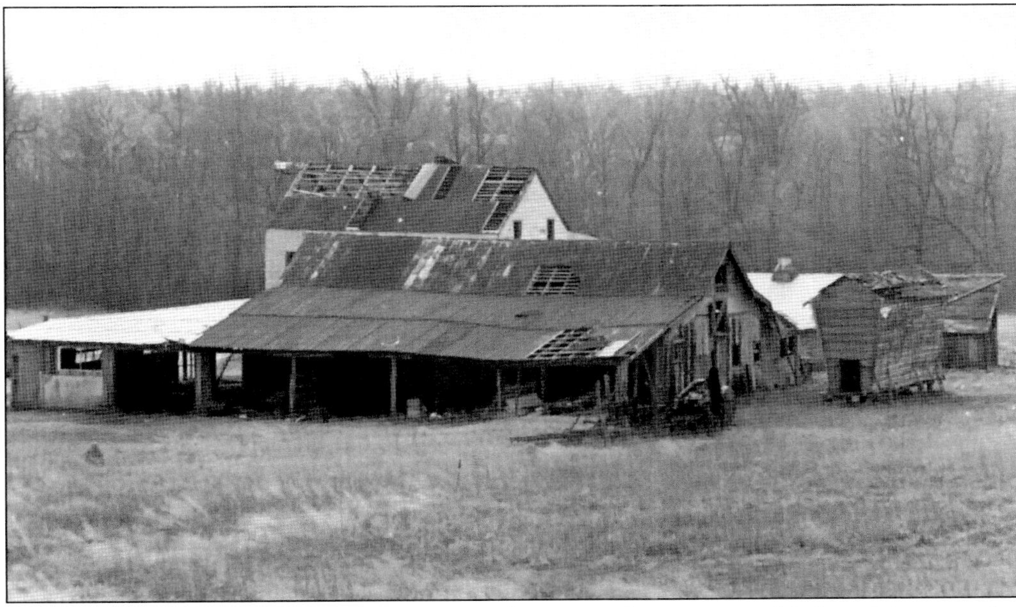

The barn complex at the Murray farm contained an array of structures usable for a dairy operation through c. 1970, but examination by the Poricy Park Citizens Committee, which occupied the place in 1975, revealed little of historic merit worthy of preservation. The two-story structure, however, dated from Joseph Murray's time. The township began demolition in January 1976 following about three years of pleading due to its deteriorating condition.

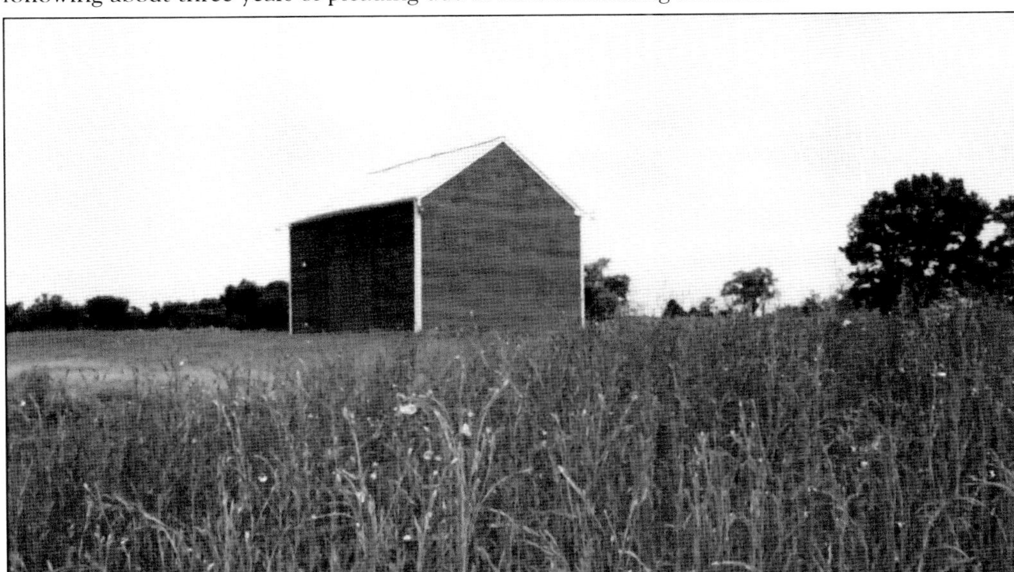

The restoration project was led by noted restoration architect Charles Detweiler. A sketch in William Nelson's *The New Jersey Coast* provided a guide, an illustration that includes a western wing, no longer part of the structure. The barn's fine, restored condition is the result of long, ongoing work, including a recent re-roofing. It is used for a variety of historic and nature programs, including the planting of flax, as evidenced in this 1995 photograph by Paul "Pete" Brady.

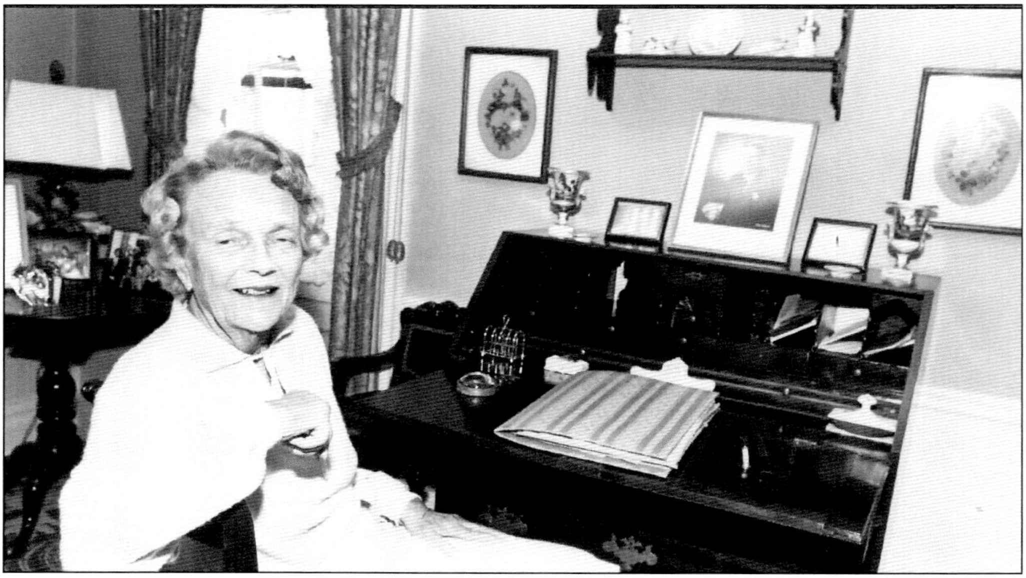

Katherine K. Neuberger, born a Kridel in New York City in 1907, married Harry H. Neuberger in 1929 and moved to Middletown from Long Island after their 1933 purchase of Sunnyside Farm. She began political activity at the local level, rising to prominence at the national level of Republican circles at a time when the party embraced liberals. Neuberger was a 1927 graduate of Barnard College and had a life-long interest in education, long serving on New Jersey's Board of Higher Education in one of her numerous public appointments. She died in 1982.

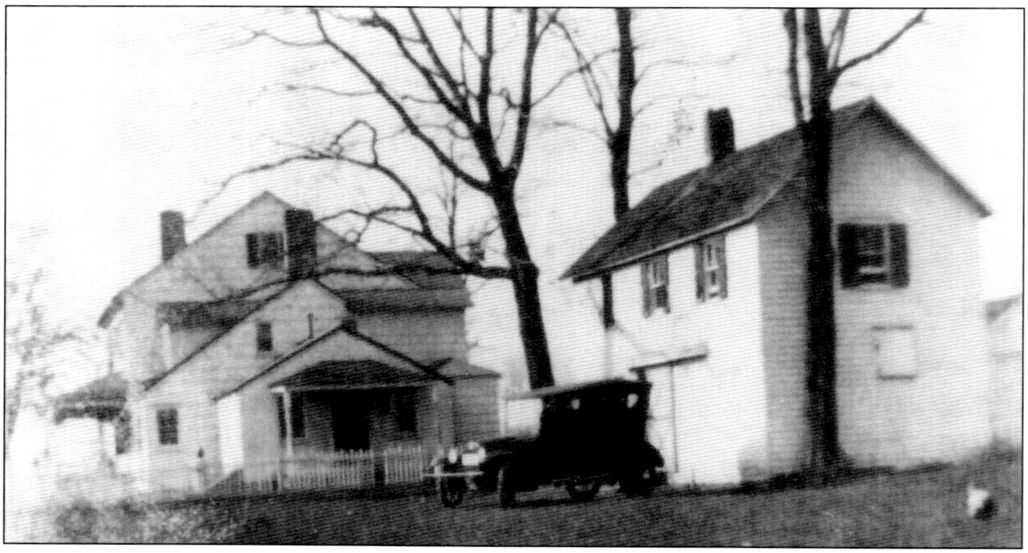

John H. Vernell farmed Sunnyside, the place known recently as the Neuberger Farm and historically as the Grover-Johnson Farm, from 1909–1926. This *c.* 1920 view is west of the main house at 600 Middletown-Lincroft Road, seen in Volume I on p. 20 before and after 1933 buyer Harry Neuberger's remodeling. The barn no longer stands. The car could be the 1918 Buick John gave his daughter Elizabeth A. Vernell before she or anyone in the family could drive. (A Monmouth County Park System copy print furnished by Elizabeth Burbank.)

Elizabeth V. Vernell, a serious amateur photographer, took this self portrait in the hall of the Sunnyside house c. 1920s, her visage marred by the lengthy exposure time needed to capture the dark hall. The Neuberger remodeling changed the fixtures and paper, but the stairs, paneling, and floors are in a fine state of preservation. Vernell's father gave up farming Sunnyside around 1926, the year his wife died. (A Monmouth County Park System copy print furnished by Elizabeth Burbank.)

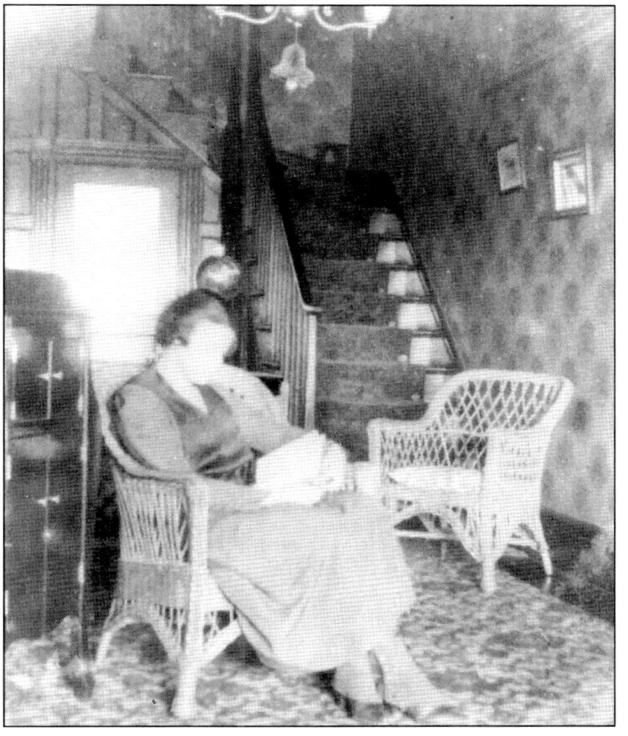

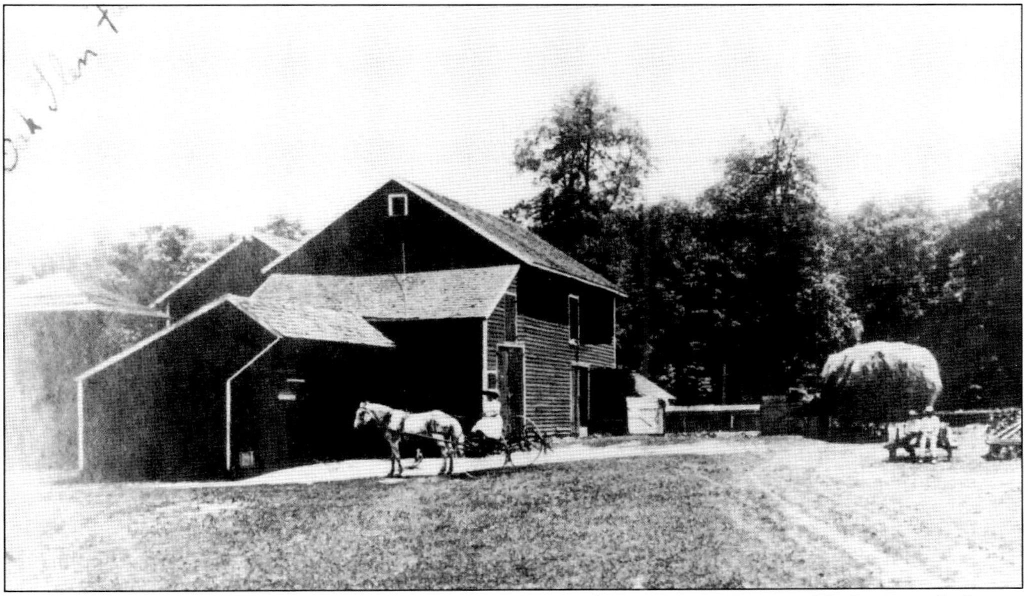

James F. Crawford, a later owner of the Grover-Johnson Farm, assembled several farms, distinguishing his holdings by calling each a traditional name. His Oak Glen farm was northwest of Sunnyside, beyond Nut Swamp Brook; this ground is now covered, in part, by the Bamm Hollow golf course and the Garden State Parkway. Eleven-year-old Elizabeth Vernell was photographed in 1908 on a cultivator in front of a no-longer-standing barn. (A Monmouth County Park System copy print furnished by Elizabeth Burbank.)

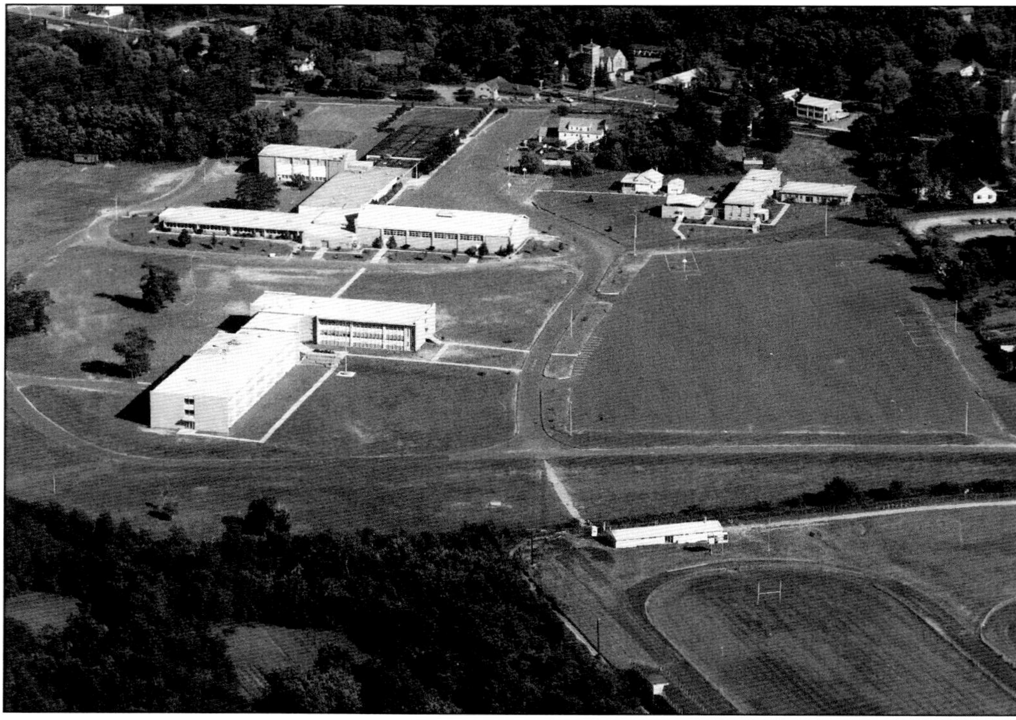

St. Mary's Roman Catholic Church is at the top of this *c.* 1969 aerial, with its educational and other buildings in front of it. Mater Dei High School, dedicated in 1965, is the L-shaped building in the center of the picture in front of St. Mary's School. It opened in September 1953 and has been altered a few times since. The one- and one-half-story building in front of the church is an old barn, earlier remodeled into a convent and now a nursery school. A new convent is to the right.

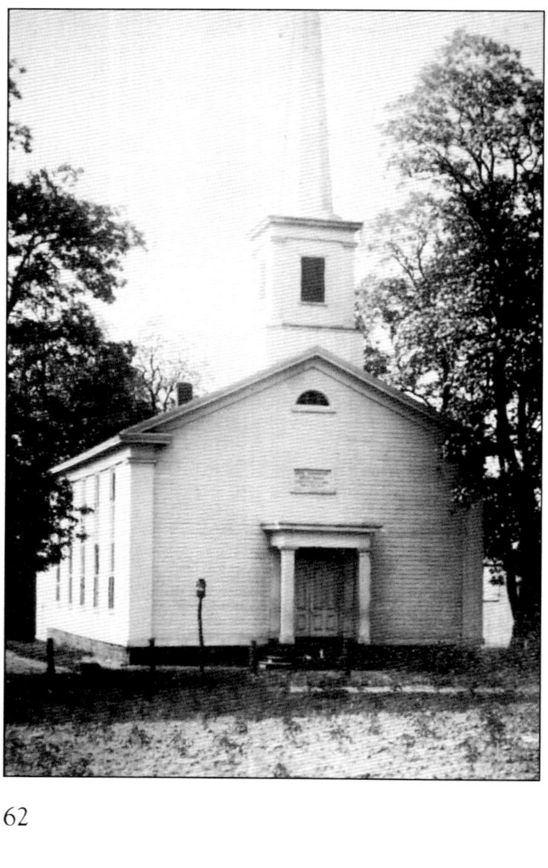

The New Monmouth Baptist Church, at the southwest corner of New Monmouth and Cherry Tree Farm Roads, was built in 1855 following its April 28, 1854 organization. The well-preserved church is readily recognizable today, but one major change distinguishes this *c.* 1910 image from that on p. 73 of Volume II: the absence of the Sunday school addition built in 1916.

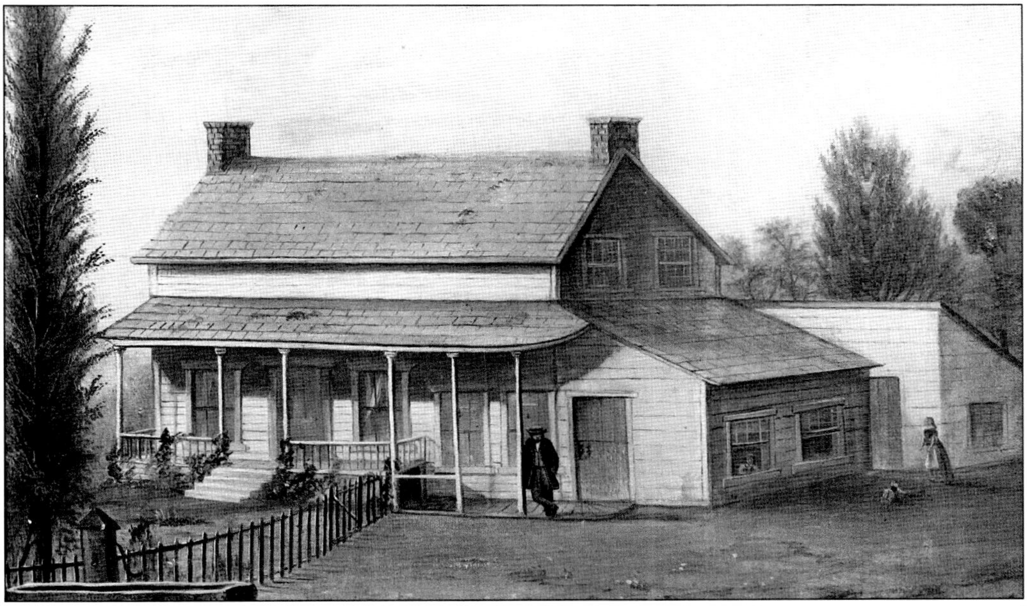

This is an unidentified artist's conjectural sketch of the eighteenth-century appearance of 1 Cherry Tree Farm Road, long a Morford residence and once the seat of a large farm. It may also have been the site of William Morford's store. Old posts and beams reflect its early origins, which the house's lore attributes to 1765. The house rests on a stuccoed, hollow-tile foundation, dating from the moving of the building when the road was widened, likely early this century.

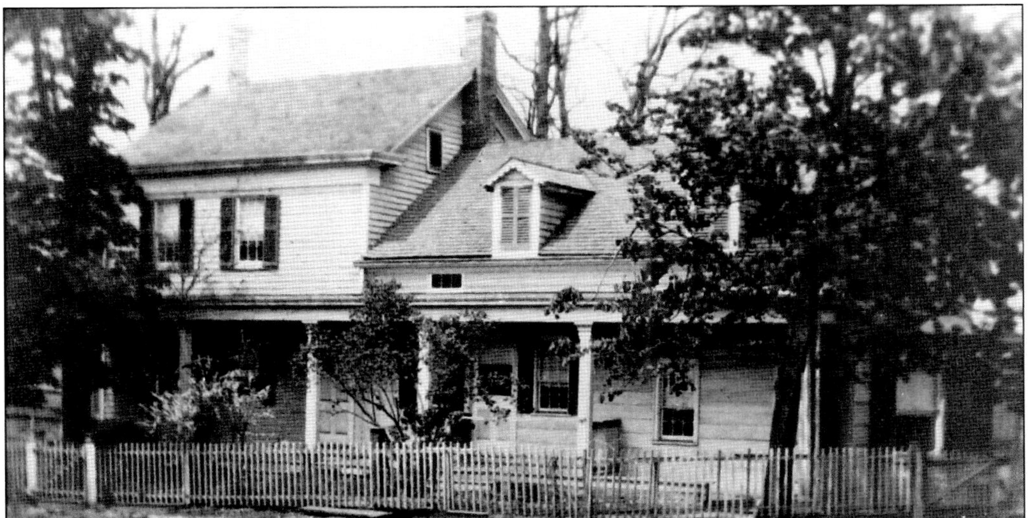

Van Pelt & Sons Insurance Agency now owns 1 Cherry Tree Farm Road. Accepting the artist's conjecture, the west end was built up to two and one-half stories, as seen in an apparent late-nineteenth-century image. Changes since that time include one larger dormer in lieu of two in the eastern section, a new exterior chimney added in the 1960s on the west, smaller windows in the upper story, a new porch and columns, and modern windows on the first floor. The lean-to at top is gone, with a bay window added to the first floor east elevation.

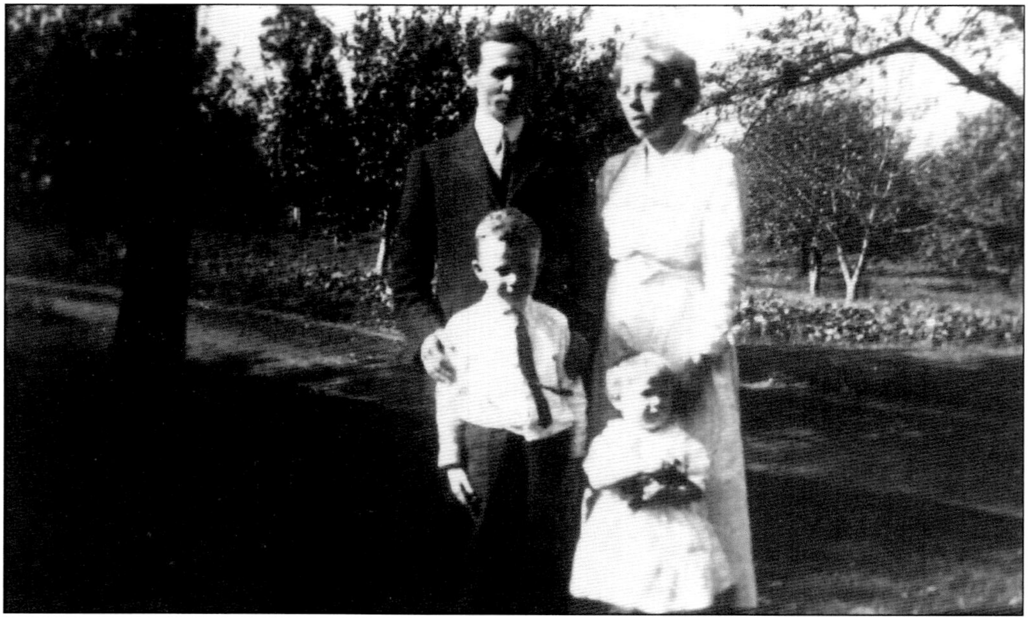

Howard W. Roberts, born in 1887 to William and Marianna Conover Roberts , married Carrie Phillips Penterman on June 20, 1912. He was a life-long resident of New Monmouth, at the Roberts Road farm as a youth and at 146 New Monmouth Road during his adult life. Howard and Carrie had two children, Frederick and Elizabeth. Roberts was valedictorian of the Atlantic Highlands High School class of 1904 but had to forgo a college scholarship. He began work as a stenographer in the law office of Charles R. Snyder, studied law with him, and was admitted to the bar in 1909.

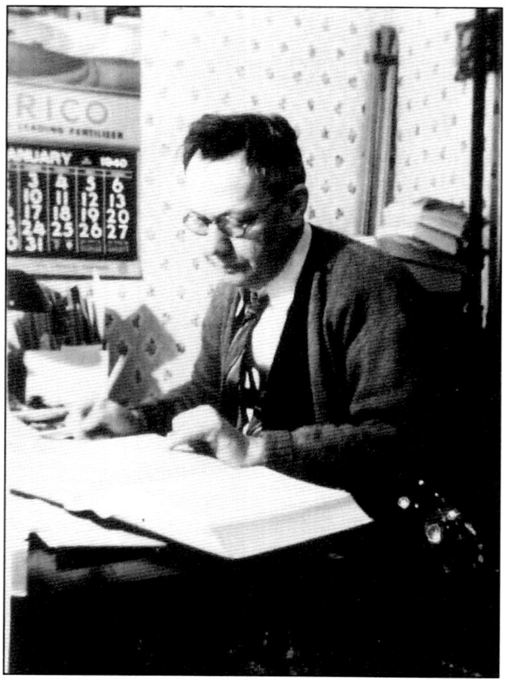

Howard W. Roberts, appointed township clerk in 1913, was regularly elected through 1926 when he assumed tenure in the office. His power grew in that unassuming position, to the point where he virtually ruled Middletown Township and rose to a number-two position in the county. His legal work and political activities intertwined, with Roberts holding numerous public counsel positions. Roberts was mindful of the electoral process and cultivated all voting groups. He was hard-working, gave his time to many organizations, and achieved great public esteem. Roberts was disabled in 1964 and died in 1966.

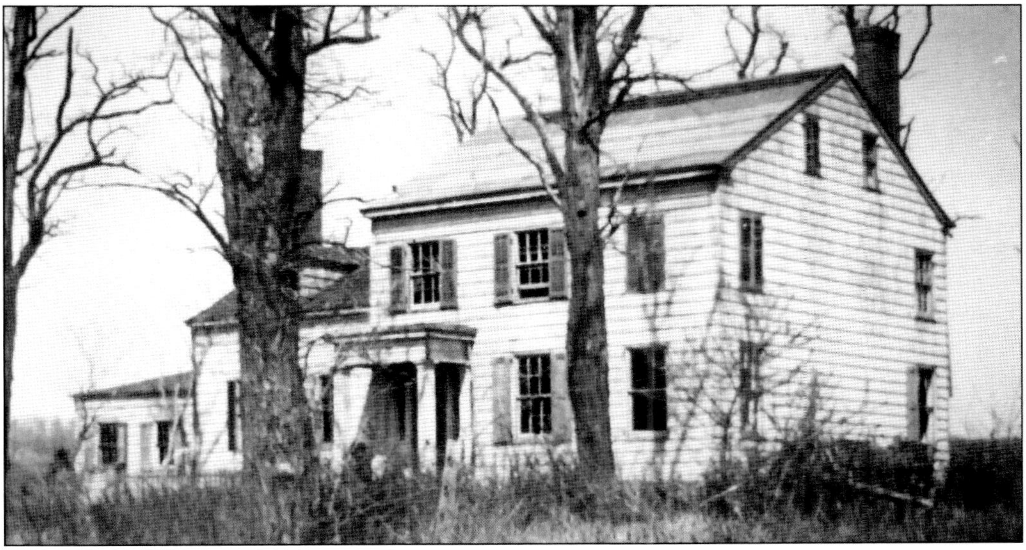

H. Norman Hoyt bought the 170-acre Dr. Edward Taylor farm between Chapel Hill and Sleepy Hollow Roads in 1937. Perhaps dating from the second quarter of the nineteenth century, the farmhouse's then run-down condition is reflected in this late 1930s photograph. Hoyt did not keep the place long, perhaps discouraged by the difficulty of obtaining building material during the war; he sold it to Robert W. Crawford in 1945.

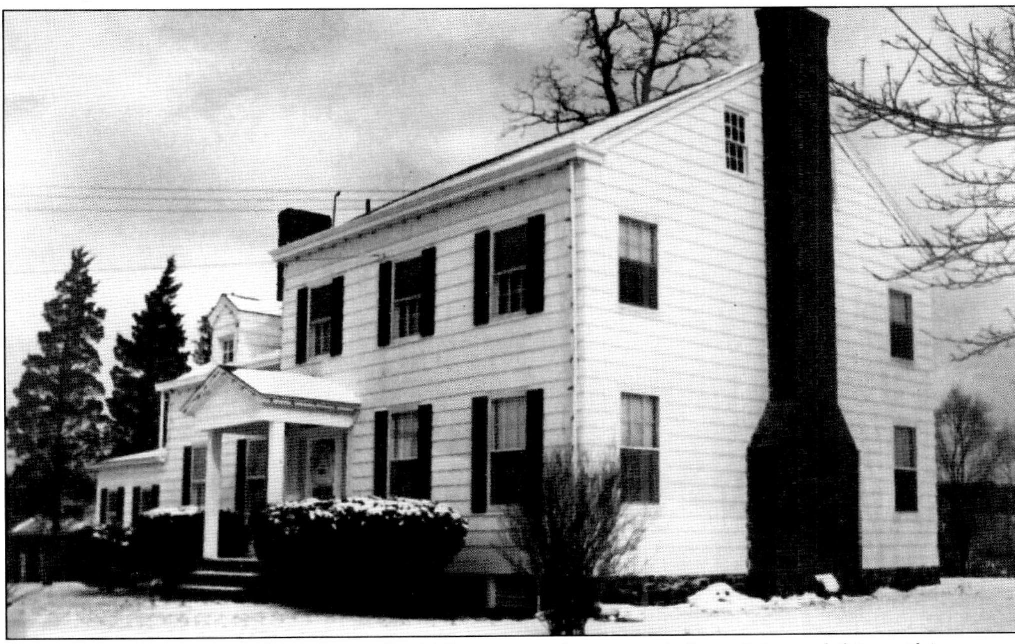

Crawford named the place Garryford Farm, a title created from his and his wife's names (his wife's name was Garretson). Crawford, an experienced building manager in New York, repaired and restored the house. This c. 1965 image reflects a new chimney and entry porch and a spruced-up appearance. The farm was developed in 1993–4 by Thomas and Ruthanne Morford—Ruthanne is Crawford's daughter—when the entrance was relocated from Sleepy Hollow Road to a development street. Its new address is 22 Garryford Drive.

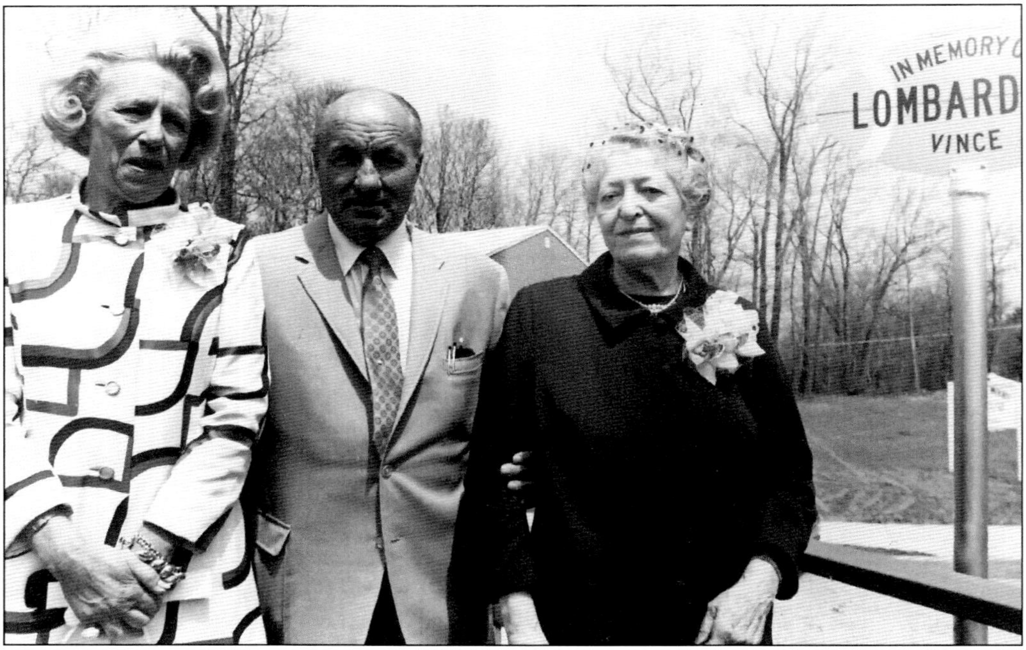

Legendary football coach Vince Lombardi, a former Fair Haven resident, died in 1970 and is buried at Mount Olivet Cemetery on Chapel Hill Road. Lombardi Court, a street running west of Chapel Hill Road opposite the cemetery, is named in his honor. Present at the April 29, 1972 ceremony are (from left to right) his widow Marie, Angelo Speciale (the developer of Harmony Woods, the street's locale), and Mathilda Lombardi (the coach's mother). The distinctive football-shaped sign was "removed" in less than a week, and replaced by a standard sign. The Vincent T. Lombardi Council of the Knights of Columbus, Middletown Township, dedicates its work to his memory and maintains his grave site.

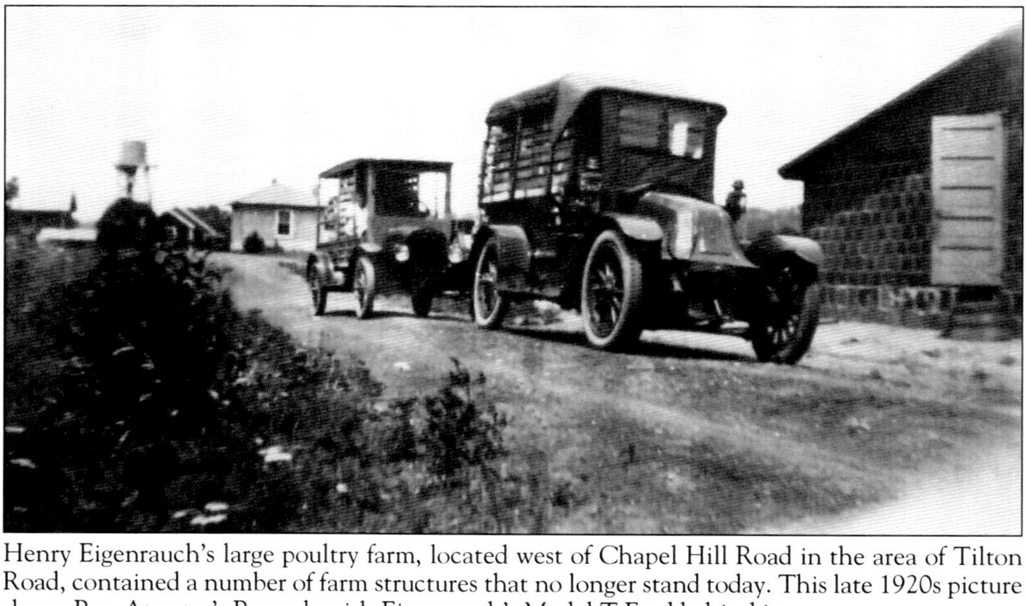

Henry Eigenrauch's large poultry farm, located west of Chapel Hill Road in the area of Tilton Road, contained a number of farm structures that no longer stand today. This late 1920s picture shows Ben Atwater's Renault with Eigenrauch's Model T Ford behind it.

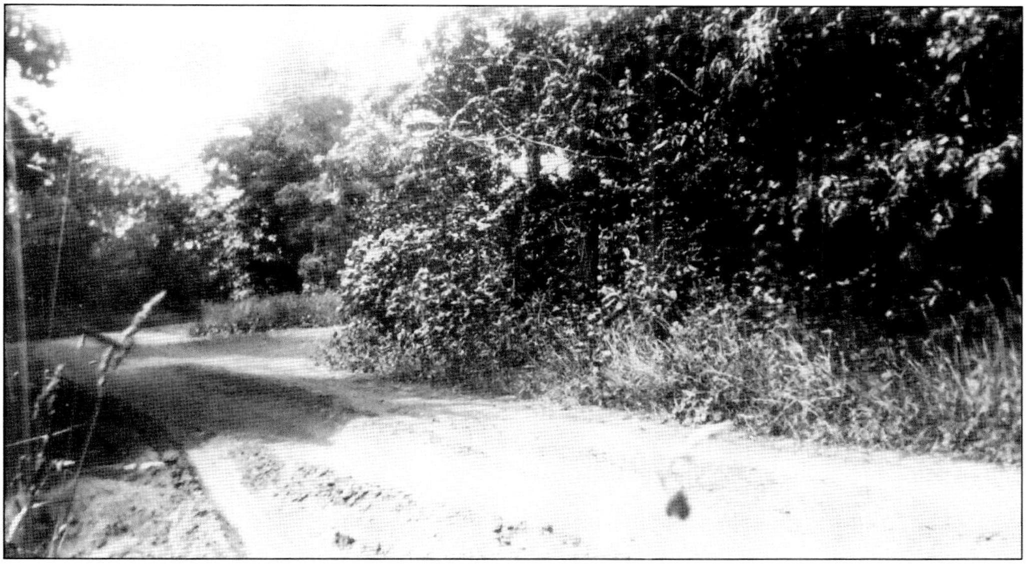

The construction of the Chapel Hill section of the Earle Naval Weapons Station cut off existing roads, explaining why Chapel Hill Road has a two-block stem south of Leonardville Road. This c. 1930s image was taken in the closed area, near Chapel Hill Road's connection with a street from the Hosford estate.

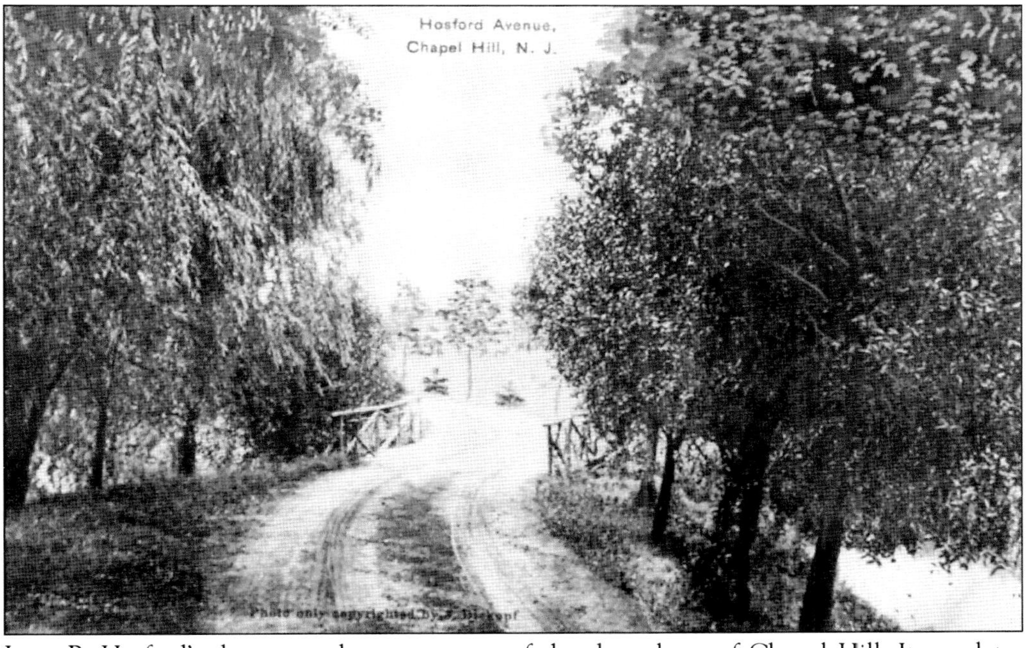

Isaac B. Hosford's three-story house was one of the showplaces of Chapel Hill. It was later a hotel, but lacking a stable future, it was destroyed by what some believe to have been an incendiary fire c. 1940s. Hosford Avenue runs south from Highway 36. This c. 1910 postcard depicts a scene likely near its connection with Stillwell Road, south of Bayview Cemetery. A picture of the house has eluded the author. Who can lend one?

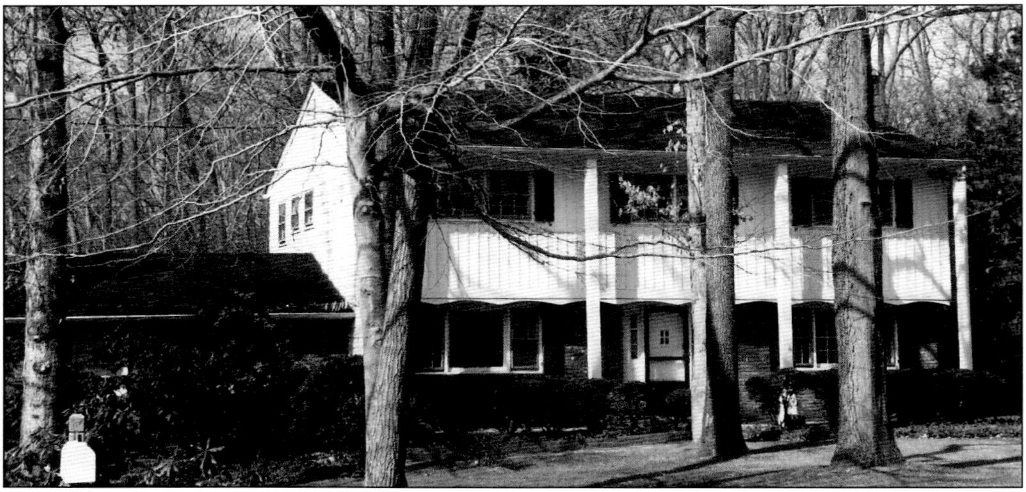

Dr. Carl Coppolino, the central figure of one of the nation's most notorious crimes of the past generation, lived at 35 Wallace Road. He was romantically involved with a neighbor, Marjorie Farber. Both Coppolino's wife and Farber's husband who lived across the street at number 50 died mysteriously in 1966. Although Coppolino was found not guilty of Lieutenant Colonel Farber's death in a Monmouth County trial, it is widely believed the verdict stemmed from a bungled case rather than innocence. Later a resident of Florida, he was convicted of his wife's murder and is now in jail.

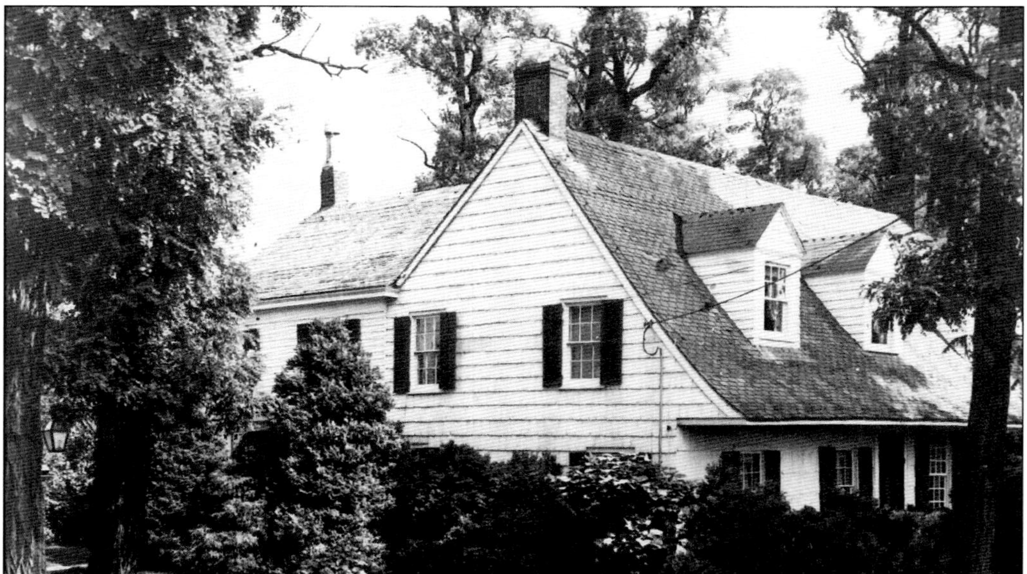

The c. 1720 Johannes Luyster house at 199 Holland Road, seen in a 1940 Historic American Buildings Survey photograph, shows the changes of the fifty-four years following the Volume II, p. 70 image. A fence is gone, mature plants surround the house, and three dormers have been built into the characteristic sloping Dutch roof. The ell in the rear is likely an addition made in the third quarter of the nineteenth century. Preserving the house, one of the township's most important homes, is one of Middletown's most urgent preservation issues at the time of this publication.

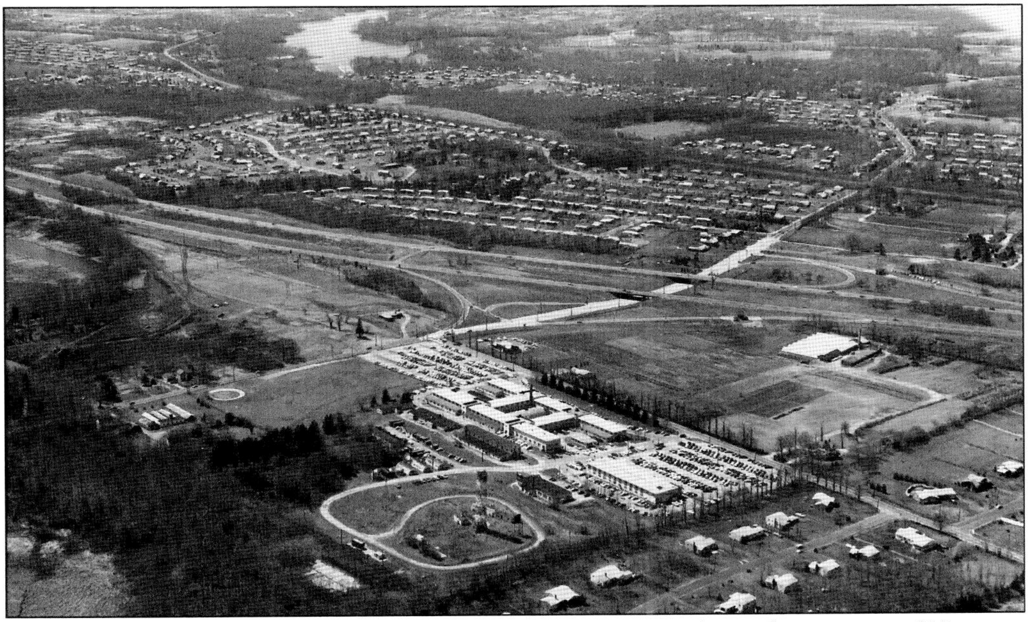

The foreground of this c. 1969 Jack Lentz aerial shows Camp Coles at the juncture of Newman Springs and Half Mile Roads, dedicated October 1, 1942, in honor of Colonel Roy Howard Coles, a World War I signal officer. Also prominent are Parkway Exit 109 and housing south of Newman Springs Road. The straight line running diagonally in the background, curving at left, is Normandy Road and the navy railroad to Earle at Colts Neck. The water in the background is the Swimming River Reservoir. Fires c. 1979–80 ravaged Camp Coles. New construction is on the site now.

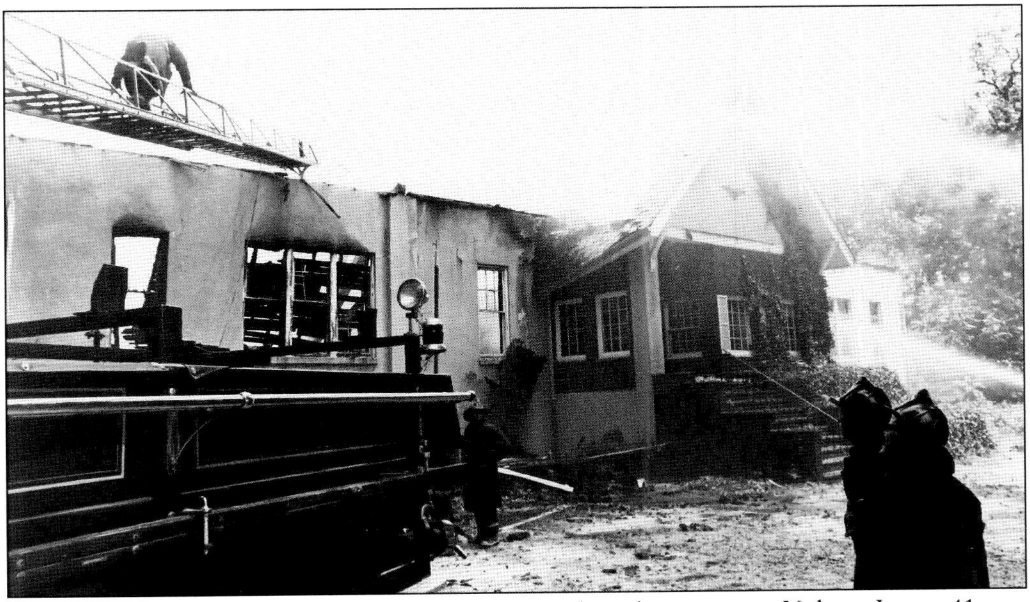

Harmony Country Club, home of Middletown's Ku Klux Klan as seen in Volume I on p. 41, was converted to industrial use. While occupied by the Miller Plating Company, the building was extensively damaged by fire in July 1974. The Shiki Restaurant is on the site now.

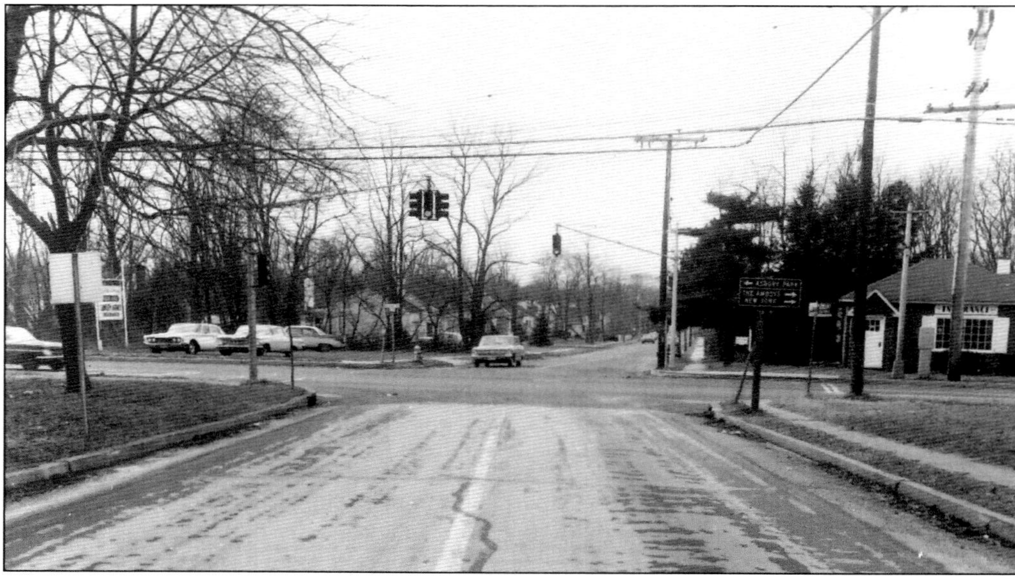

This 1961 view of Navesink River Road at Highway 35 looking west shows a narrow intersection without turning lanes, jughandles, or highway dividers. The stem west of the highway is a 1922 re-alignment of Tramp Hollow Road, then newly designated as part of Riverside Drive, the former name of Navesink River Road.

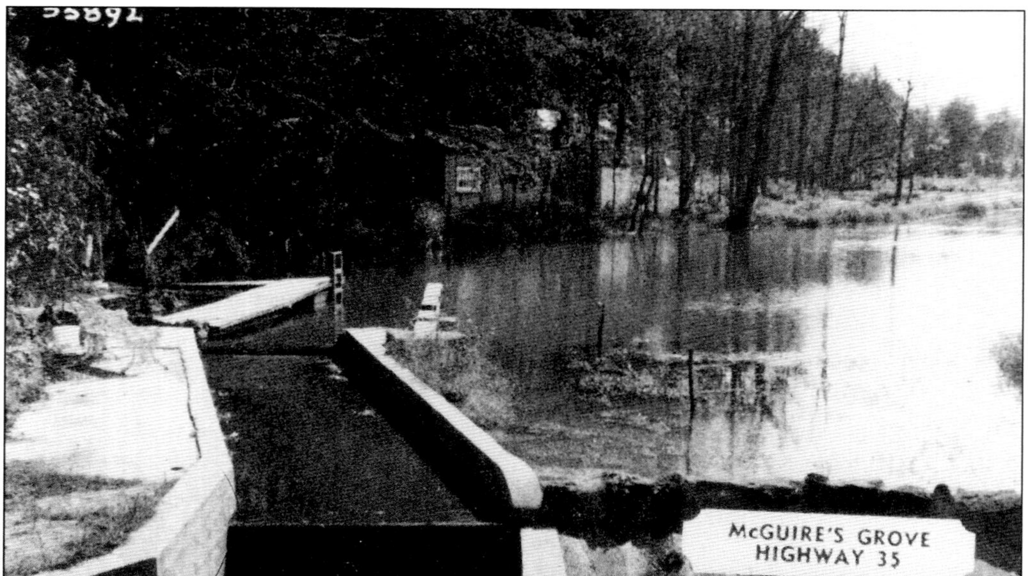

McGuire's Picnic Grove was on the south side of Highway 35 between the Navy Overpass and Oak Hill Road at the site of the present McGuire's Grove Apartments and Union Square Shopping Center. While this *c.* 1950 image may lack pictorial excitement, its message described the place well, as it was composed of 16.5 acres of playground on a 71-acre farm with 12 fireplaces, a recreation hall, a ball field, large woods, a large lake for swimming and boating, and rest rooms with running water and electric light. It provided parking for five hundred cars and was open for picnics, parties, clambakes, etc.

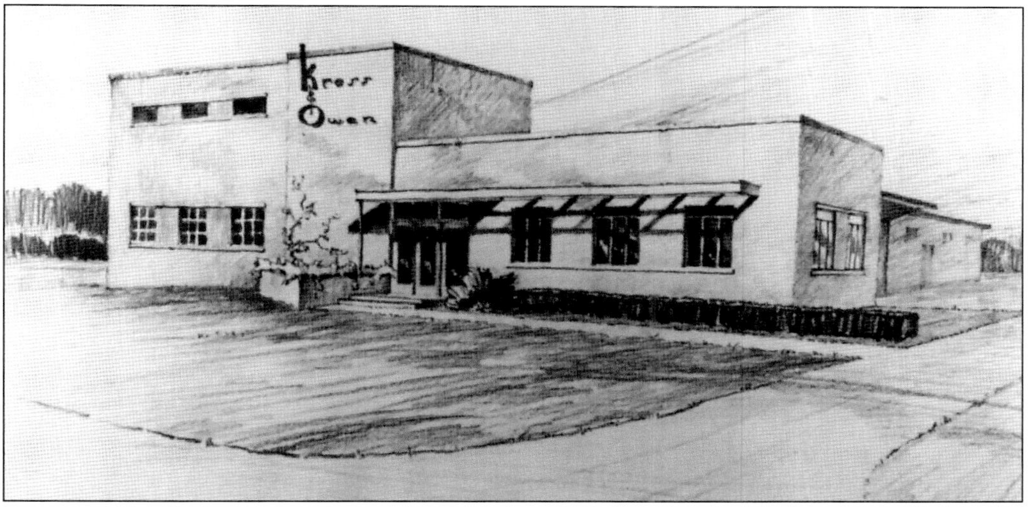

Kress & Owen built an antiseptic processing plant at 565 Highway 35, adjacent on the east to the Navy Road. The building was designed around its processing area, which had an extensive network of pipes and tanks, while offices were on the second floor. The building, seen in a 1951 rendering by architect Bernard Kellenyi, is now the Brigadoon Professional Building.

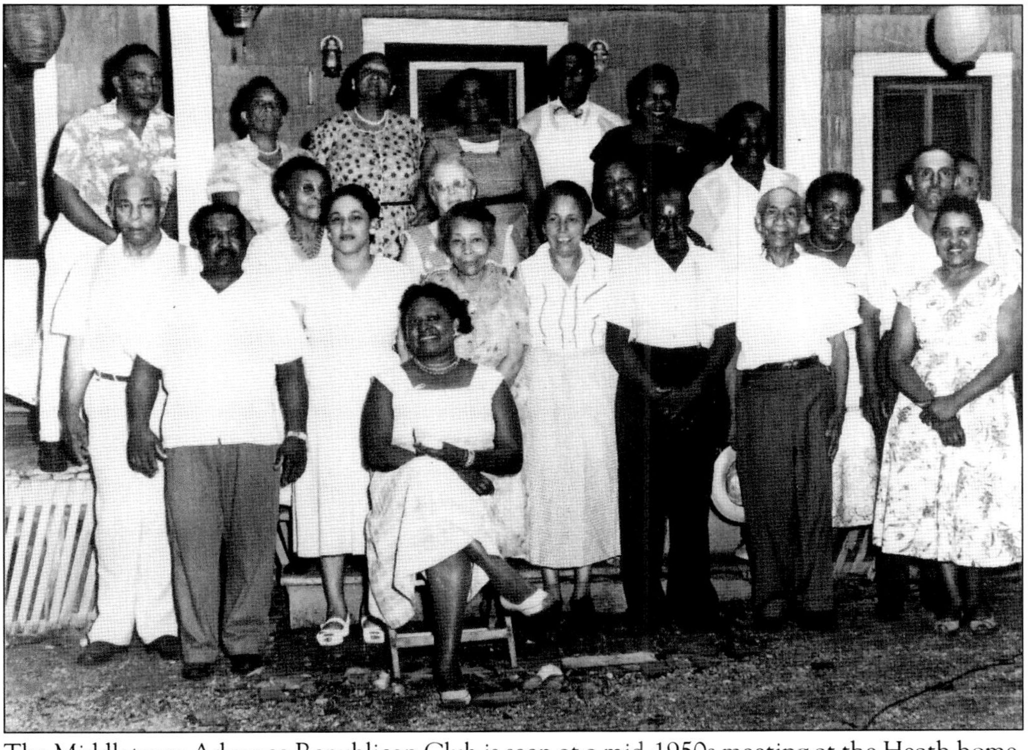

The Middletown Advance Republican Club is seen at a mid-1950s meeting at the Heath home. Maud Smack, mother of Mae Edwards (lender of the picture), is fourth from left in the center row. Rebecca Alston, keeper of the Red Hill store, is in the back row and third from left, while club president Ernest Jackson has the responsibility of supporting the porch post in the back row on the left.

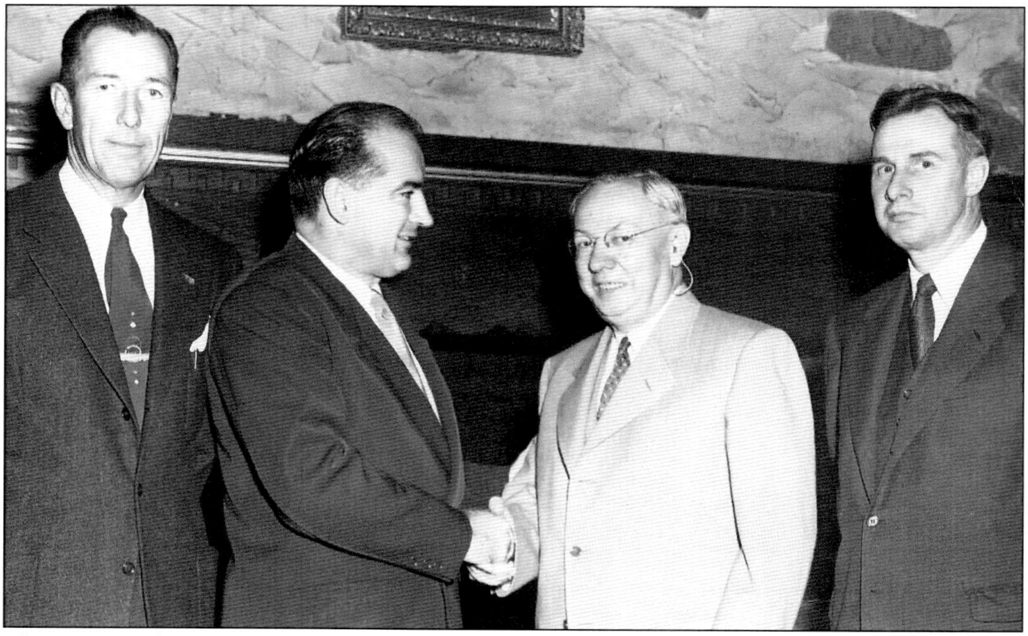

The nation's foremost Cold War demagogue, Senator Joseph R. McCarthy of Wisconsin, was visiting Fort Monmouth in October 1953, investigating an alleged spy ring. He gave an anti-Communism speech at Leonardo Grade School on October 21, attracting an over-flow crowd, part of whom listened in the street over loudspeakers. McCarthy's downfall was accelerated by the next year's U.S. Army hearings. He was censured by the Senate in 1955 and died in 1957. Freeholder Joseph Irwin stands next to McCarthy, who is shaking the hand of Township Clerk Howard W. Roberts while Mayor Lawrence A. Carton Jr. looks on.

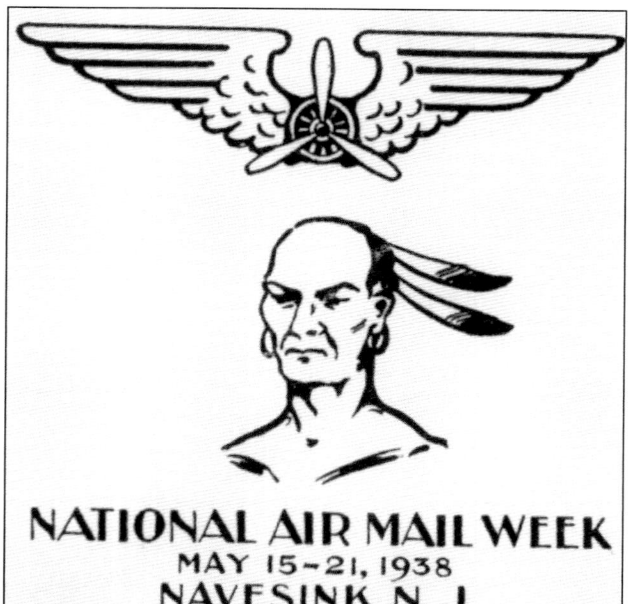

National Air Mail Week was a nationwide promotion encouraging the use of airmail, which was then a premium priced service. It began one day after the release of the attractive 6¢ bi-colored eagle airmail stamp during an era of single-color postage adhesives. Thursday, May 19 was New Jersey Day, with a ceremonial transport of airmail made to the Red Bank Airport. Many local offices issued special cachets for stamping on that week's airmail. This example is from an unmailed souvenir envelope.

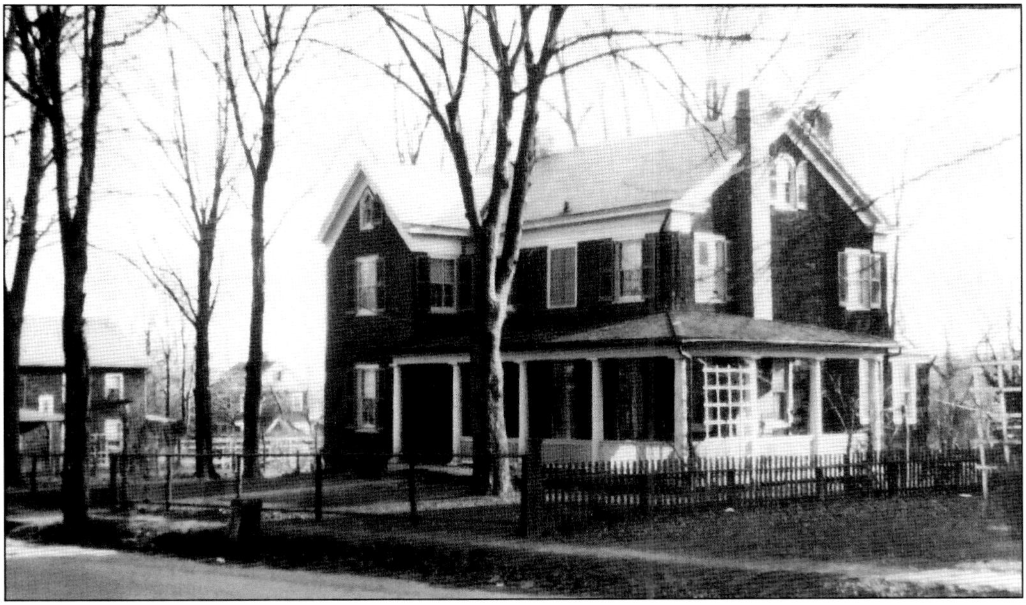

The view from the street of 206 Monmouth Avenue is little changed since this *c*. 1930 picture, which may disguise the house's reported origins in first half of the nineteenth century. A second chimney was added to the west end, while some windows were changed. Both doctors Russell Andrew (father and son) practiced medicine here (see pages 78–79). The younger's widow married William Keeshan, a retired chemist who became Navesink's postmaster.

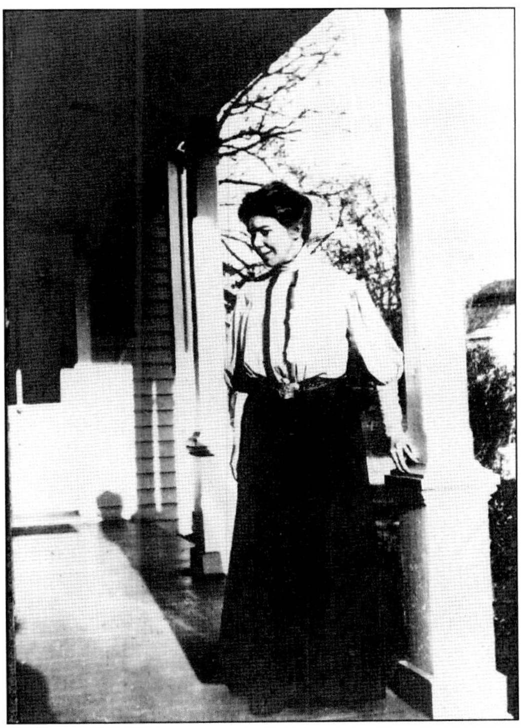

Norma Lippincott Swan, daughter of Webster and Eliza Mount Swan, was born *c*. 1873 in Navesink and is seen here *c*. 1910. She graduated from Goucher College in Baltimore and did graduate work at the University of Chicago and at Oxford University in England. Miss Swan taught and wrote extensively on history, dictating in her later years to overcome the effects of multiple sclerosis. Two of her most useful works are the indexes compiled for Franklin Ellis' *History of Monmouth County* and Thomas Henry Leonard's *From Indian Trail to Electric Rail*. She was a member of the Navesink Methodist Church and died at Navesink in 1957.

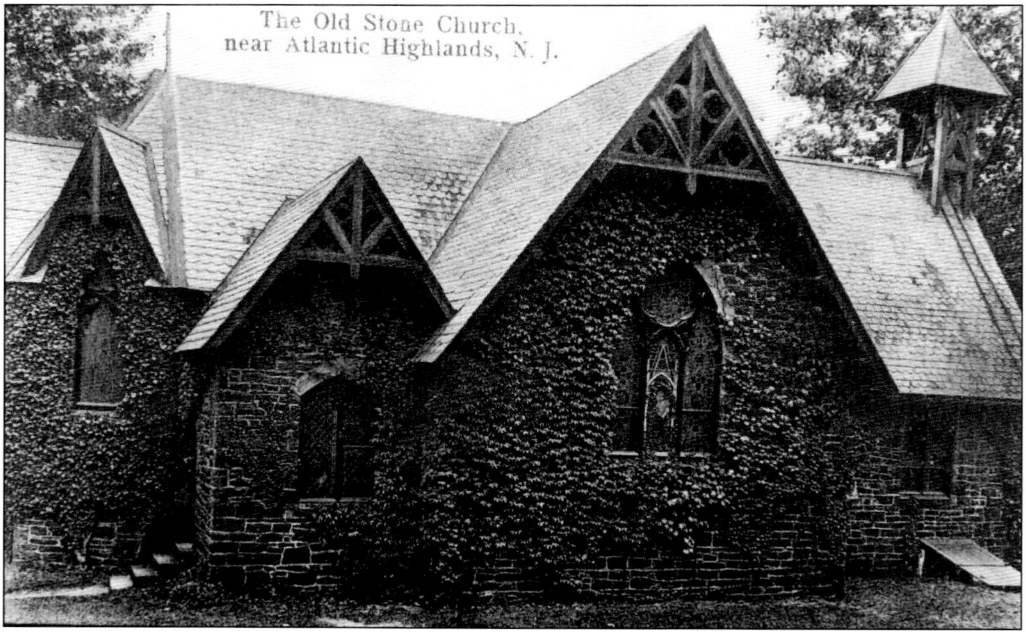

All Saints Memorial Church, an English Gothic design by Richard Upjohn, is so little changed since its September 23, 1864 consecration that careful examination of this *c.* 1910 postcard is required to spot two additions to the exterior. The corner at the shorter gable was built out for a sacristy, while the basement stairs at right are covered now with a gable-roofed enclosure. The church is built of local peanut stone and has a slate roof.

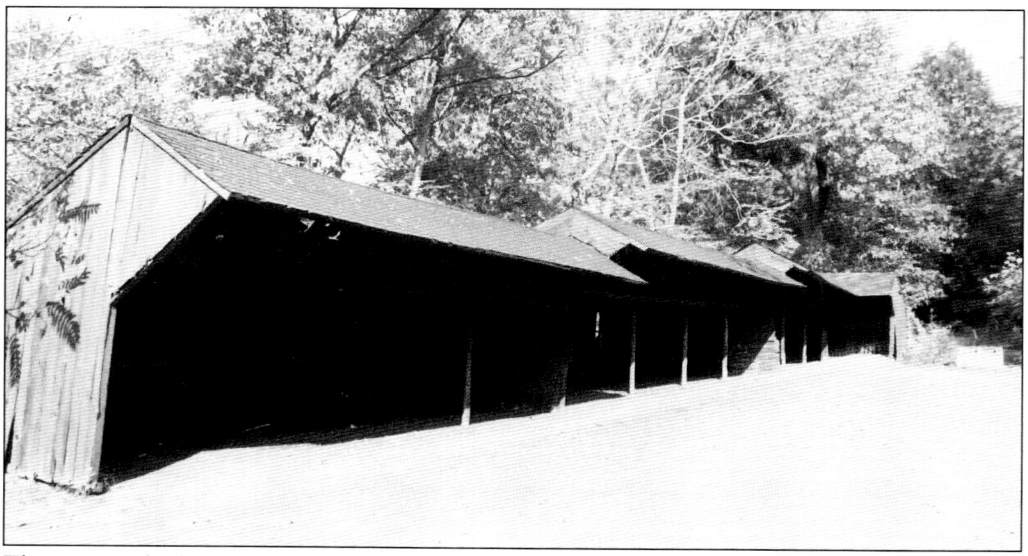

The wagon sheds at All Saints, built in 1907, are rare survivors of a type of utility building often lost to "progress." Seen here in 1982, the church's present appearance is enhanced by the control of surrounding vegetation. All Saints attained designation as a National Historic Landmark in 1988, partly because its network of buildings is intact. The All Saints National Landmark Trust has been established to aid maintenance, recognizing the church's role as a community asset.

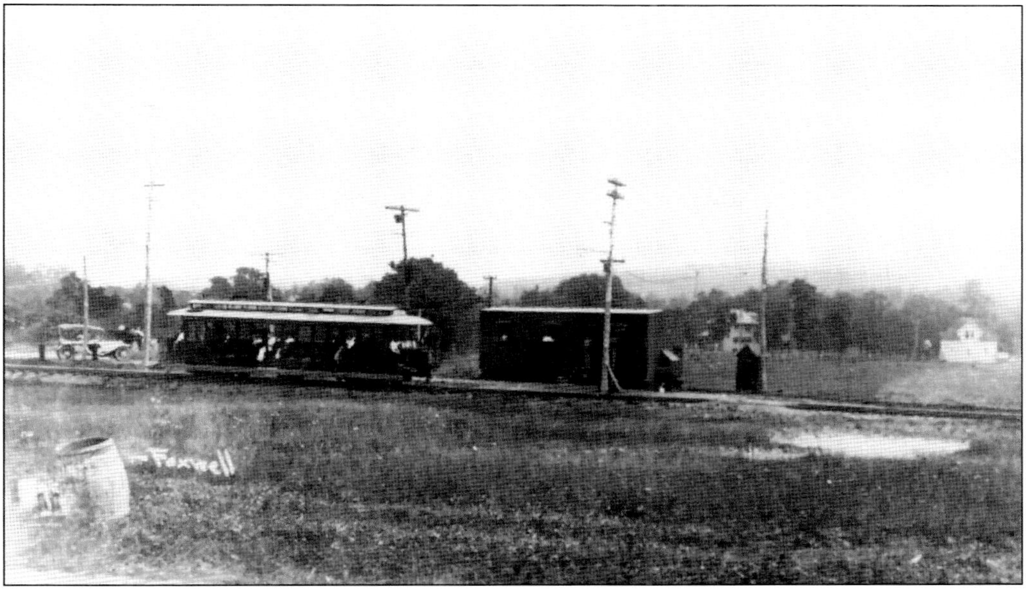

The Jersey Central Traction Company trolley line from Campbells Junction to Highlands utilized track built by the Central Railroad for its Stone Church line. Open car no. 31 is seen in a *c.* 1910 Foxwell photograph at the portable substation no. 101. The name "Stone Church" was apparently coined for use as a rail stop, although it was more widely used to designate the corner and the church property. (Collection of Joseph Eid.)

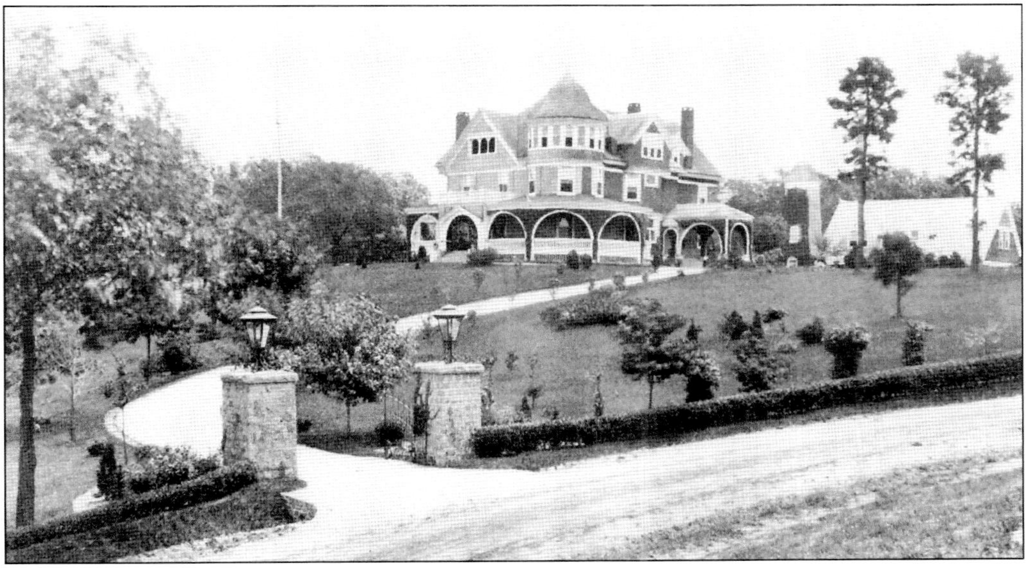

Colonel Ephraim Tillotson of Chicago built this large Queen Anne style house in 1894 on Serpentine Drive in the Hillside section of Navesink using an unidentified Chicago architect. The assemblage of his property included the purchase of the lot belonging to the A.M.E. Zion Church, to whom he paid an additional $100 for removing remains from their graveyard. The foundation was reported to include nearly 100,000 bricks. Tillotson had scant time to enjoy the new house, as he died in January 1895. This *c.* 1900 view is from William J. Leonard's *Seaside Souvenir.*

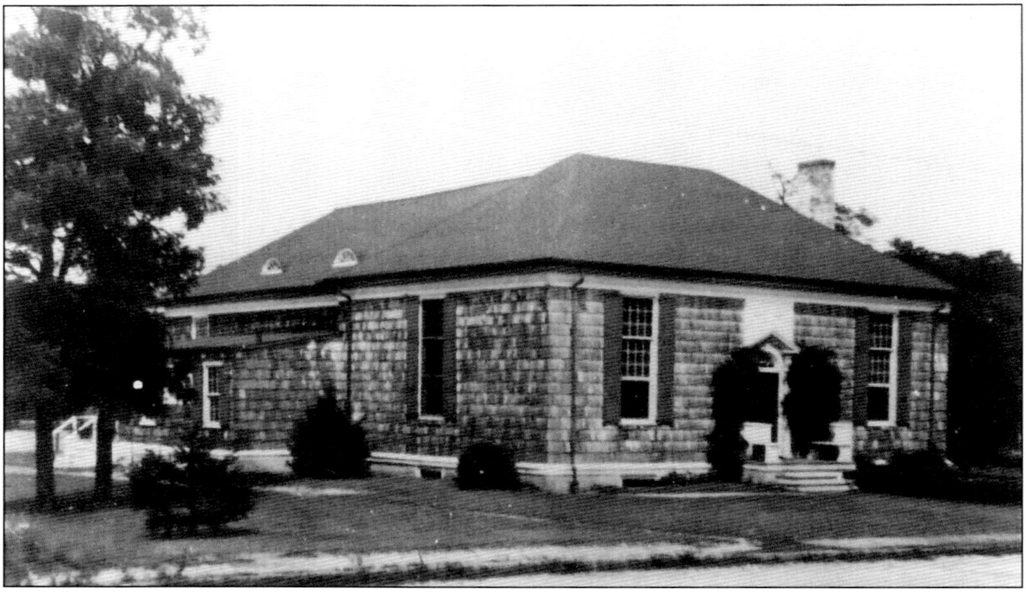

The Navesink Library on Monmouth Avenue, built in 1917 as a memorial to Herman B. Duryea by his widow Ellen, retains the basic appearance of its design by William L. Bottomley, but several changes are noticeable. Siding covers the shingles, while the side entrance has been built out. The rear of the building is a theater, with a back-stage area added since this c. 1920s postcard was issued. Sconces are adjacent to the door, and the shrubs are lower. The library is one of the township's finest Colonial Revival public buildings. (Collection of John Rhody.)

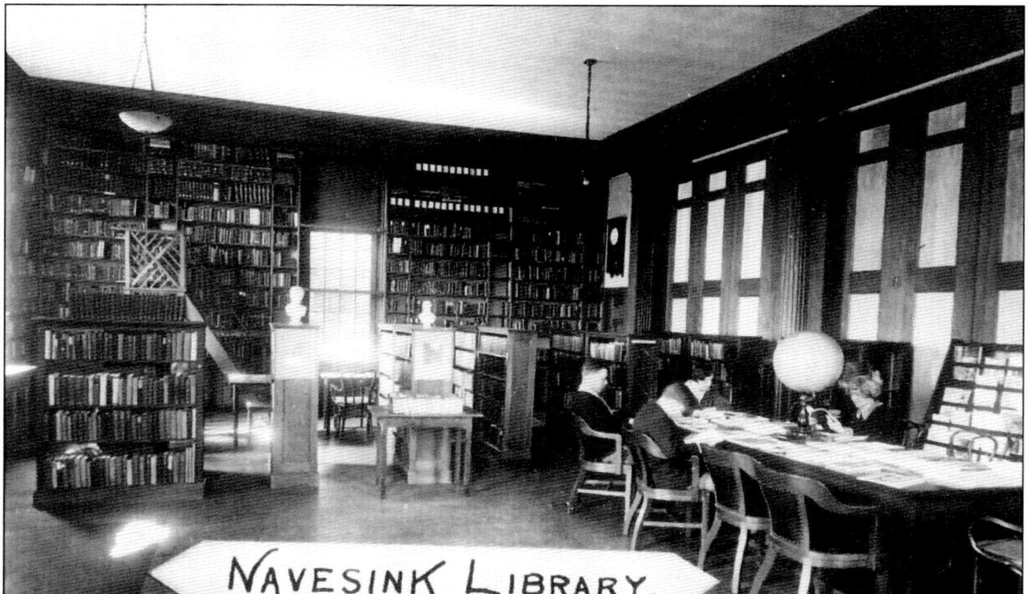

Library furniture was added between the Volume I, p. 11 photograph and this c. 1930 image, and much more since. The interior is little changed, however, with the exception of the painting of the columns on the north wall separating the library from the theater behind it. (Collection of John Rhody.)

The Reverend Bromwell Andrew was for twenty years the circuit preacher of the northern part of the eastern Monmouth Methodist community, eventually retiring to his Navesink home. A number of active Methodists campaigned for a church, raising $ 3,000 for the erection of one in 1854, a structure that was remodeled into this edifice in 1889. A fire in December 1962 caused extensive damage. The rebuilt church bears a resemblance to this *c.* 1920s image, although there are some pronounced changes. (Collection of John Rhody.)

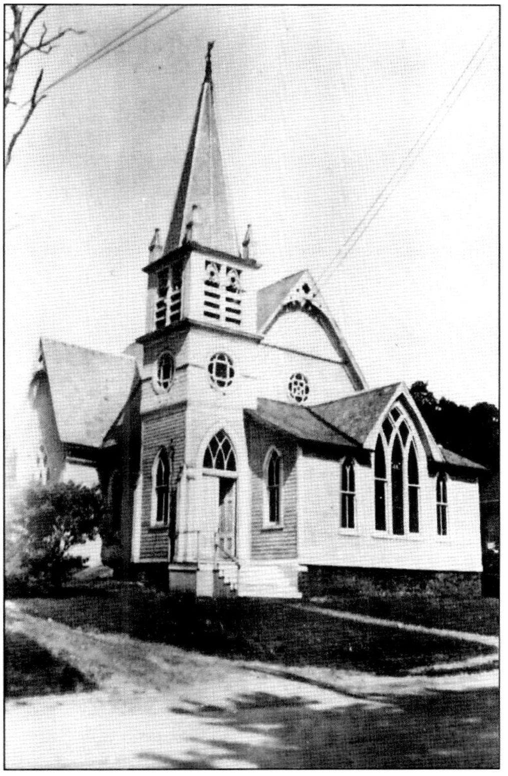

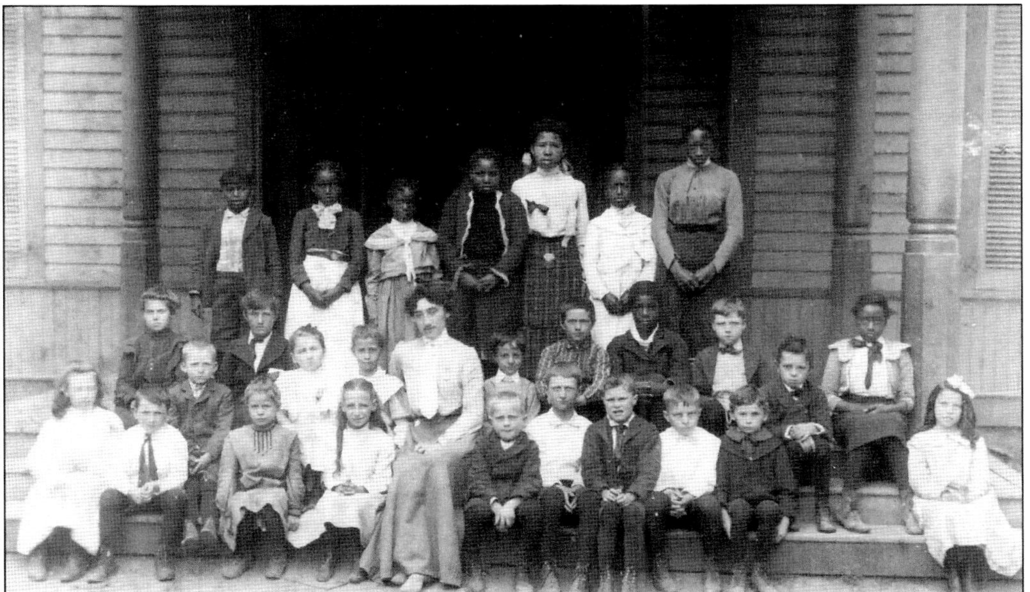

We are accustomed to non-smiling faces in early group photographs, but rarely is the group as disagreeable-looking as this one at the Navesink School *c.* 1900. Mike Cassone's original is marked "Benie Maxwell's class." Where's Benie? He is likely more in the open than Waldo, but less recognizable.

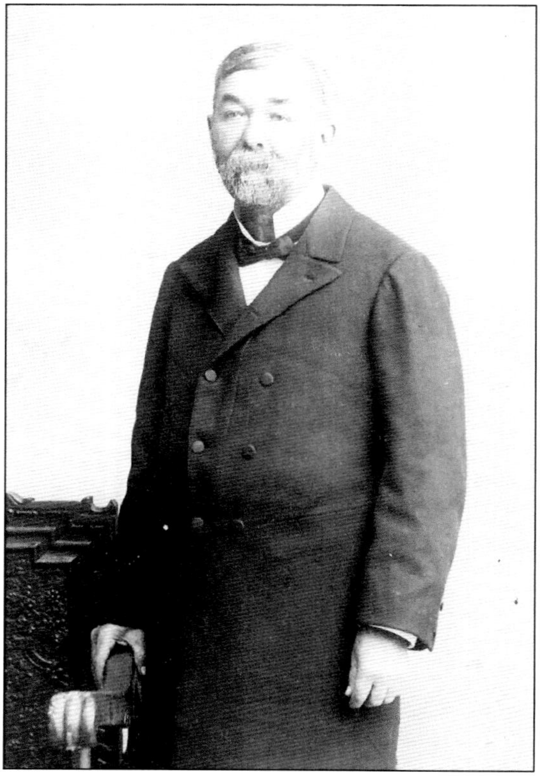

Russel G. Andrew, born c. 1840 at Barnegat, New Jersey, graduated from Albany Medical College in 1866. He settled in Navesink, where for years he was the only physician. Andrew built a large practice there and earned esteem as one of the village's most respected citizens. He collected colonial artifacts and presented to the Monmouth County Historical Association at least one paper on ancient Middletown settlers, which presumably he wrote. Andrew died in July 1909.

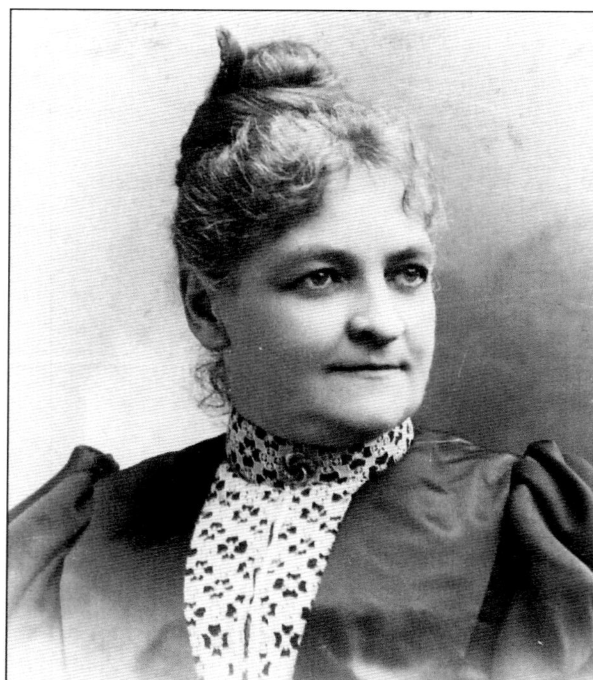

Susan Johnson was born c. 1847, presumably around Navesink. She married Dr. Russel G. Andrew and had one daughter, the future Mrs. C. Albert Mount, and one son, Dr. Russel G. Andrew Jr. Mrs. Andrew died in 1917.

Russel G. Andrew Jr., born 1873 at Navesink, studied at the University of Pennsylvania and the Medical and Surgical College of Philadelphia. He practiced medicine first at Atlantic Highlands and later at Highlands. Andrew was elected coroner as a Democrat in 1902, serving his full three-year term. He caught pneumonia from a chill he suffered after sitting up all night with a patient while wearing damp clothes and died in 1906.

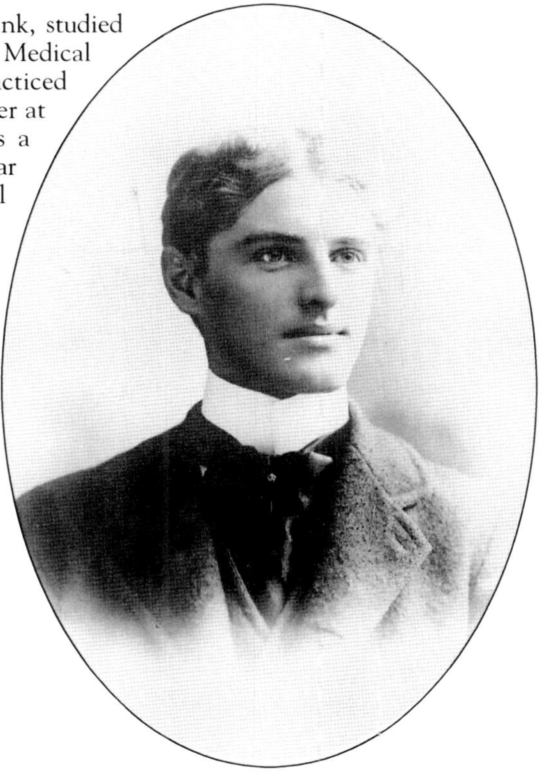

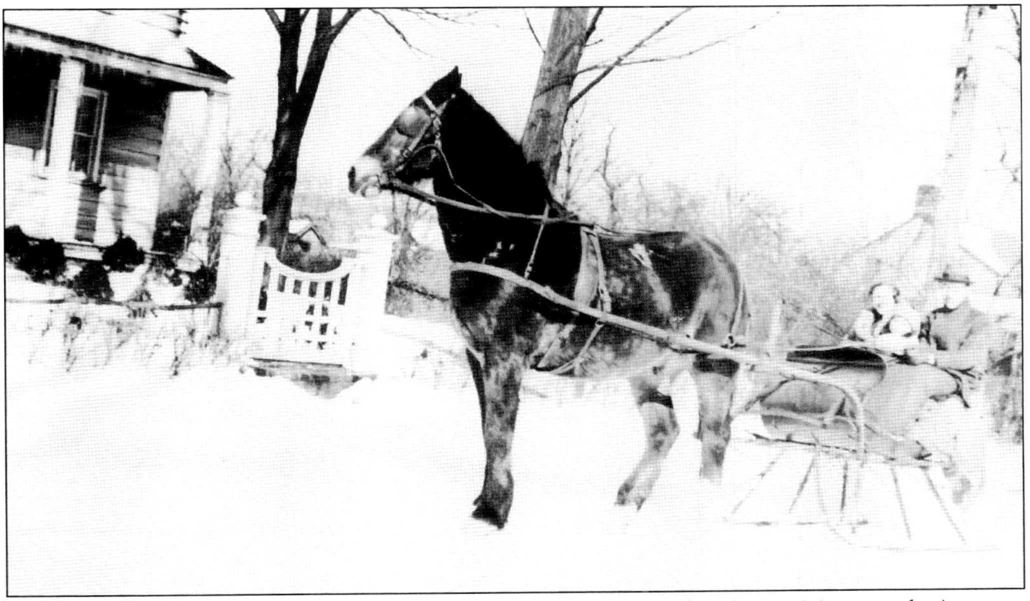

The Rathemachers, Andree, John, and August, appear around 1930 on Monmouth Avenue, on the block east of Navesink Avenue. The Rathemachers would later move to Atlantic Highlands, buying one of the borough's most distinguished residences: the Oscar Unz house on Ocean Boulevard (*Atlantic Highlands*, p. 71). A later son, Richard, lent this picture.

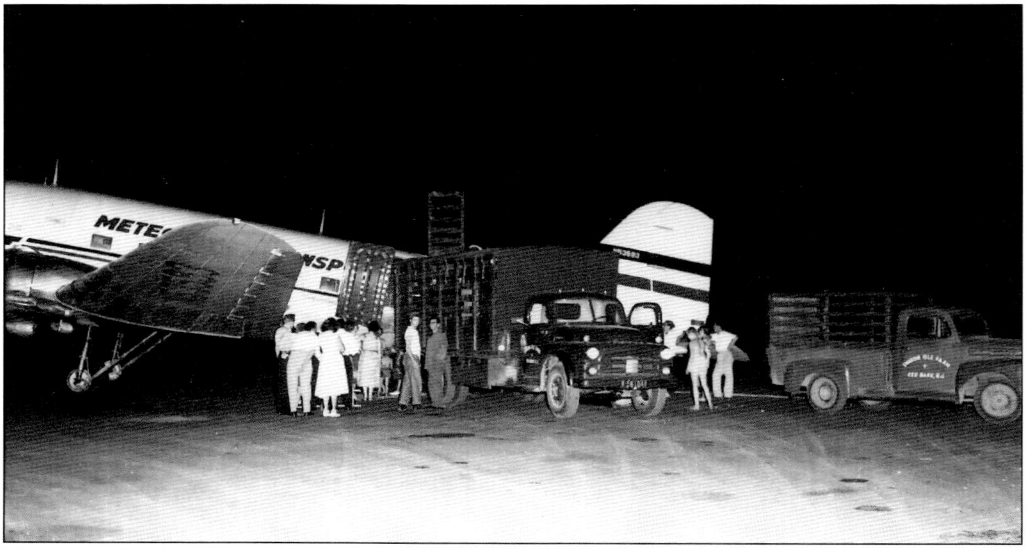

The annual sale of prize black Aberdeen-Angus cattle, one of the most impressive events in the industry, took place September 12, 1953, at Dr. Armand Hammer's Shadow Isle Farm in River Plaza. Visitors from thirty-eight states and three other nations paid $260,400 for sixty-one head of thoroughbred Angus. Hammer was selling half-shares of the very costly ones, and those animals spent six months on each owner's farm or ranch. Two prize bulls, Prince Sunbeam 249th and Prince Sunbeam 328th, were flown in from Texas.

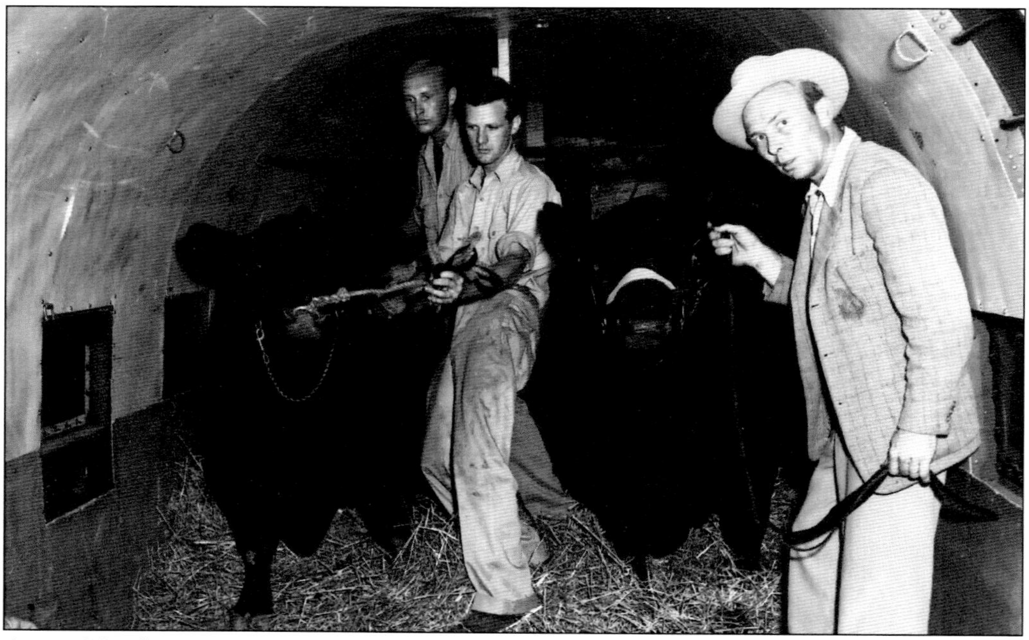

Austin Moody, assistant manager of Shadow Isle, is escorting the valuable bulls from the plane. Their half-interests brought $100,000 and $60,000. The Angus breed is prized for its great quantity of prime meat. If one is tempted to leave this chapter dreaming of the joys of being a prize stud bull, then that someone should be mindful that most of their reproductive responsibilities were accomplished by artificial insemination.

Three

The Bayshore

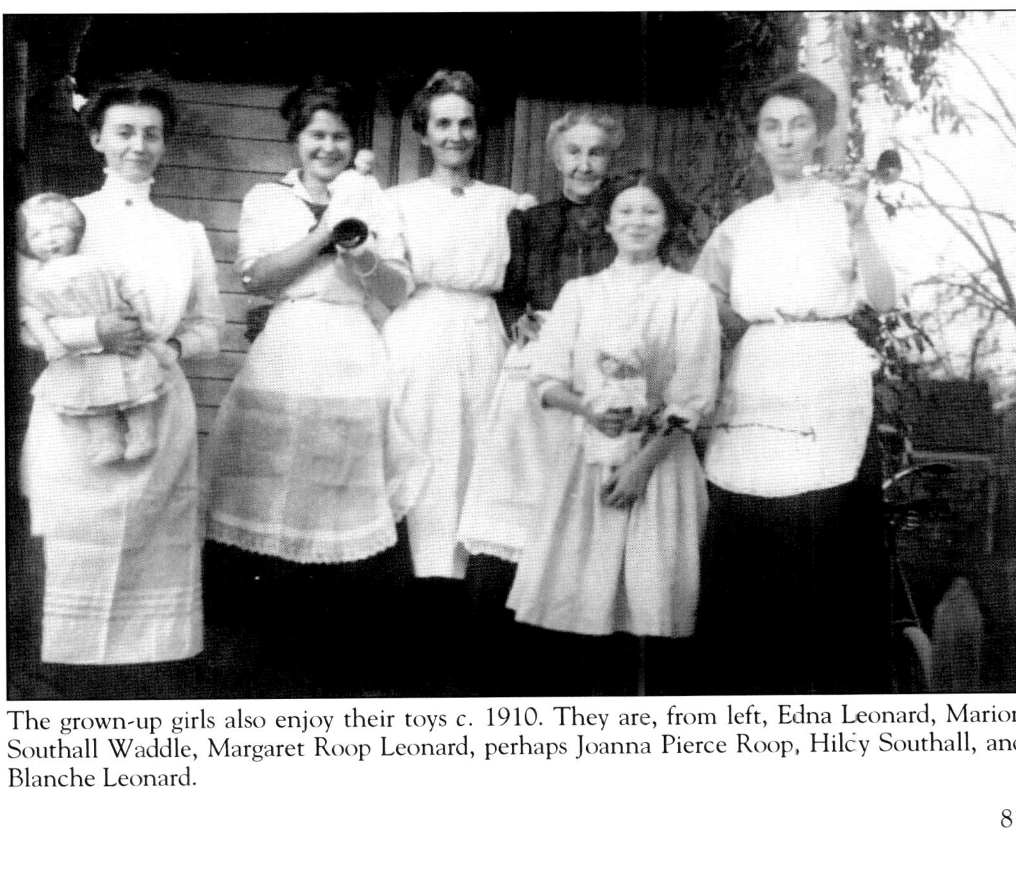

The grown-up girls also enjoy their toys c. 1910. They are, from left, Edna Leonard, Marion Southall Waddle, Margaret Roop Leonard, perhaps Joanna Pierce Roop, Hilcy Southall, and Blanche Leonard.

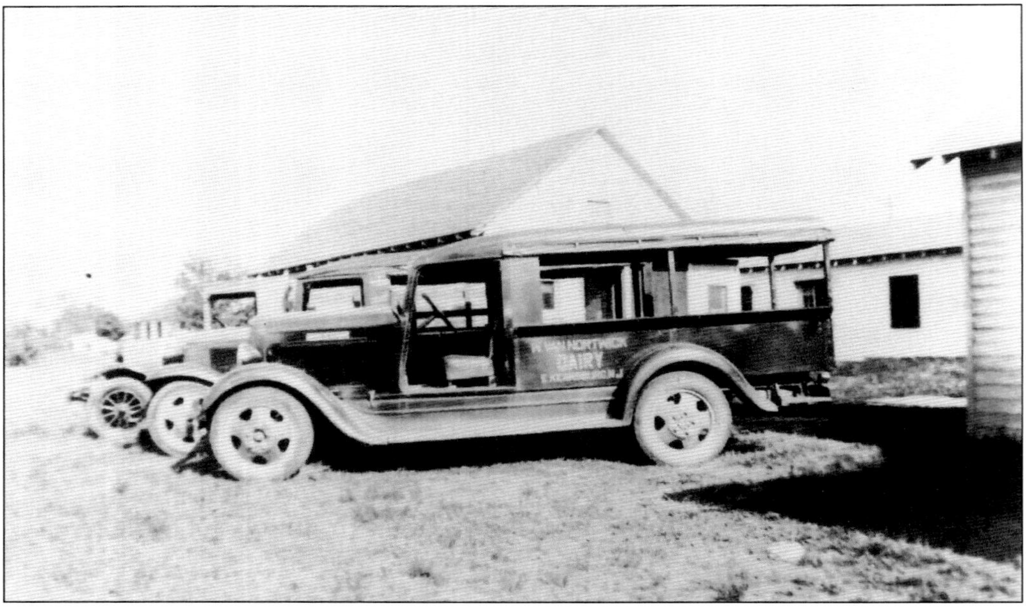

Walter Van Nortwick moved to the township from Newark *c.* 1930, beginning a dairy in the bayshore area *c.* early 1930s. That dairy's equipment is pictured here in 1936. The dairy continued to operate until *c.* 1970, when it became a casualty of changing milk-buying practices. The pictures and background information are courtesy of Peter Van Nortwick, Walter's great-grandson.

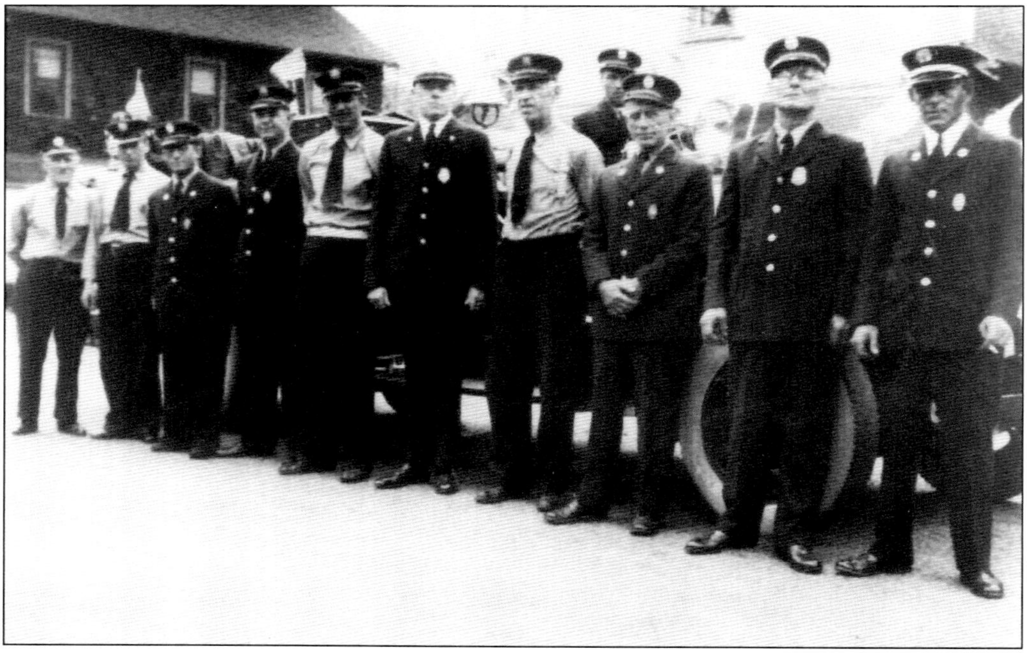

The East Keansburg Fire Company , the township's fifth, was formed in 1922. The occasion of this 1935 gathering is unknown. Walter Van Nortwick is third from the left, while the chief, Gene Reardon, is sixth; driver Ned Hammond is at right.

Frank and Walter Van Nortwick began the Van Nortwick Bros. bus line around 1953, building this garage on the south side of Highway 36 c. 1954. The building is located behind a recognizable landmark, the Polar Cub soft ice cream stand. This aerial pre-dates the late 1950s relocation of the house in the rear.

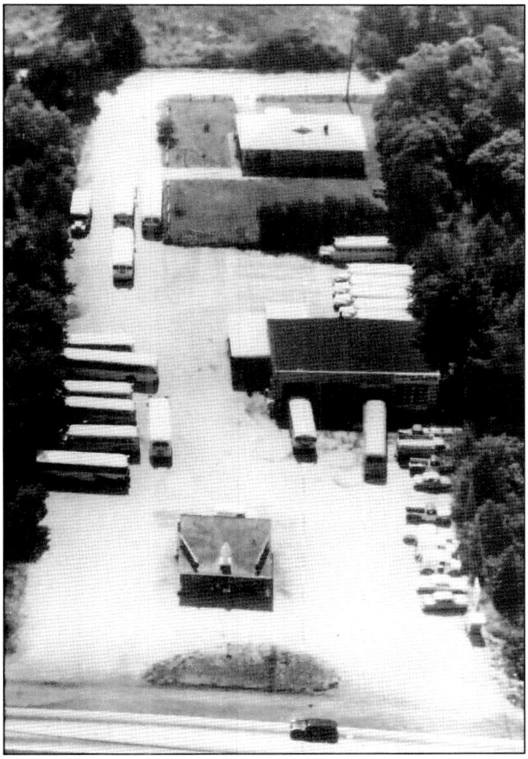

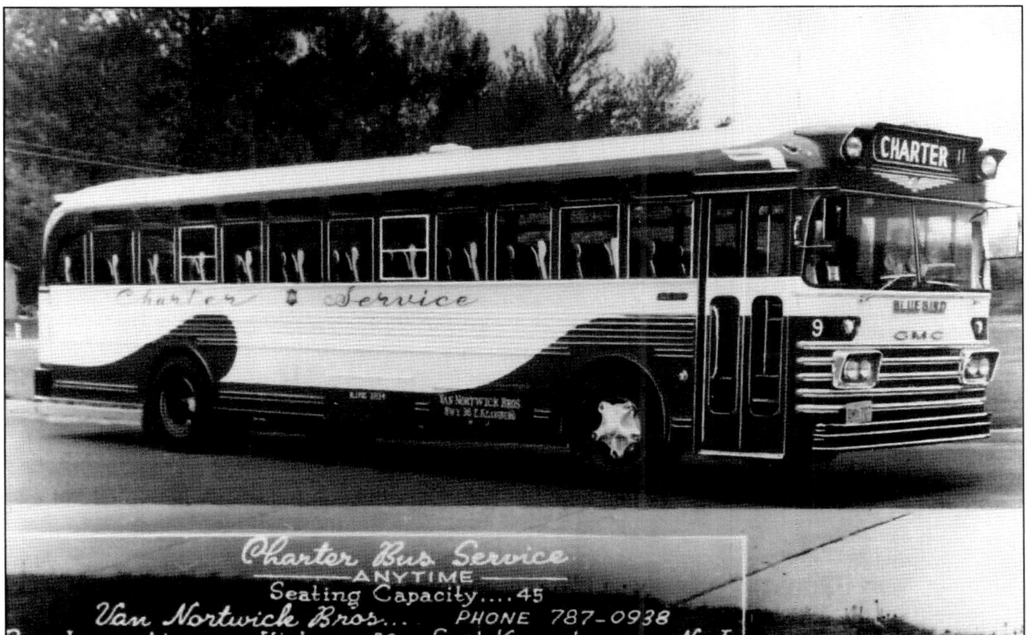

Van Nortwick initially ran school buses only, later adding a charter service. The former business was sold to Michael Loori in 1986, while the charter service moved to Toms River in 1980. This is a 1961 charter coach, a run sold to Shamrock Stagecoach in 1996.

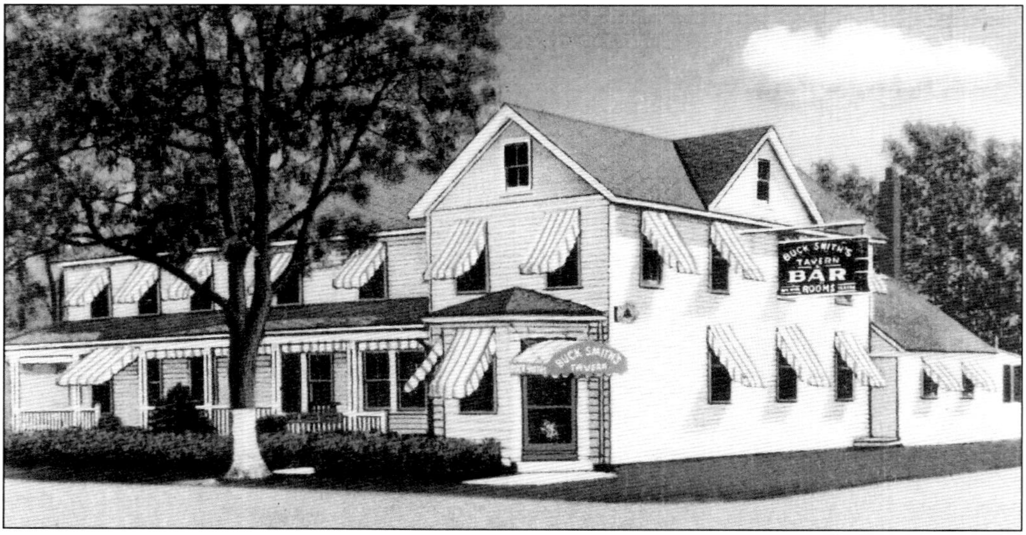

Charles "Buck" Smith, a native of Newark and a member of that city's slaughterhouse family, worked as a union organizer and butcher prior to unexpectedly acquiring the fading Christiansen Boarding House in 1934 (Vol. II, p. 86). This *c.* 1930s view of his bar shows little change from the structure's boarding house days, other than the building of a door at the former bay window. The building, at the southeast corner of Palmer and Thompson Avenues, is now enveloped by expansions. (Collection of John Rhody.)

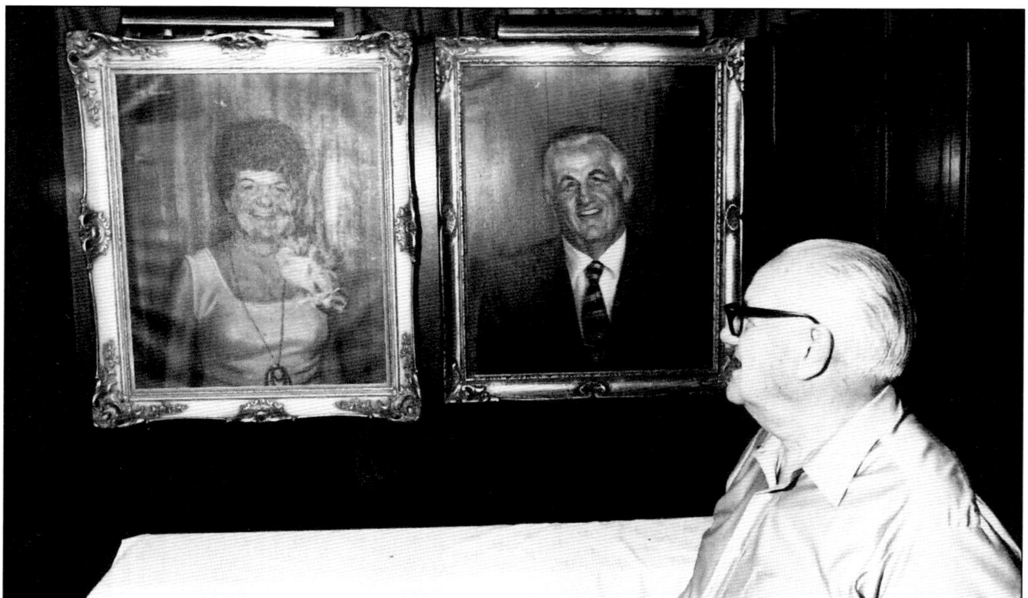

Charles "Buck" Smith, seen in 1979 ten years prior to his death, was widely known and respected for his hospitality at the establishment that became known as his "House of Brides." The name stemmed from his dedication to Catholic nuns, for whom he offered an annual party. The catering facility was host to a wide variety of guests, with its universal popularity implied by simultaneous use by rival political organizations. Buck Smith was known for his community benefactions, now continued in a memorial scholarship fund.

The thirty-year absence of a bridge over Pews Creek to connect Port Monmouth on the east (toward the left), and East Keansburg or North Middletown, on the west, may make this 1960s image appear to be part of ancient history. The picture was taken by *The Courier* when questions of property ownership were delaying jetty extension plans. The marina on the east bank has expanded in recent years.

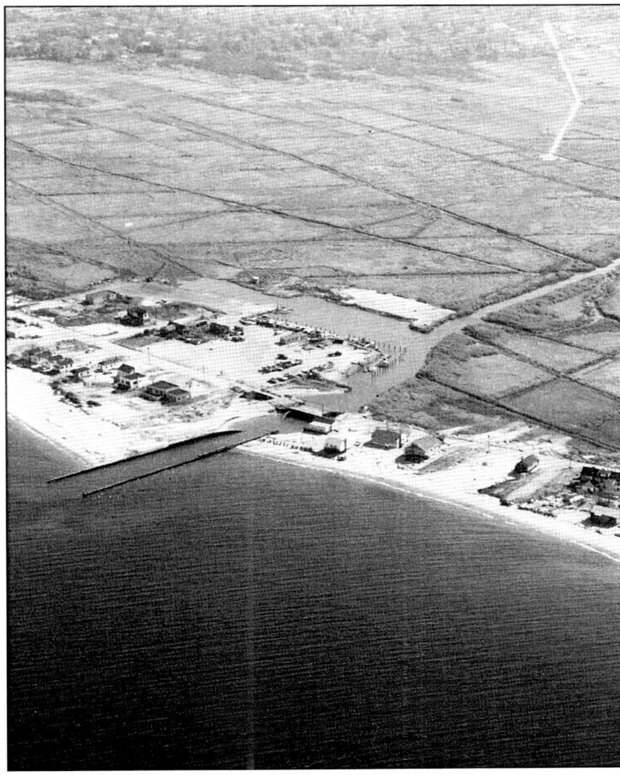

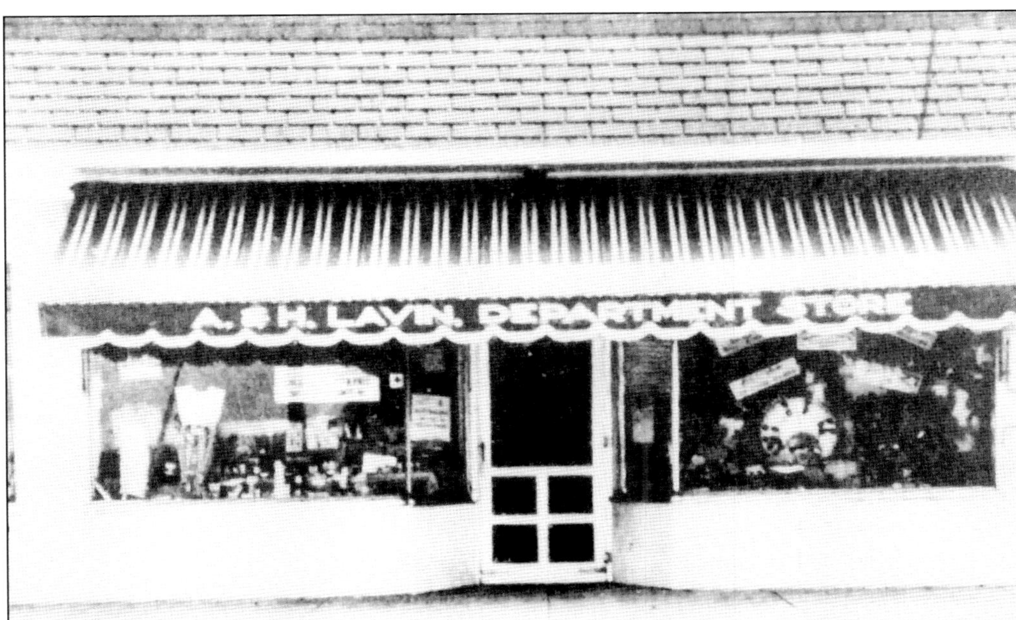

The store built by Fred Freibott—shown here *c.* 1930s—has had a number of tenants, including the builder's office. The A&H Lavin Department Store is seen in a *c.* 1940s postcard. The place at 177 Main Street in Port Monmouth is now occupied by pet grooming and manicurists' shops.

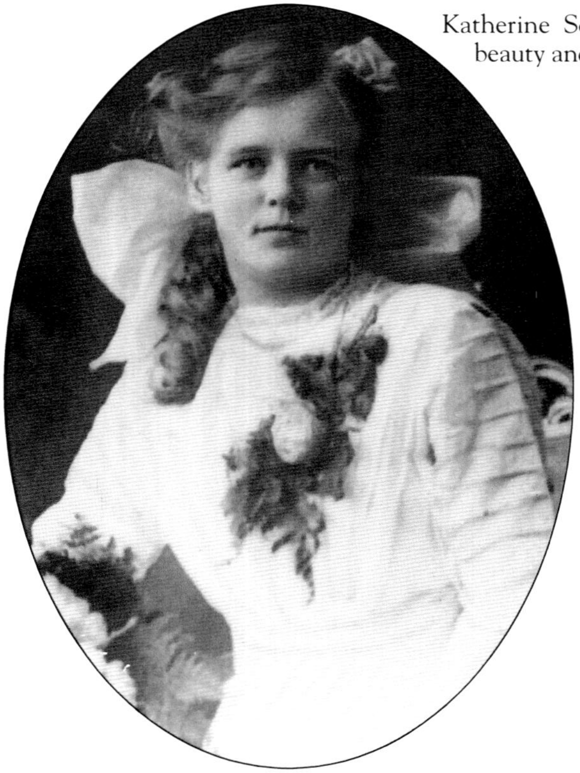

Katherine Soehlke Meyer smartly conveys timeless beauty and early-century costuming.

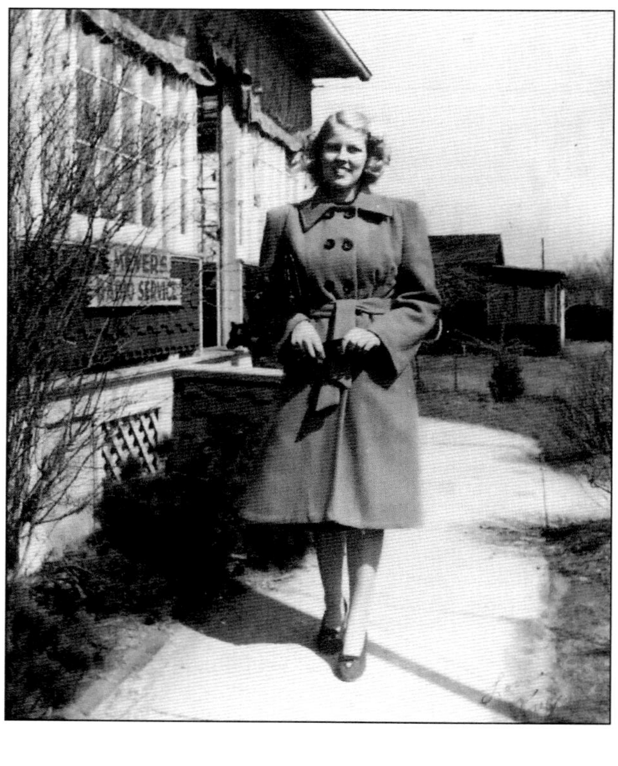

Katherine B. Meyer Richards, daughter of Katherine Meyer, is outside Charles Meyer's radio shop on Highway 36 in Port Monmouth. Her daughter, Sandi von Pier, lender of the photograph, has a strong resemblance and continues the family tradition of beauty.

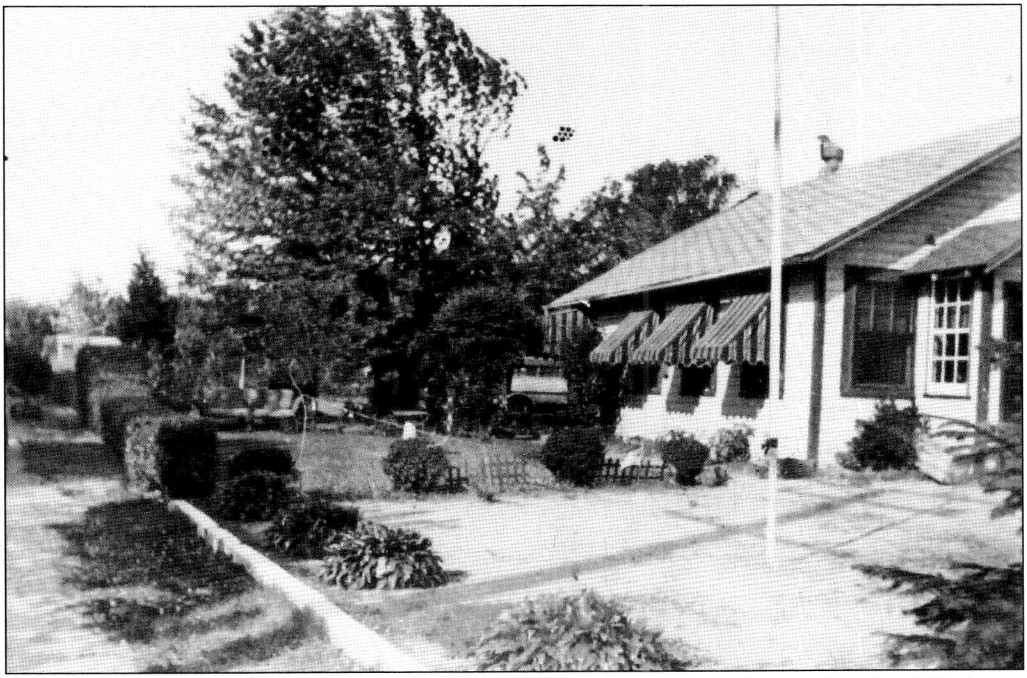

The Charles Meyer radio shop was located in the family home on the north side of Highway 36, near Main Street in Port Monmouth. This *c.* 1950s photograph conveys open, attractive ground that later fell to "progress" when the house was destroyed for the 1960s widening of the road.

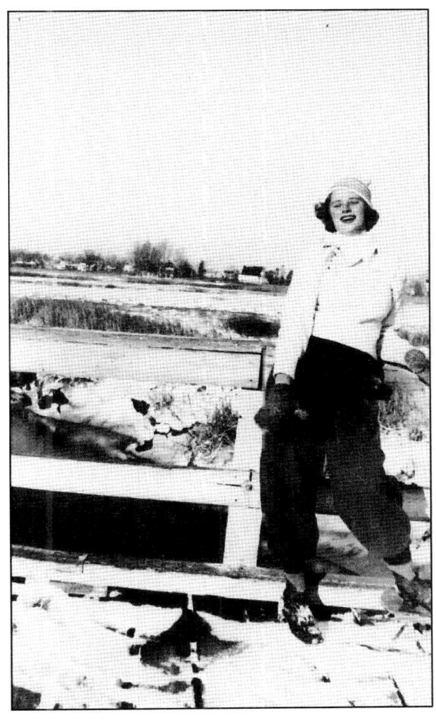

Louise Elton Kruger, cousin of Katherine (opposite) provides an appealing image for viewing the Port Monmouth marshes in May 1942.

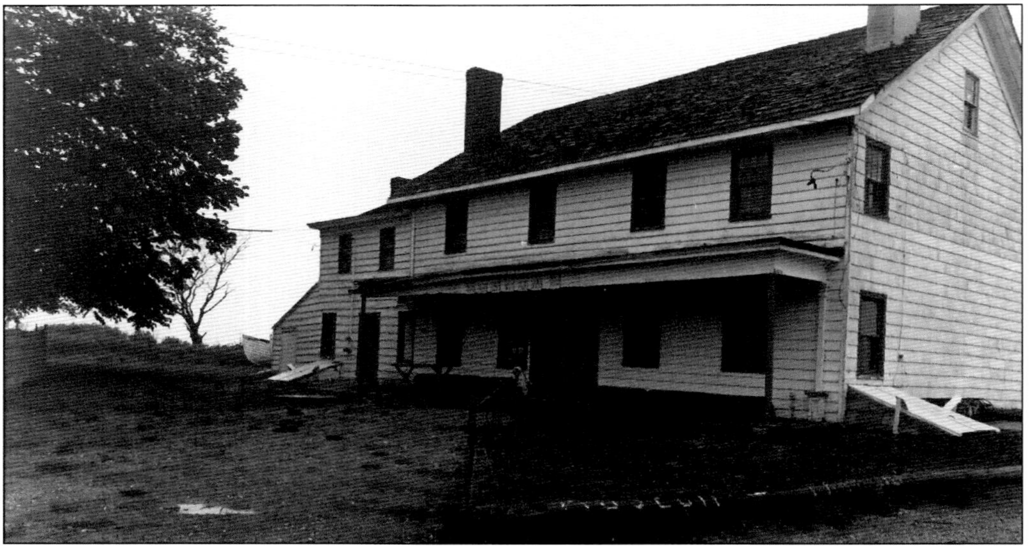

The Whitlock-Seabrook-Wilson House, seen in Volume I on p. 18 as the Reverend Wilson's house and in Volume II on p. 88 as part of the Spy House complex, is viewed here in 1971, around the time of its acquisition by the Township of Middletown. The building was refurbished and "restored," initially through the efforts of the Middletown Township Historical Society and in time by various organizations headed by Gertrude Neidlinger. It operated for many years as a "folk museum of the bayshore people," with a new interpretation now evolving.

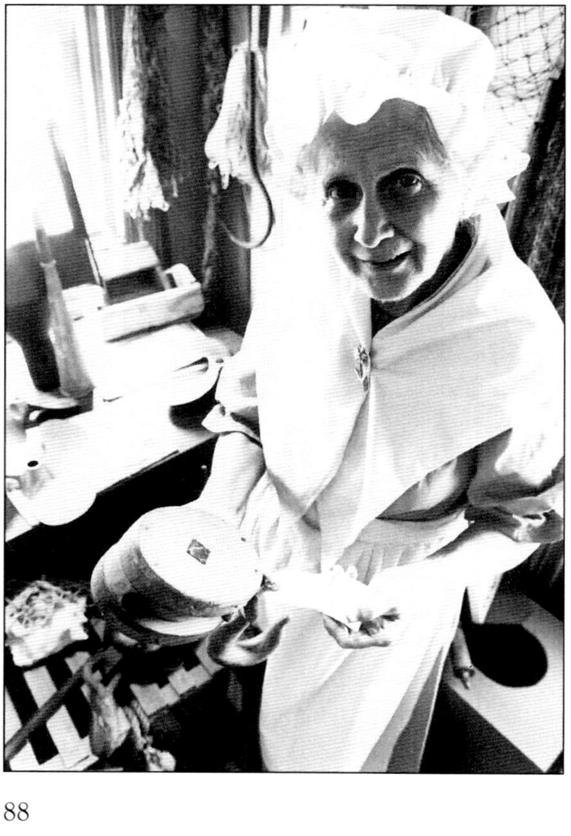

Gertrude Neidlinger, born 1910 in Montclair and a member of a family that long summered in Leonardo, was trained as a singer and enjoyed an entertainment career that embraced *comedia del arte*. She is best known locally for nearly a quarter century of single-minded devotion to the Spy House and its folk interpretation. Miss Neidlinger has left the museum at the township's behest over interpretive and policy matters but has a proud, distinguished record as the force most responsible for its preservation.

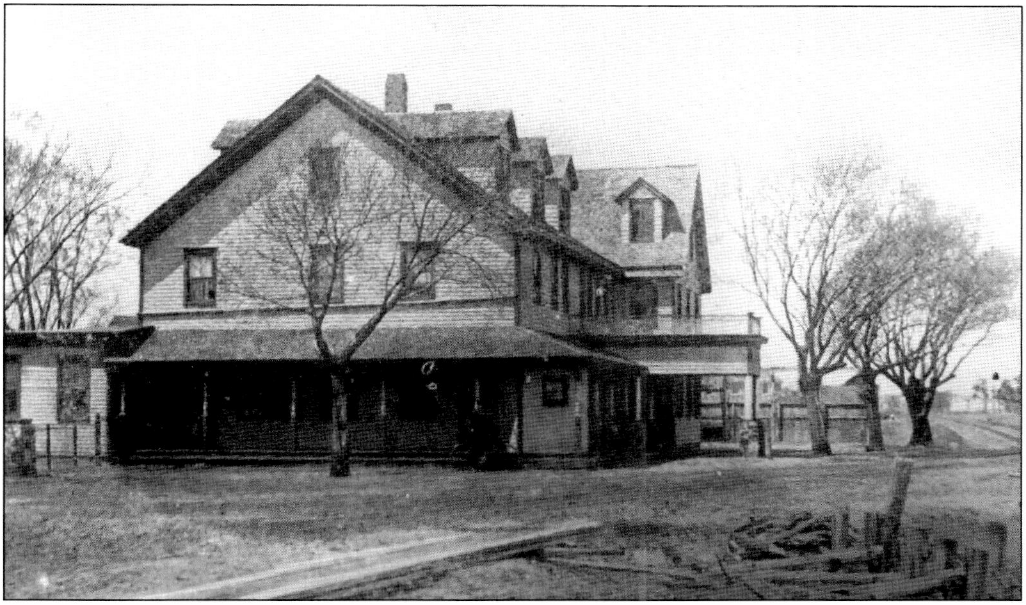

The Hotel Shoal Harbor, seen in a *c.* 1910 postcard view, was located on Port Monmouth Road, initially in close proximity to the fish factory (Vol. II, p. 92), but later inside the factory's property after Port Monmouth Road was relocated a short distance to the south. It was long operated by James Carroll and was alternately known as Carroll's Hotel. It was demolished *c.* 1990 along with the long-idle plant, which is awaiting development.

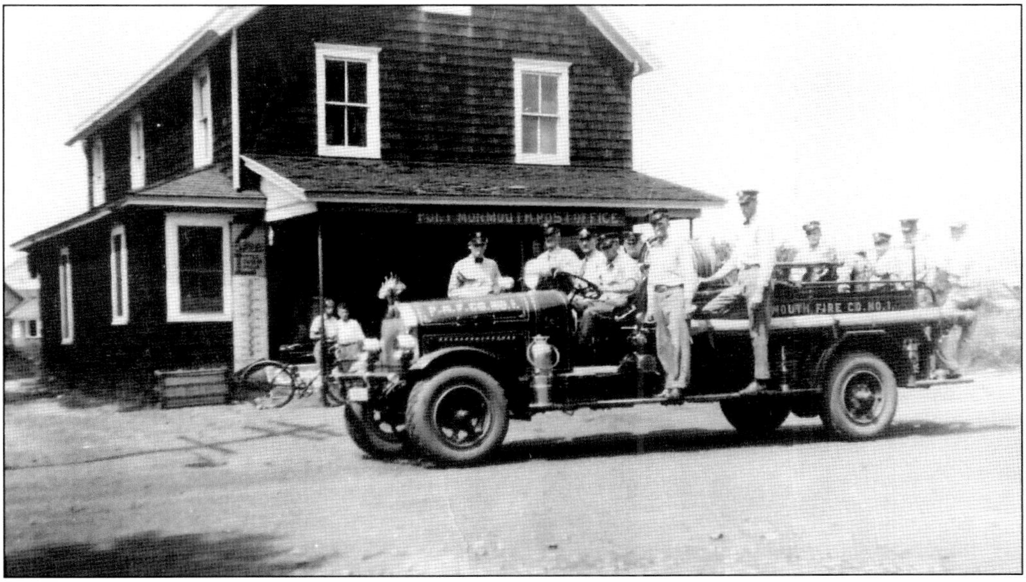

The Port Monmouth Fire Company is seen in front of the former post office, now the Bayshore Branch of the Middletown Public Library at 168 Main Street, *c.* 1930. The driver is Henry Pulsch, the first chief of the Middletown Township Fire Department. Jack Morrell is standing next to him. (Collection of Ed Banfield.)

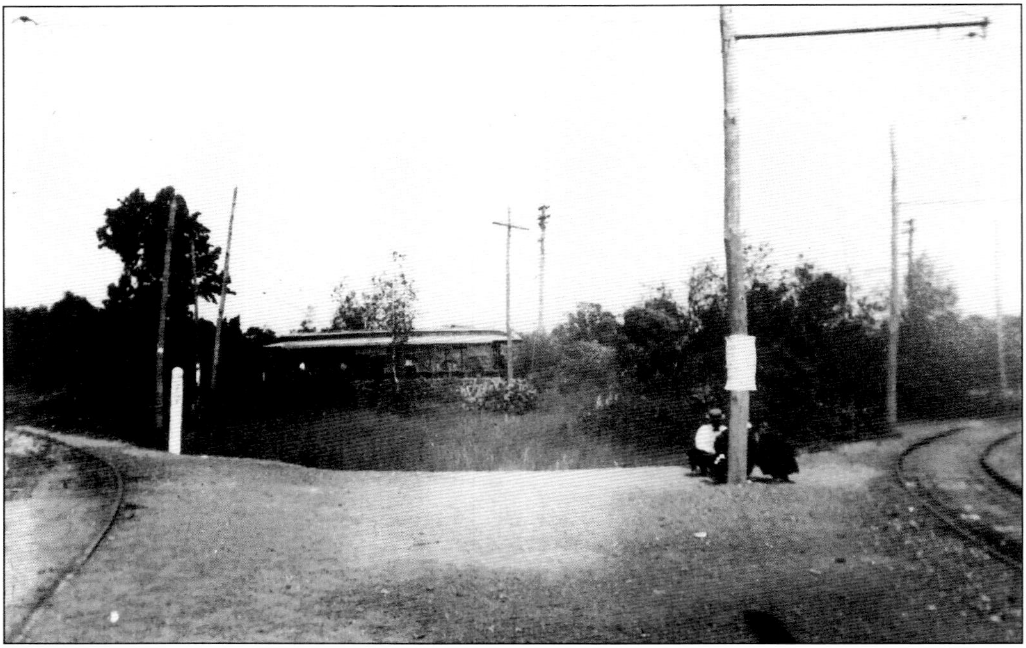

Campbells Junction, the juncture of trolley lines running to Highlands, Red Bank, and Keyport, was built on Derek Campbell's corn field, although this *c.* 1907 image shows a field of brush. The frequently illustrated station soon gave the site a look of permanence, leading to its status as the township's first commercial district.

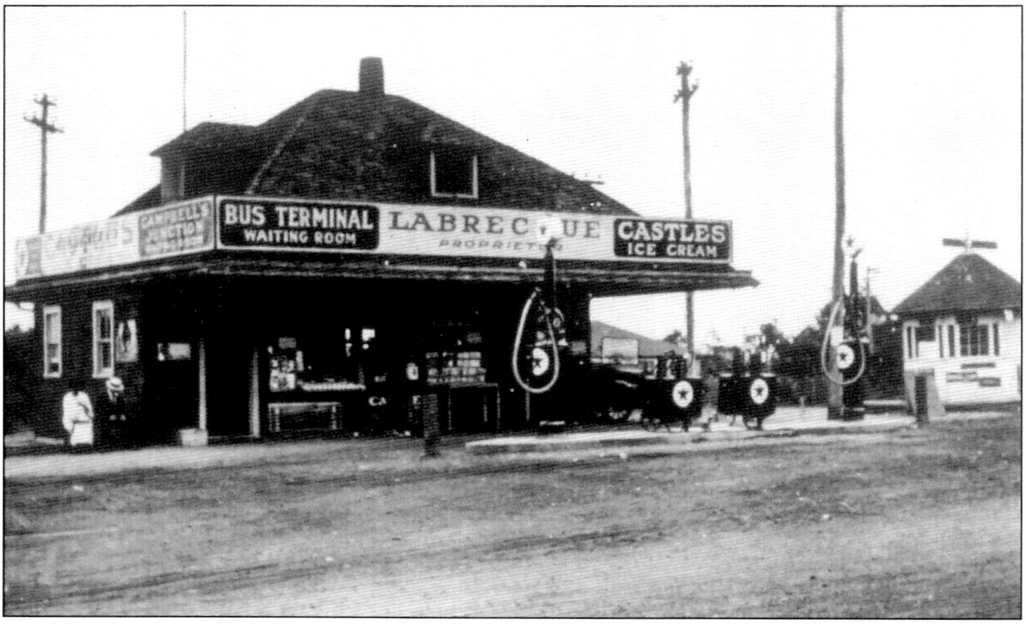

The Campbells Junction waiting room adjusted to reflect the replacement of trolleys by buses in 1923. Motor vehicles, winners of an unstated transport "war," could fill up with gasoline here *c.* 1920s. Herman Labrecque, who initially kept the waiting room, became a real estate investor, developing much of the immediate area.

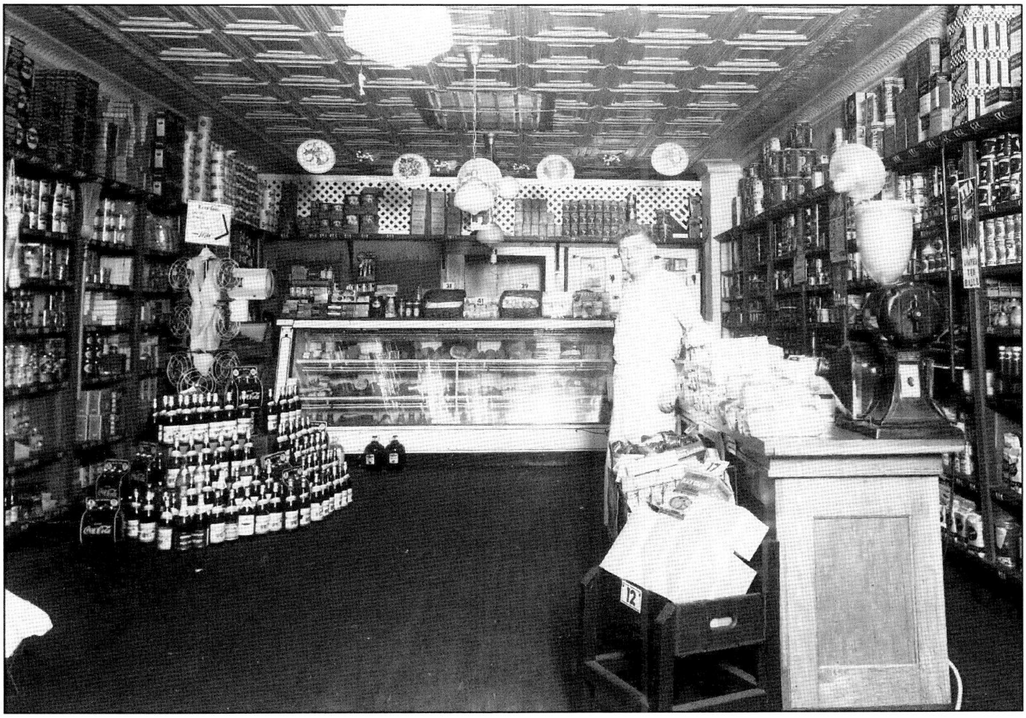

John Lentz bought the Butler grocery on the northwest corner of Main Street and Morris Avenue in Belford in 1939, converting it to a United store, seen here *c.* 1939–40, perhaps in summer if the fans for sale are an indication. A later rearrangement placed the counter on the other side, with the meat case aside it, the rear freed for a Weston bulk cookie display. Lentz sold the business in 1954, joining son John in his auto body shop ("It's Lentz for Dents"). A grocery with light food service is still on the site.

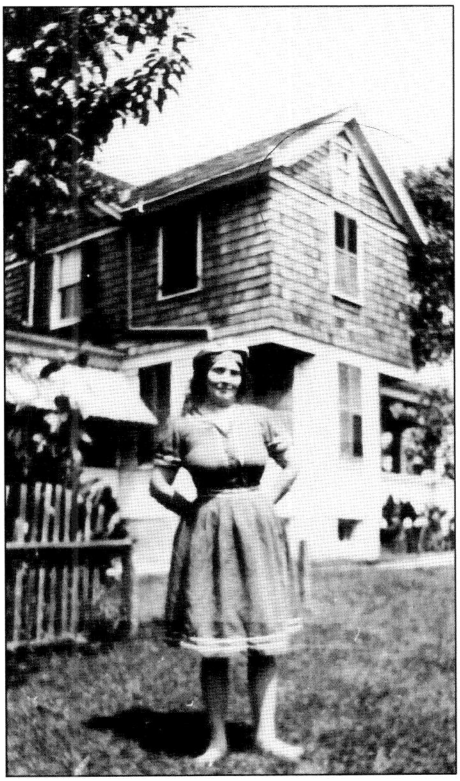

Lois Bodtmann had no details about the pictured Aunt Olive, but she cut an attractive figure by the family's Belford home in 1908.

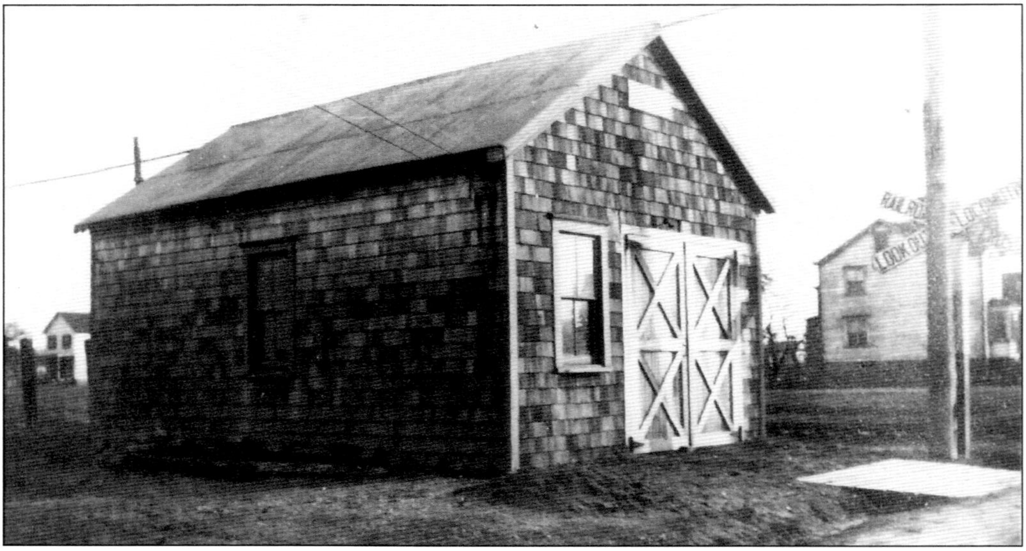

The Belford Engine Company, originally the Belford Chemical Company No. 1, organized in 1916. The first officers were Harold Willett (chairman), Frank Yarnall (secretary), and Joe Hyers (president). Their early equipment was stored at this building on Church Street at the railroad, which became Dickie Walling's garage. The photograph is, perhaps, *c*. 1920.

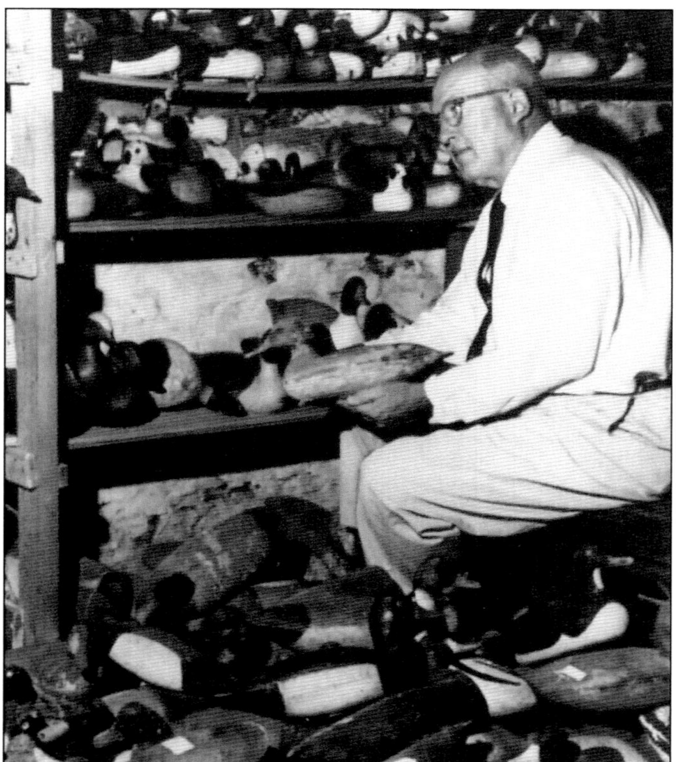

William J. Mackey Jr. of Belford, seen here in 1967, was a foremost collector and student of American bird decoys. His home was lined with thousands, with Mackey regarding each as a distinctive work of art. His 1966 *American Bird Decoys*, published by E.P. Dutton & Co., is a much sought-after work on the subject. He befriended the old-time decoy makers, hunting and living with them during travels along the Atlantic coast. Mackey also gained a reputation for his interest in conservation. (Special Collections and Archives, Rutgers University Libraries.)

Captain Arthur Lindland, a Norwegian fisherman, lived in Atlantic Highlands and docked at Belford. His vessel, the *L.J. Dayton*, a name that came with the ship, is seen moored there *c.* 1930s.

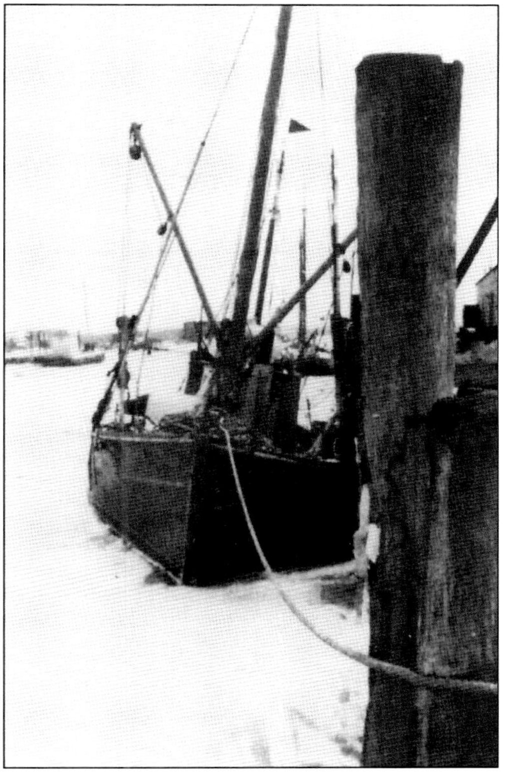

Captain Arthur Lindland, left, is seen with helper Hans Tonnesen, hauling in a load of blue claw crabs. They dredged the bottom for the fattened, hibernating crabs, which although awakened, lacked their seasonal fighting spirit. They brought $1-$2 per bushel in the 1937 market.

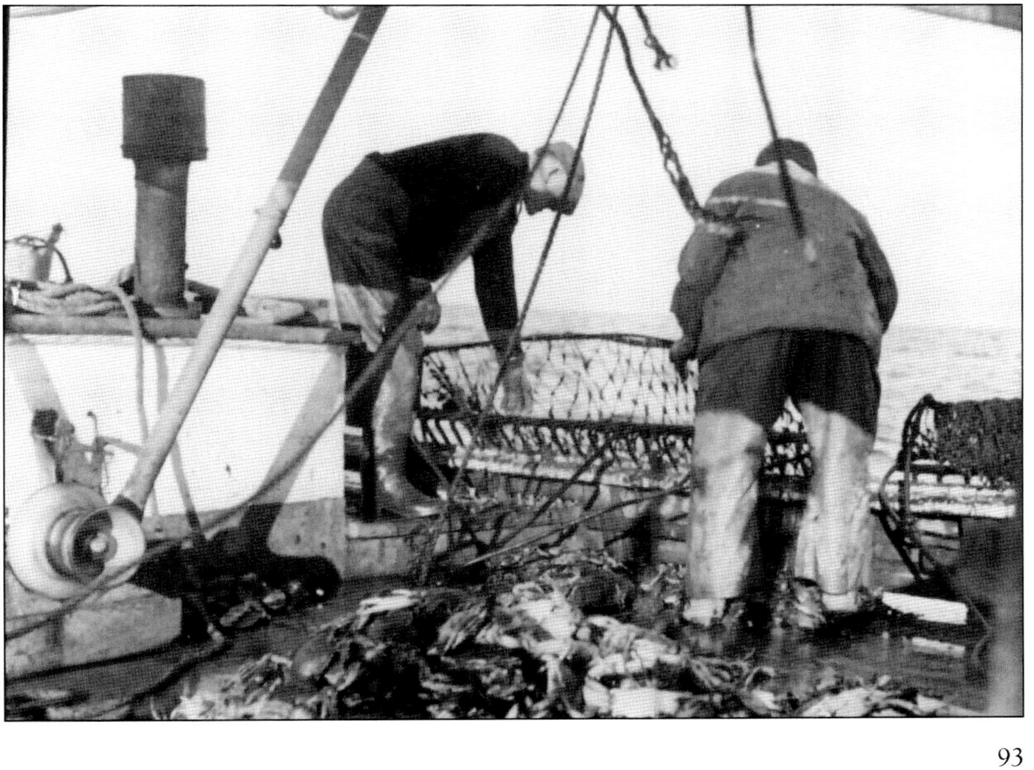

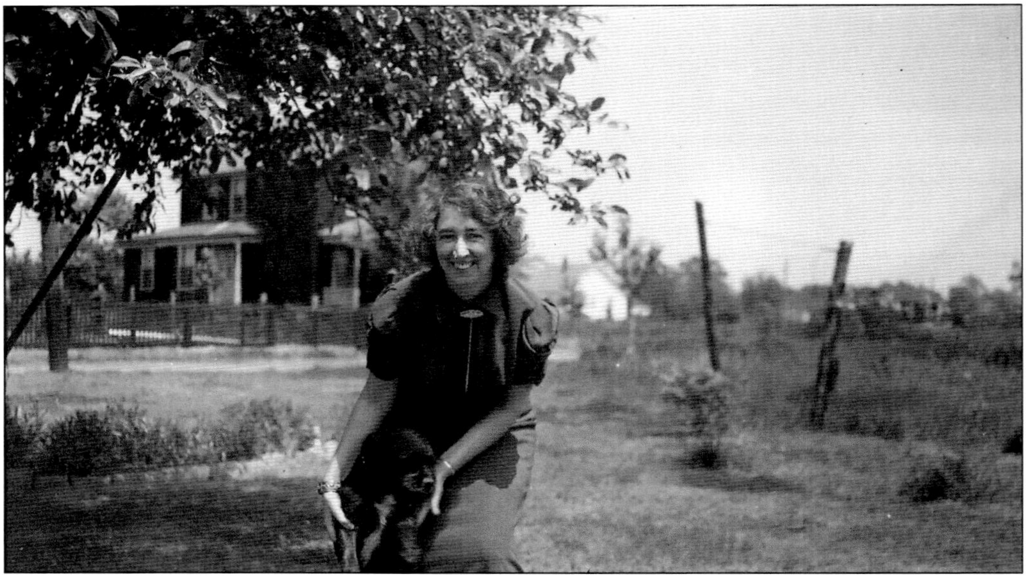

Mary and Lester B. Walling built this house on Church Street in Belford near the present site of number 211 *c.* 1907. Their daughter Alva is seen in front of it *c.* 1930 after the house was moved to Garnsey Place for a street construction job.

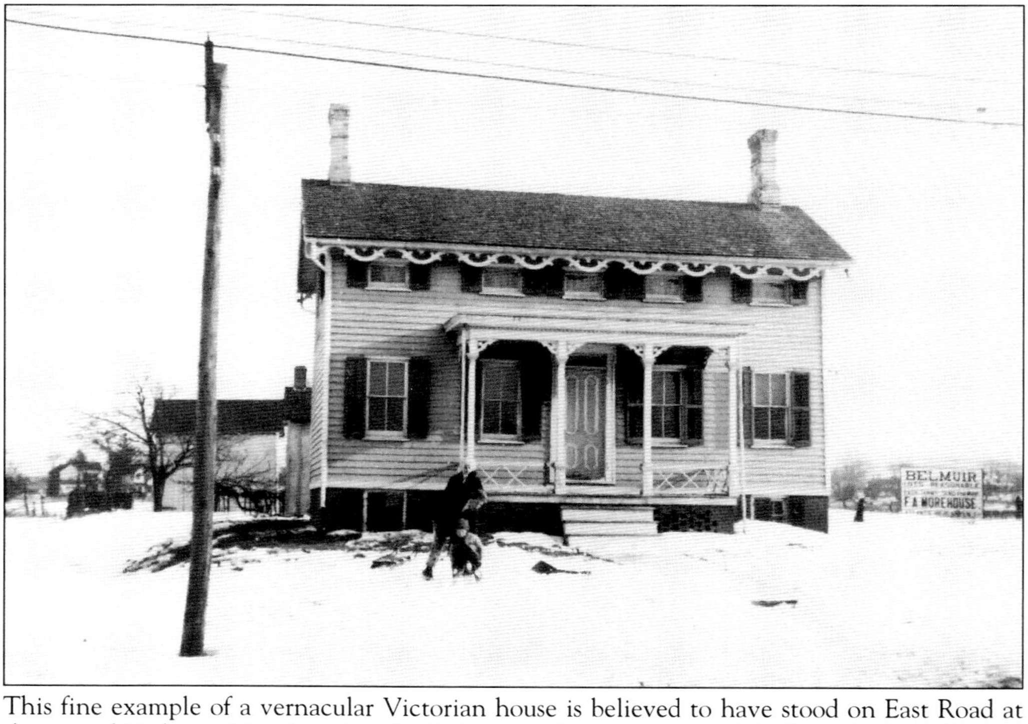

This fine example of a vernacular Victorian house is believed to have stood on East Road at the site of Highway 36, a location the Belmuir real estate sign would affirm. It likely dates *c.* 1870 and is exceptional for its five bays. The image is *c.* 1920s; the house's present location has proved elusive.

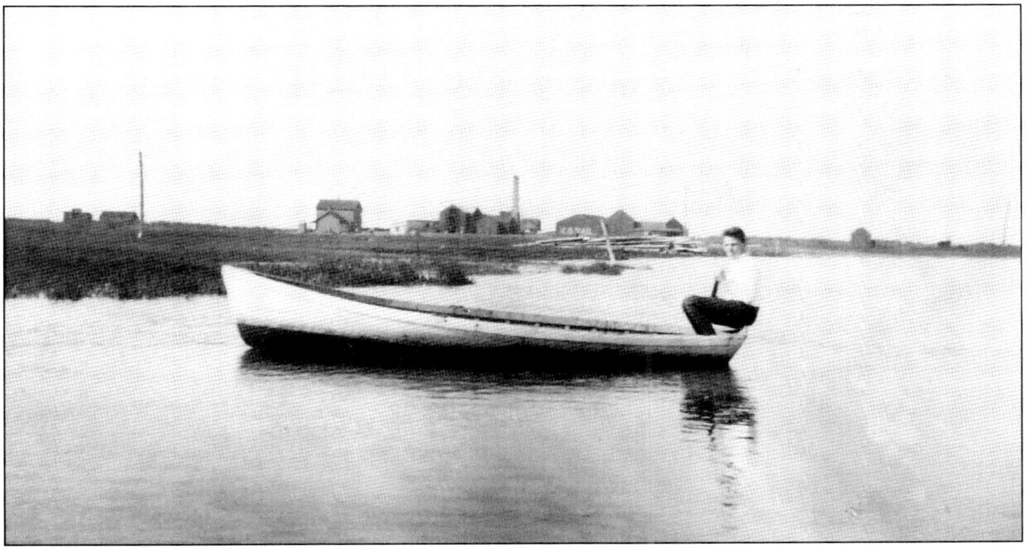

John Tarnow Reichman is seen *c.* 1910 on Compton Creek, with the fish factory visible in the background.

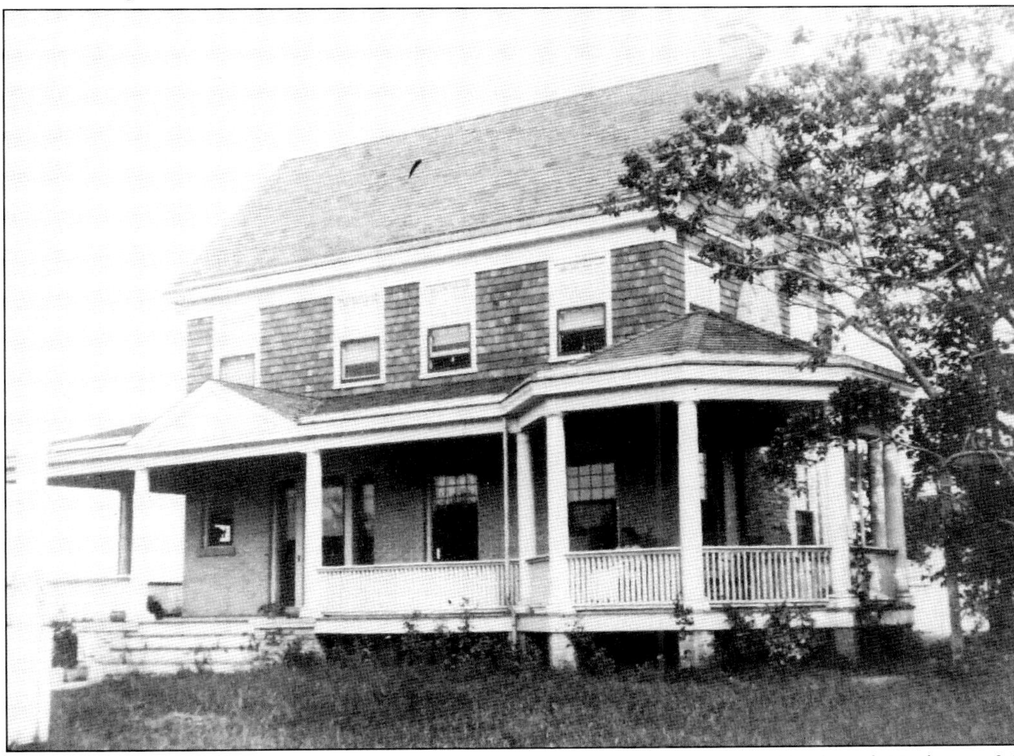

John Reichman's house at the northeast corner of Main Street in Belford and Highway 36, which was seen before the highway was opened in Volume I on p. 94 , was built *c.* 1910. This handsome, minimally decorated Colonial Revival home is little changed today, although siding covers the shingles. Reichman was an engineer, long in charge of the Central Railroad's marine division.

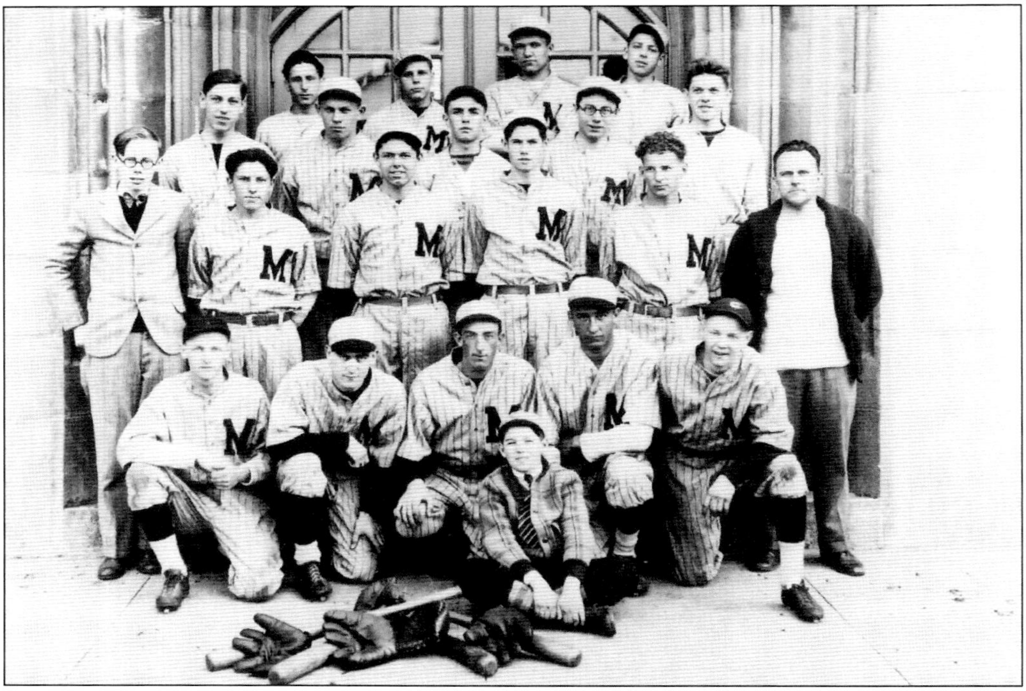

This image of the Leonardo High School Baseball Team appears to have been taken *c.* 1930s. Only coach Lewis Blood is identified.

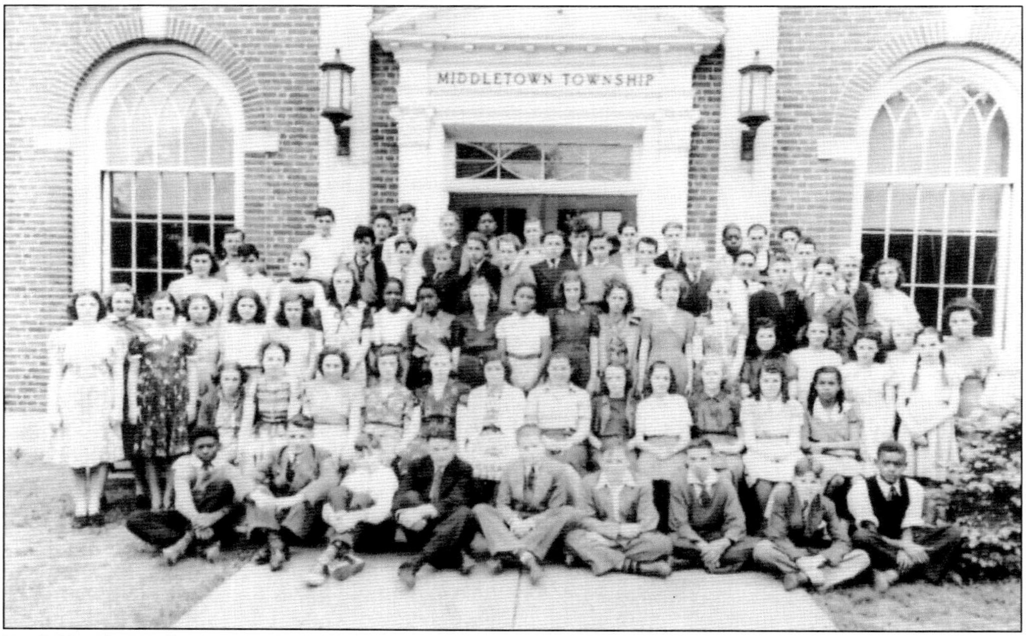

Red Bank architect Ernest Arend's Georgian Revival designs, including the Leonardo Grade School, are among the county's finest locally-produced examples of Colonial Revival architecture. The Class of 1939 was the first to attend all of its elementary years at the school, which opened in 1931.

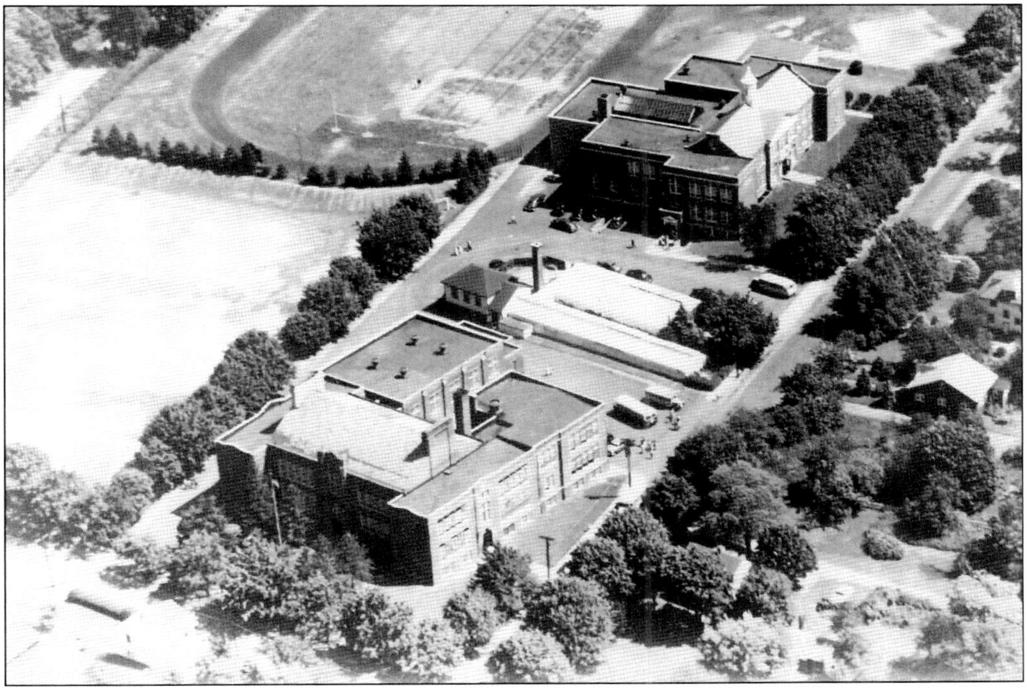

This c. 1940 aerial looking south from the corner of Leonardville Road and Hosford Avenue shows the former township high school at bottom and the Leonardo Grade School at top. The high school, completed in 1913 to a design by New York's Brazer and Robb, was largely destroyed by fire in 1963; part of the old school was incorporated in the replacement structure now known as the Bayshore Middle School. The Leonardo Grade School, completed in 1931 to a design by Red Bank's Ernest Arend, still stands but needs work to preserve it. The greenhouses between them no longer stand, and the schools have been expanded.

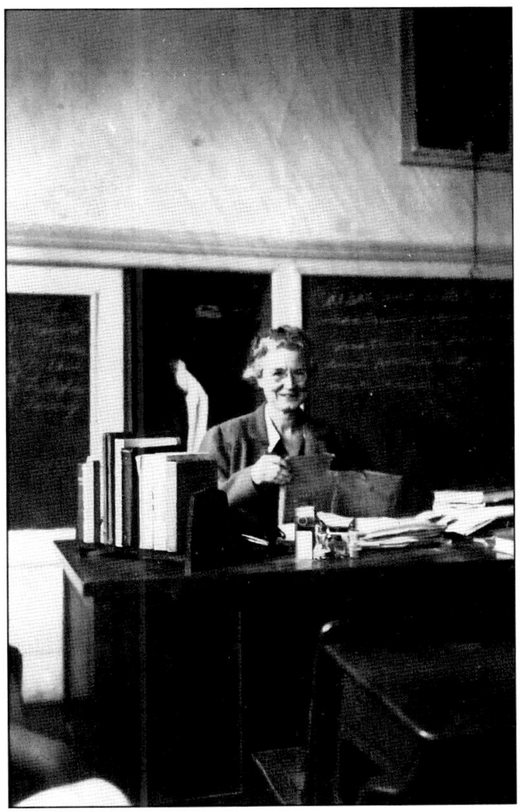

Martha R. Pennington, from Millington, Maryland, seen c. 1940, was a graduate of Washington College. It was said she wondered why her Problems of American Democracy classes became increasingly smart as the day progressed; she was apparently unaware that the day's issues were break-time topics among the eager student body.

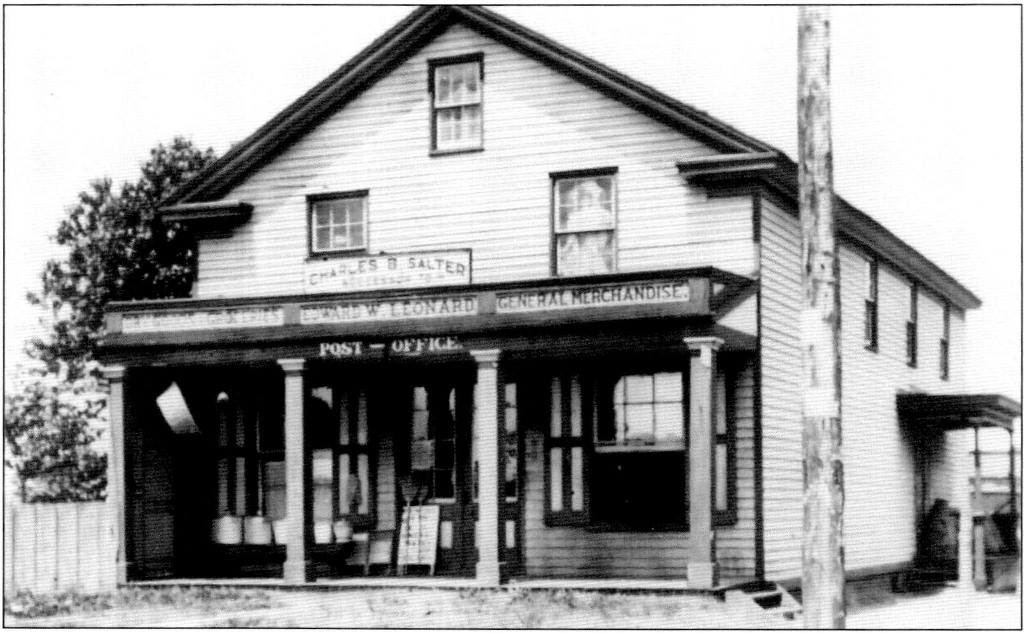

Leonard's store at the northwest corner of Leonardville Road and Avenue D, seen perhaps in the early 1900s, was long a local commercial center. At one time, it contained the post office; the 1897 establishment of an office under postmaster Charles T. Leonard effected the beginning of the use of the name Leonardo, in lieu of Leonardville. Note the shadow of the woman in the window at right, who is perhaps giving the photographer a suspicious look, the type that the author knows well.

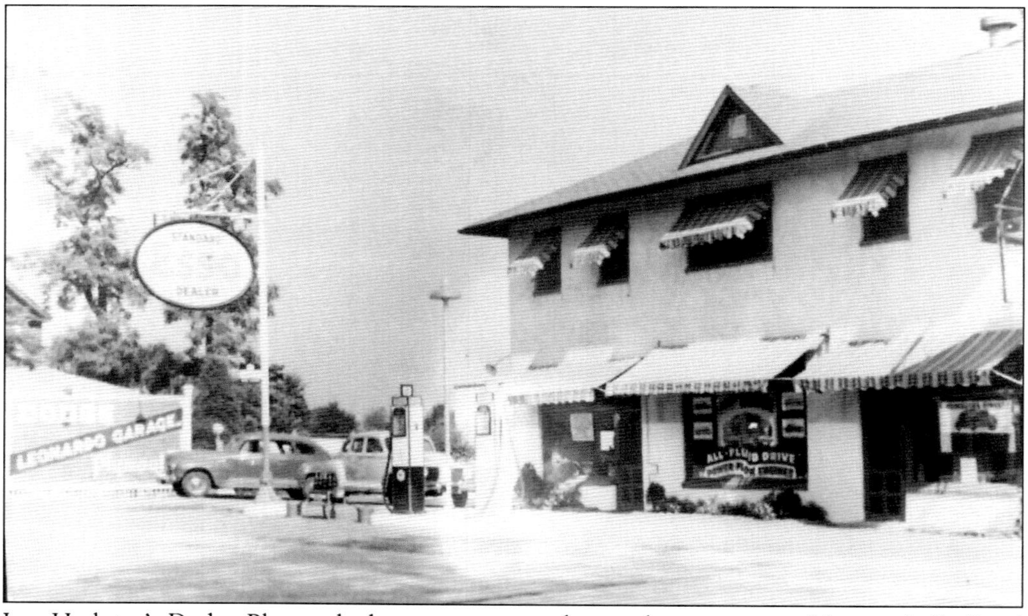

Leo Herbster's Dodge-Plymouth showroom was at the northwest corner of Leonardville Road and Appleton Avenue. Seen here in the 1940s, it was later the Leonardo Garage and is now occupied by a light manufacturing operation.

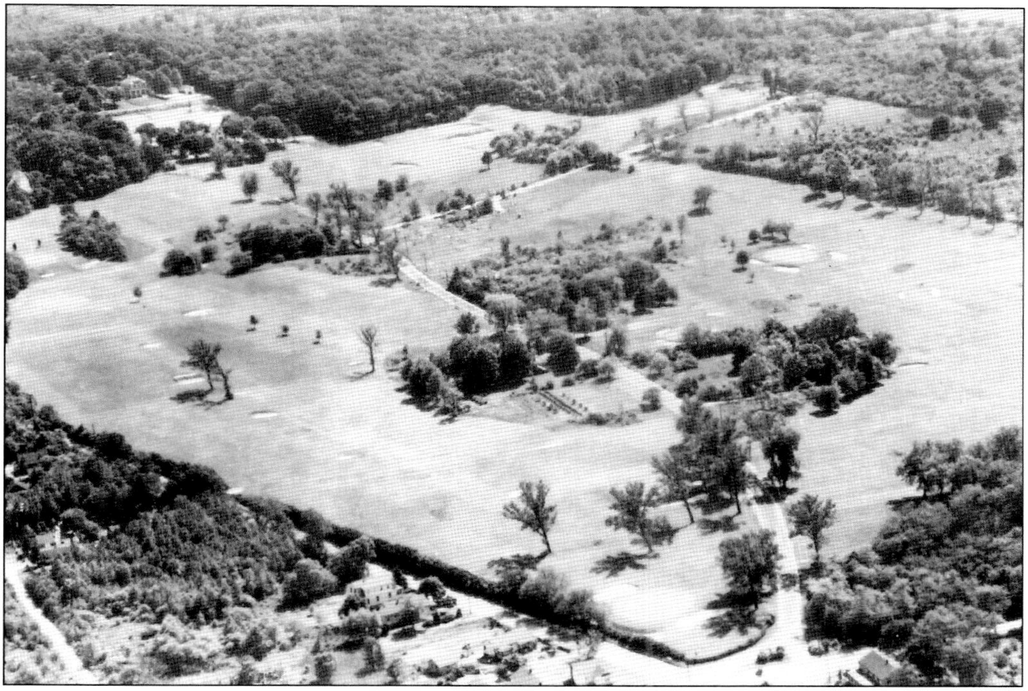

The Beacon Hill Country Club, viewed *c.* 1970s looking northeast, began when early cottage owners at Highland Park sought permission from the developer to build "golf links" in the midst of their houses. Lot sales had been lagging, so the owner thought golf could enhance the property. A 9-hole, 3,029-yard course was in use by 1899. The course, now 18 holes, has changed over the years. See Volume I, p. 99 for an early image.

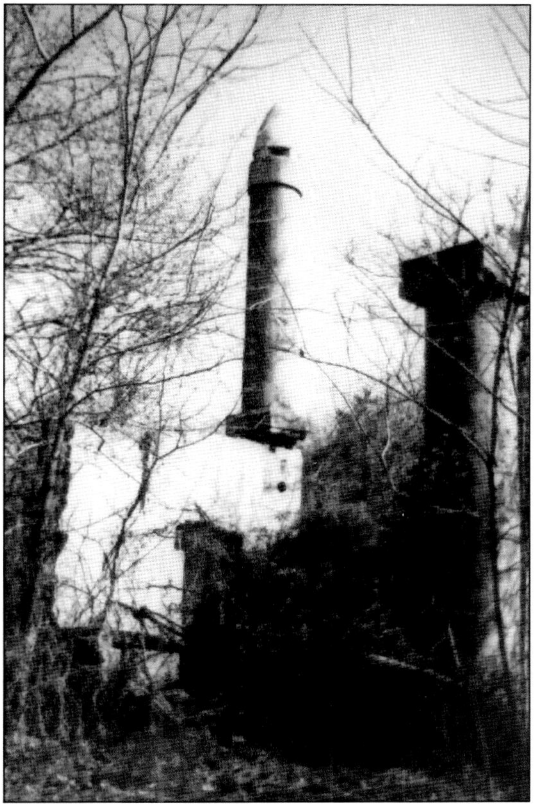

The caption to the Volume II, p. 101 illustration of the William J. Leonard house, popularly known as "Willy's Castle," noted it likely had greater appeal as ruins. A column and a minaret of the house, located south of Leonardville Road behind Croydon Hall, are shown here at an unspecified date. The oldest part reportedly dates to the eighteenth century, although various later expansions were made. Leonard's house included a central portion enclosed with glass, which allowed first- and second-story sun rooms. The house was destroyed by fire in September 1936.

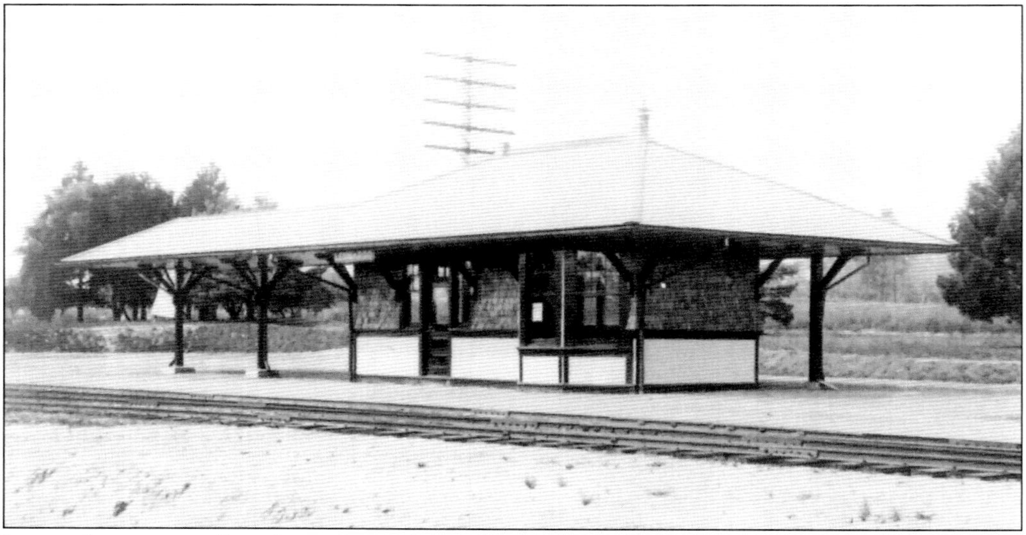

Leonardo was initially a flag stop on the Central Railroad's Atlantic Highlands branch known as Leonard Avenue, but that demarcation was replaced by this structure in 1910. Dehart and Letson, Red Bank photographers who had a summer branch in nearby Atlantic Highlands, took this image apparently when the building was new. The station, long in a state of disrepair, came down after the branch closed *c.* 1963.

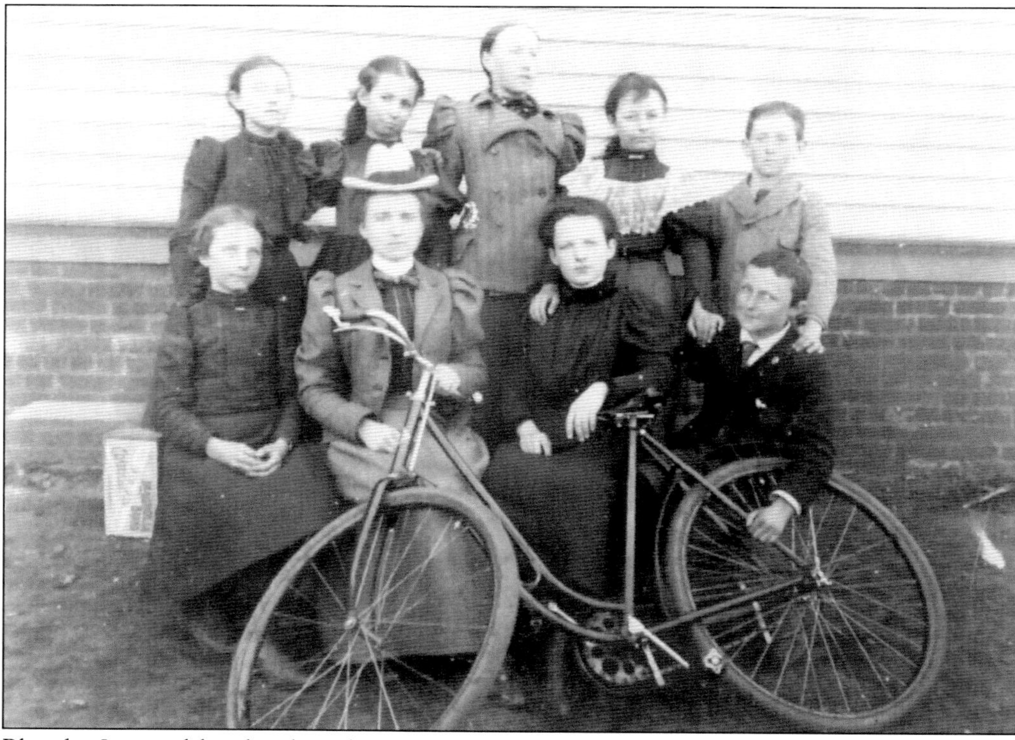

Blanche Leonard has her bicycle at the Leonardo Grade School. She is posing with several students, some of whom appear to be smirking, perhaps because of her hat. Ashley Roop is at right in the front row in this *c.* 1902 photograph.

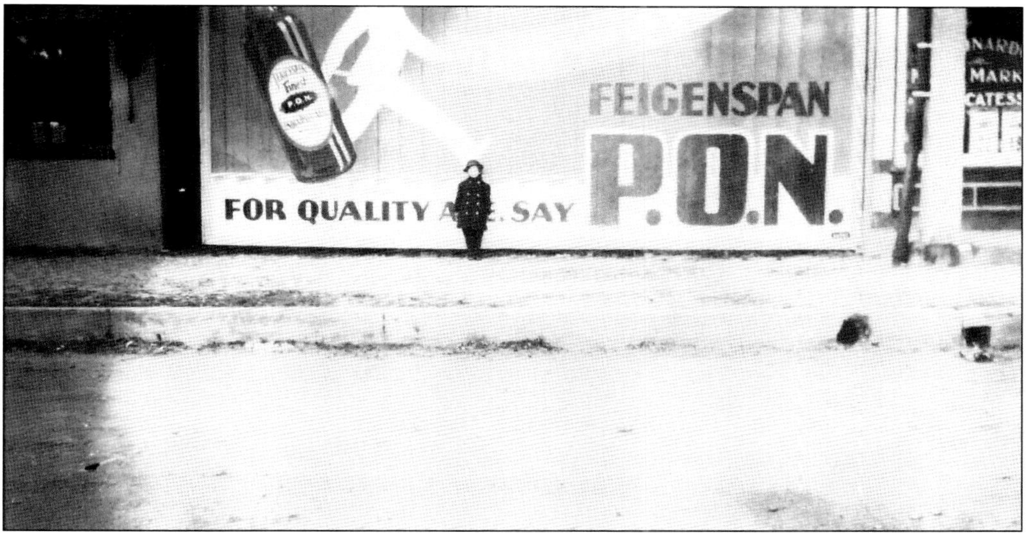

The figure and letters on the sign make the youthful Mae Fisher seem even more diminutive than her approximately five-year-old size in this *c.* 1934 image. Christian Feigenspan's Pride of Newark beer had a local tie, as he was a summer resident of Rumson. It also had a family tie, as Mae's grandfather James W. Shannon of Atlantic Highlands was a distributor.

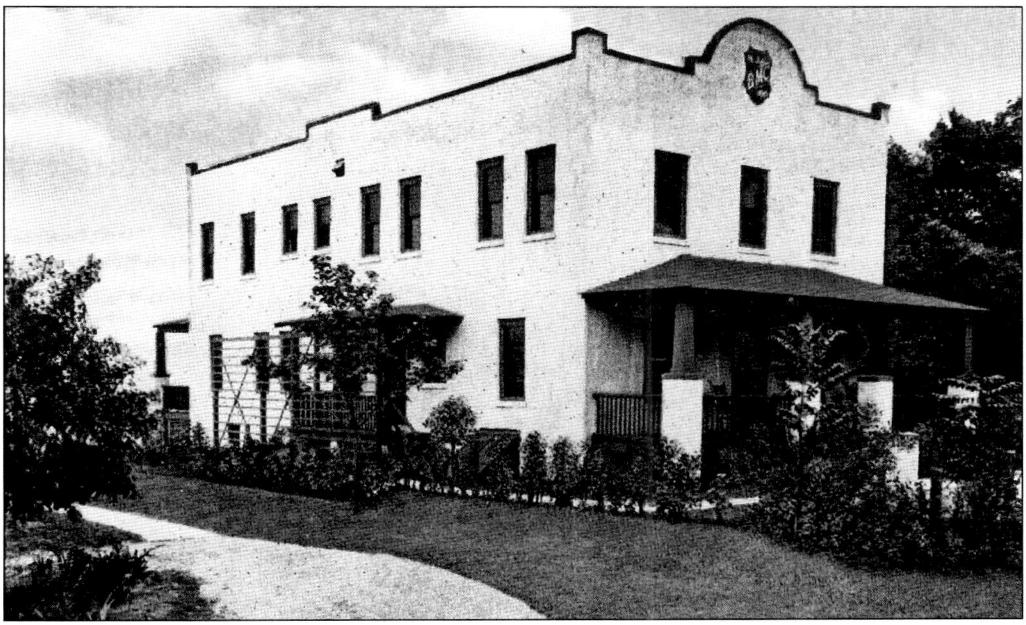

The New Jersey Blind Men's Club built Camp Happiness as a summer vacation home for the blind. New quarters were erected in 1930: a two-story, stucco, hollow-tile structure at 27 Burlington Avenue on Sandy Hook Bay. The building, now named Adicks Hall for co-founder William Adicks, was paid for with the proceeds of Frank Hall's widely-produced play, *Blind Life*. The image conveyed in this *c.* 1930s postcard is little changed today, although the porch is now enclosed and a driveway has been built around the entrance.

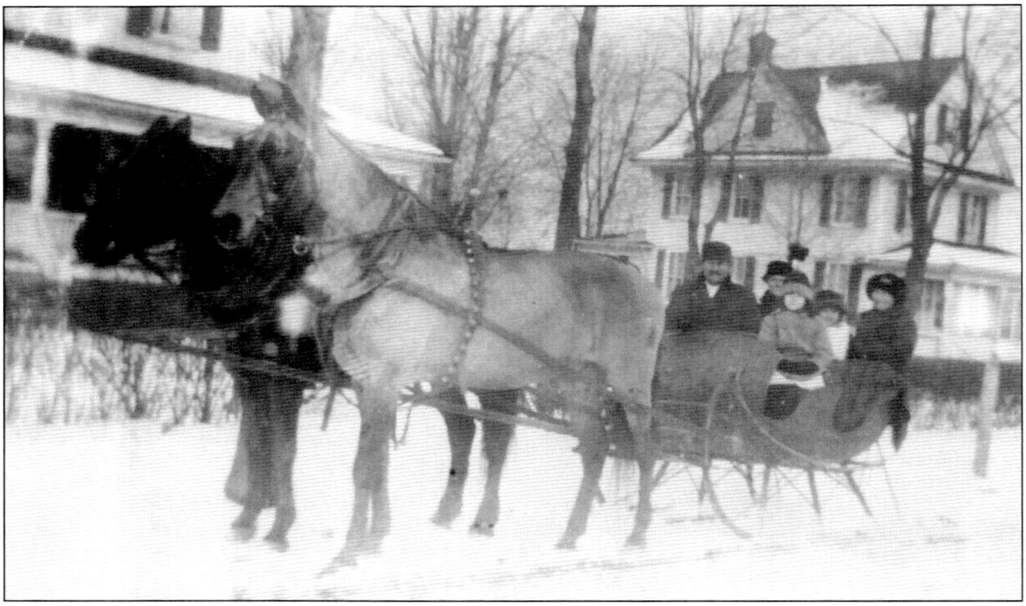

The house at right, 955 Leonardville Road, provides a recognizable focal point for this vintage image, but it is believed the subjects are unidentified members of the Frost family who owned the house at left. Later, the building became a nursing home, but was then destroyed by fire in the early 1960s; luckily, the home was empty at that time. The lot is now vacant.

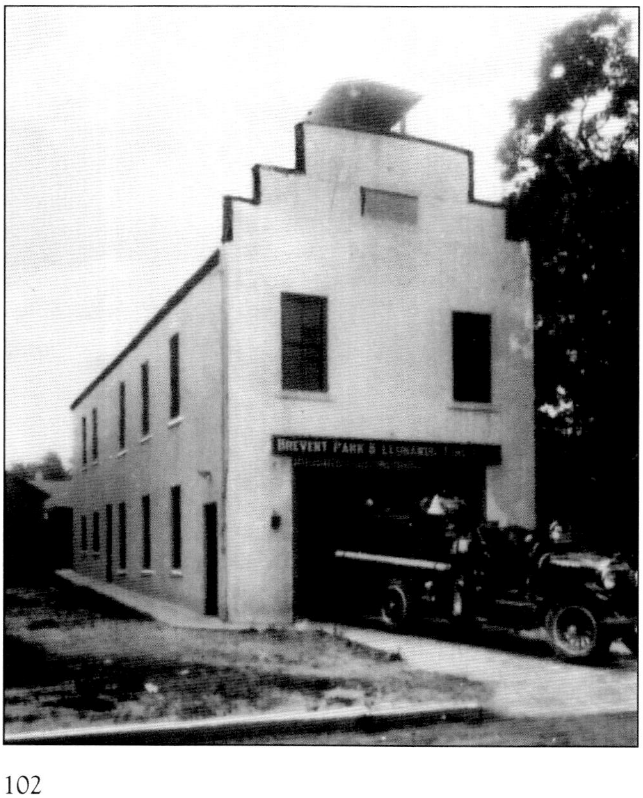

The stone marker on this stucco-clad firehouse on the north side of Center Avenue west of Brevent Avenue indicates the Brevent Park and Leonardo Fire Company was founded in 1903, with the building erected in 1914. The present appearance is changed from this *c.* 1930s image by the elimination of the step gable and the erection of a two-bay addition on the east, or left.

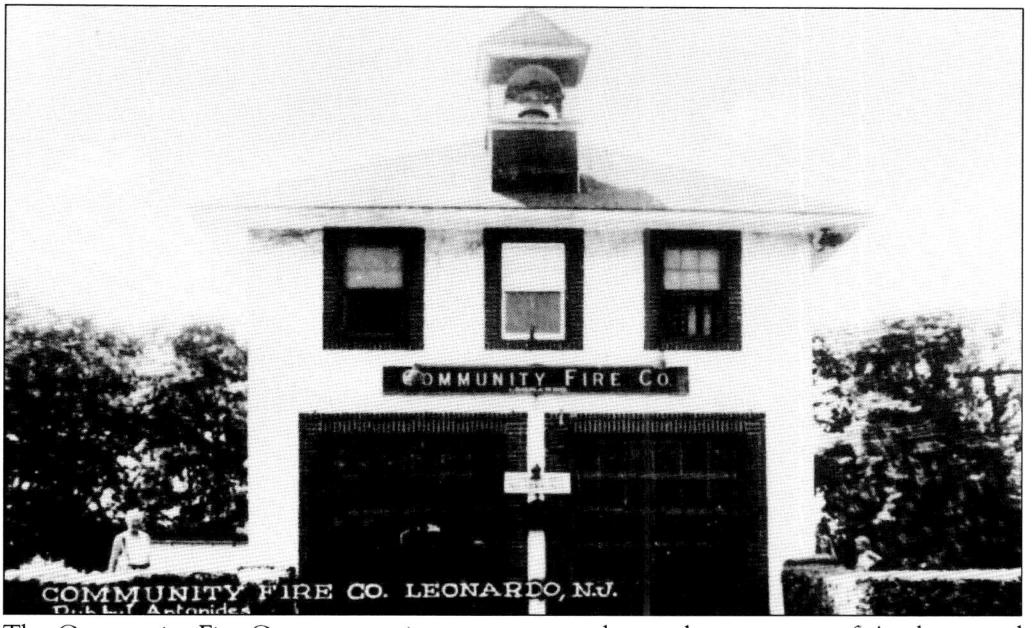

The Community Fire Company station was once at the southwest corner of Appleton and Highland Avenues in this 1925 building, to which a wing was added on the south, at left, in 1955. The fire company now has a new building on Appleton, just south of Highway 36. This structure was remodeled as the Little Chief Engine Company Pre-School, which opened in 1992. The doors are bricked-up and the cupola is gone, but the building is still recognizable. (Collection of John Rhody.)

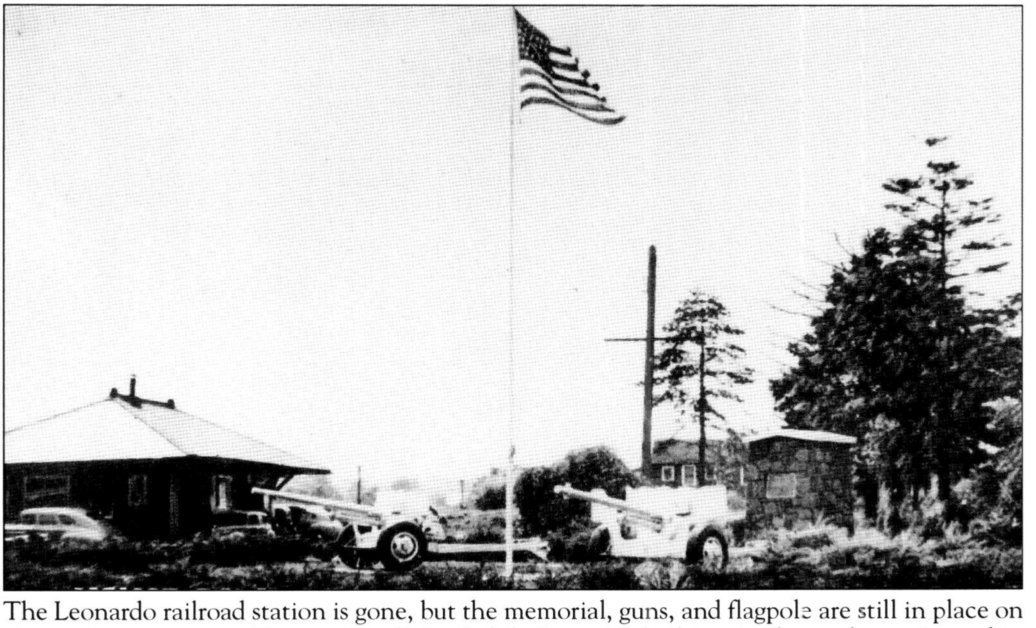

The Leonardo railroad station is gone, but the memorial, guns, and flagpole are still in place on the northwest corner of Leonard and Vanderbilt Avenues, looking similar to those pictured in this mid-1940s postcard. The plaque conveys a dedication to Arthur Josephs, Frederick Lauer, and Arnold Lisk, who made the supreme sacrifice, and to all who served in World War II.

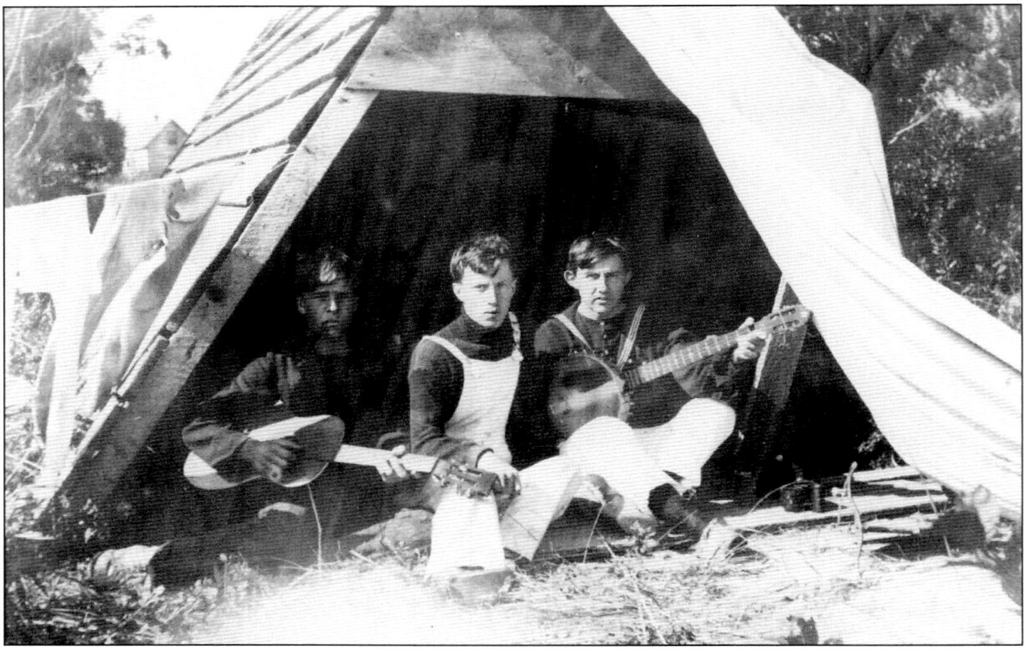

G. Charles Gunderson , center, was born in Norway in 1883 to a sea-going father, emigrating to the United States while a young boy. He developed an early love for the water and sailing, living for a while in Perth Amboy and spending recreational time on Raritan Bay. The substantial frame "tent" and clothesline imply their camping trip to the Leonardo shore around the turn of the century was planned as a prolonged stay.

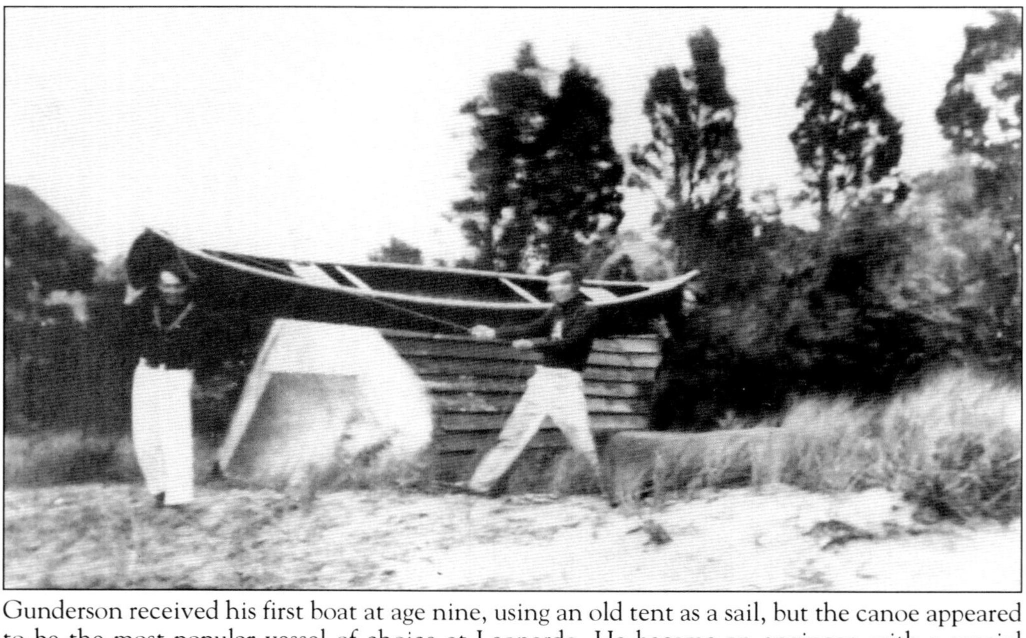

Gunderson received his first boat at age nine, using an old tent as a sail, but the canoe appeared to be the most popular vessel of choice at Leonardo. He became an engineer, with a special focus on electrical machinery. One of his inventions, the first automatic compression molding press, is owned by the Smithsonian Institution.

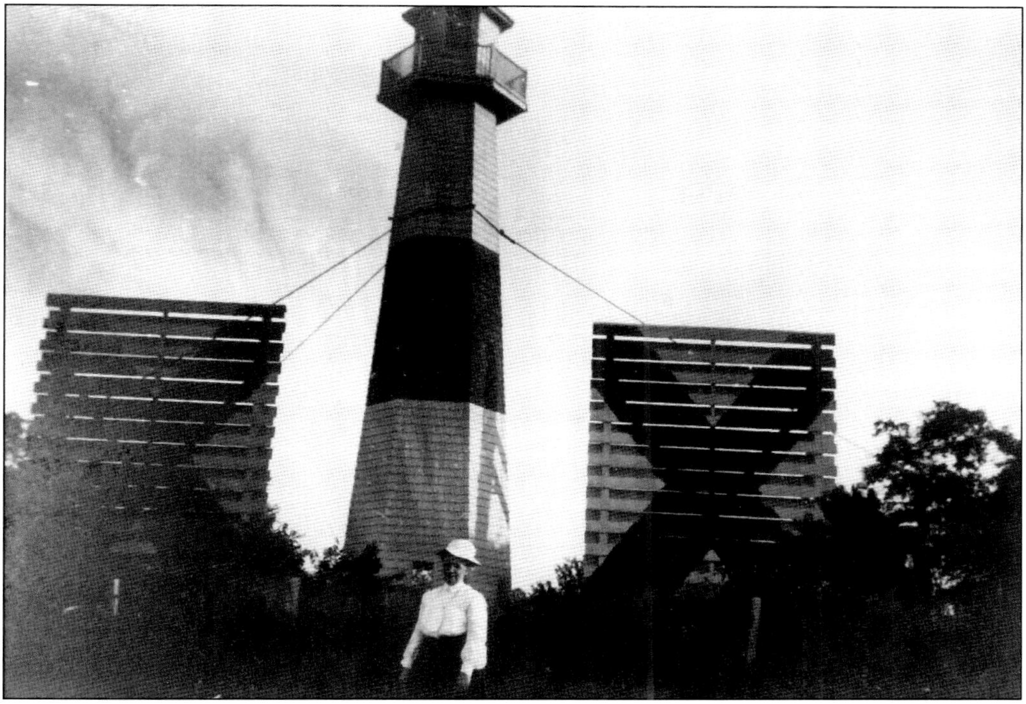

A Gunderson camping companion poses in front of the original 1856 Conover Beach Beacon with raised sideboards. This lighthouse, when aligned with the Chapel Hill Light (Vol. I, p. 81), guided the mariner to the Sandy Hook Channel. The sideboards increased visibility during daylight hours. This frame structure was replaced by a light on a steel tower light still c. 1941. Its preservation is an important public issue as this book goes to press.

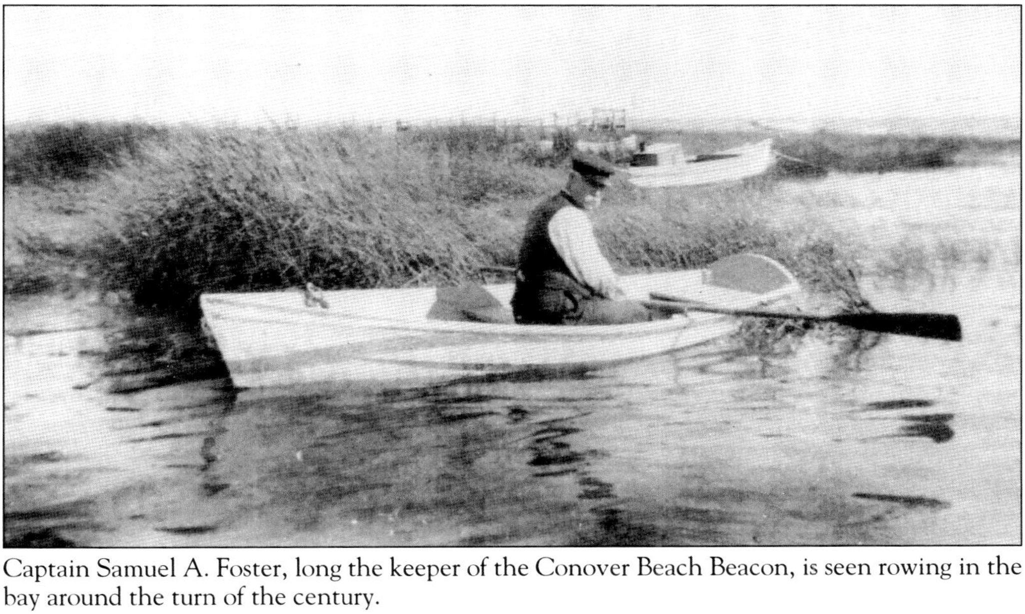

Captain Samuel A. Foster, long the keeper of the Conover Beach Beacon, is seen rowing in the bay around the turn of the century.

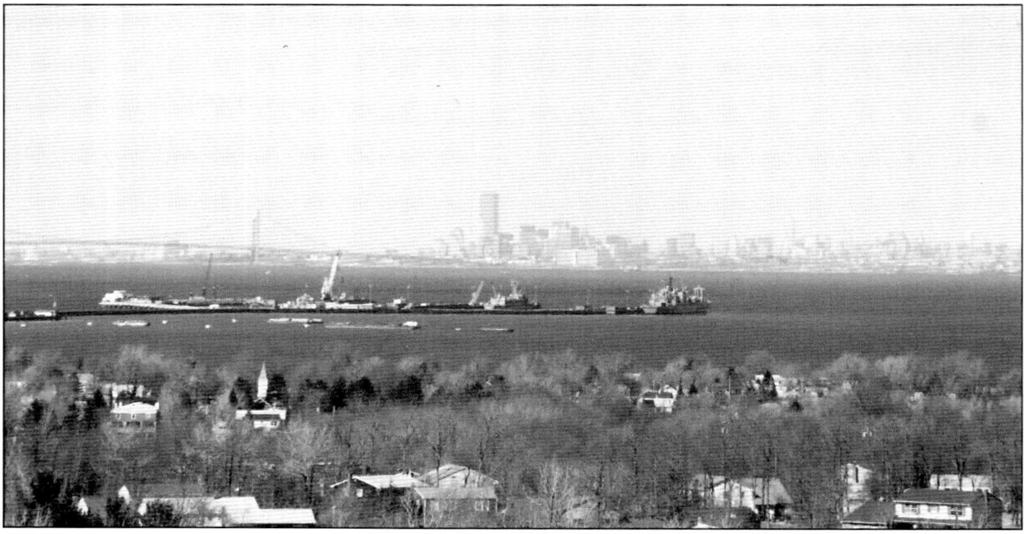

The pier at the Earle Naval Weapons Station, built in 1943–4, was the origin of much of the munitions used in the 1944 Normandy invasion. It still serves as a major supply and support facility for the Atlantic Fleet. The pier, seen in the 1980s and viewed from the Chapel Hill Lighthouse, has been lengthened in recent years. The effect of a telephoto lens appears to bring New York City closer than the 20 air miles between the pier and the tip of Manhattan.

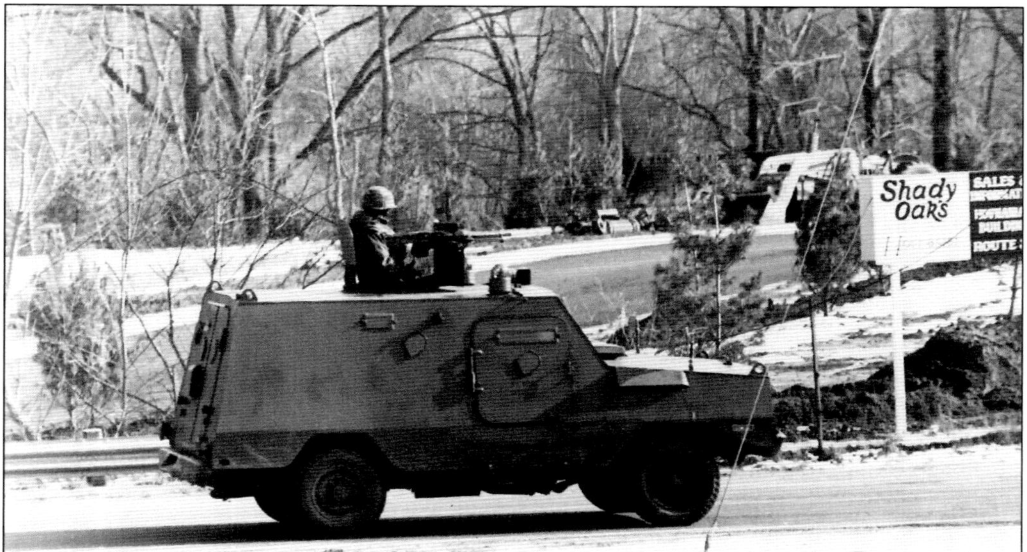

The protection given to some shipments on Normandy Road from the Earle Naval Weapons Station facility at Colts Neck to the pier at Leonardo was awesome. Armed sentries at intersections, helicopters overhead, and armed escort vehicles led one to believe they were not merely transporting gun shells. The Navy never admitted storage of nuclear weapons there, but this has been Monmouth County's worst-kept secret. The government admits they do not have there now what they never admitted they once did. This image dates from 1983.

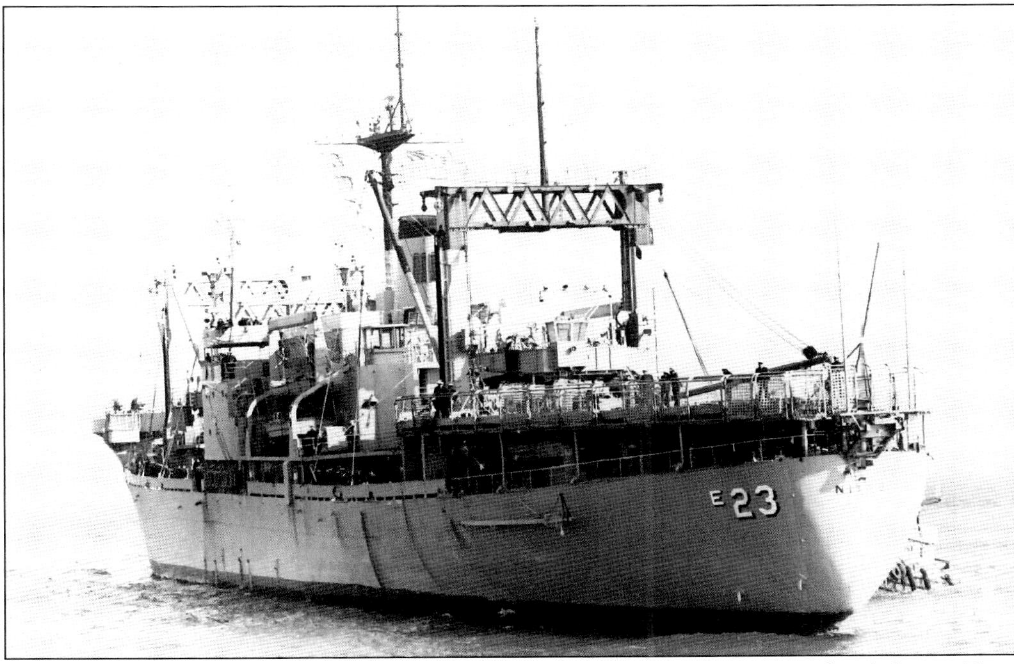

Earle is the home base for a number of supply and support ships serving the Atlantic Fleet, including the U.S.S. *Nitro*, seen here returning from an extended tour at sea in 1976. Their ships are literally floating warehouses, supplying munitions and goods of every type to the Atlantic fleet vessels.

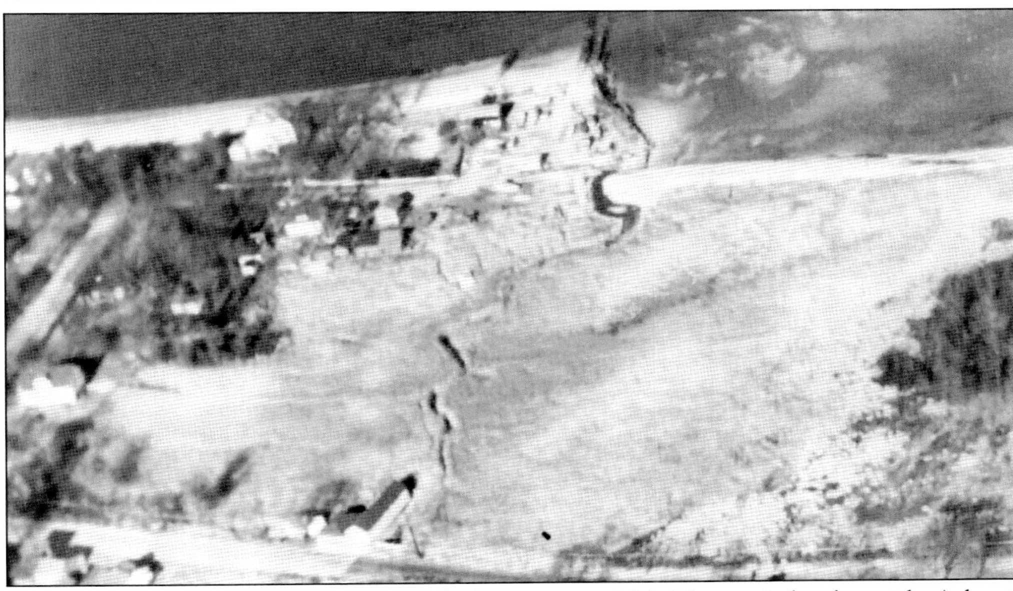

Wagners Creek, seen in a 1930s aerial, forms part of Middletown's border with Atlantic Highlands to the right, or east. The Wagners, long a maritime family there, owned the property on the Leonardo side. It was the site of the Banfield Seaskiff boat-building operation during the 1920s and is now the premises of Al Loux's Wagners Boat Yard. The shore was once covered with sedge grass (see Vol. II, p. 107).

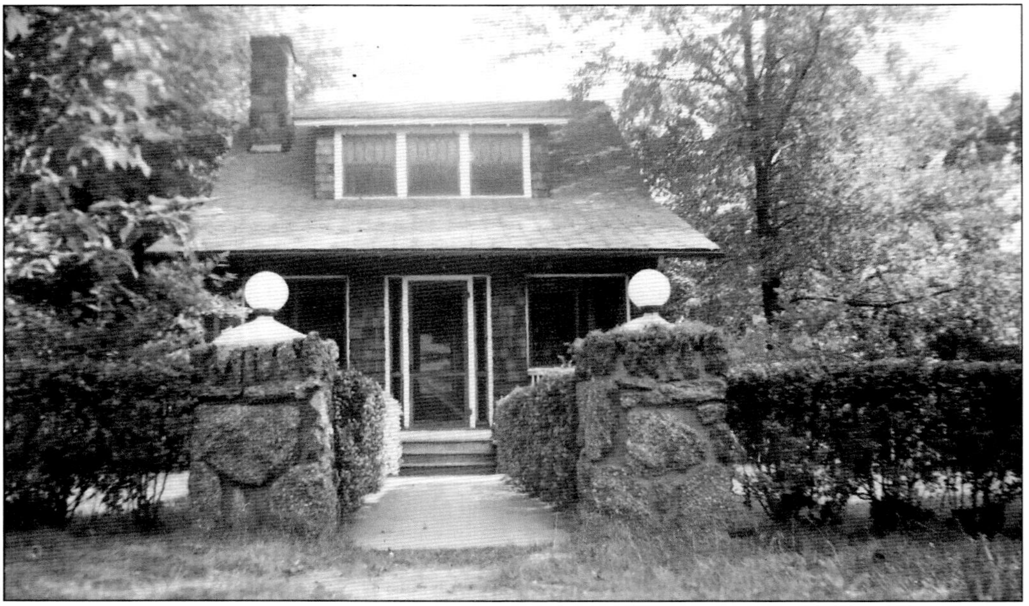

Earle Naval Weapons Station, fenced-off and closed to the public, shut off not only access but memories of a land that was a summer home to private owners. Bastable Browne bought this shingled cottage from O.G. Frake, who may have been the builder, in 1915. The front faced the bay. It was located near the north side of Highway 36, east of the Earle entrance gate, and is seen in a July 1937 photograph.

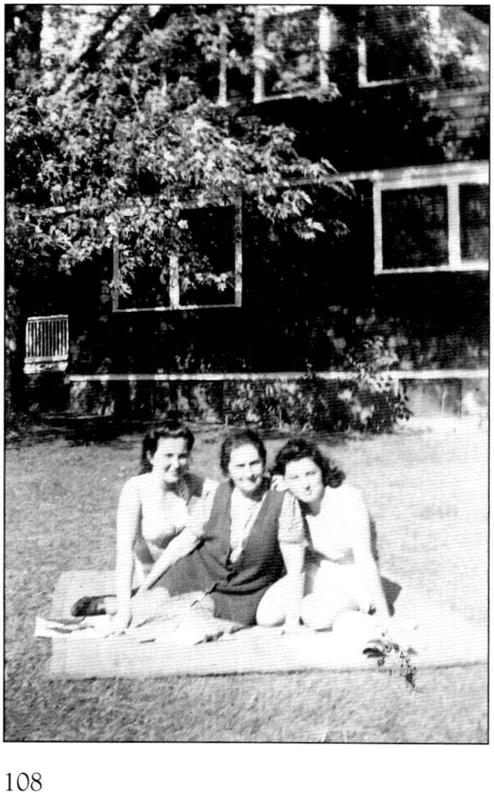

This photograph of three Brownes relaxing on the lawn in July 1940 provides an opportunity to view a house of a size belied by its entrance. They are, from left, Mary Jane "Peggy" Browne Corballis, Margaret Foley Browne, and Isabelle Browne Dugan.

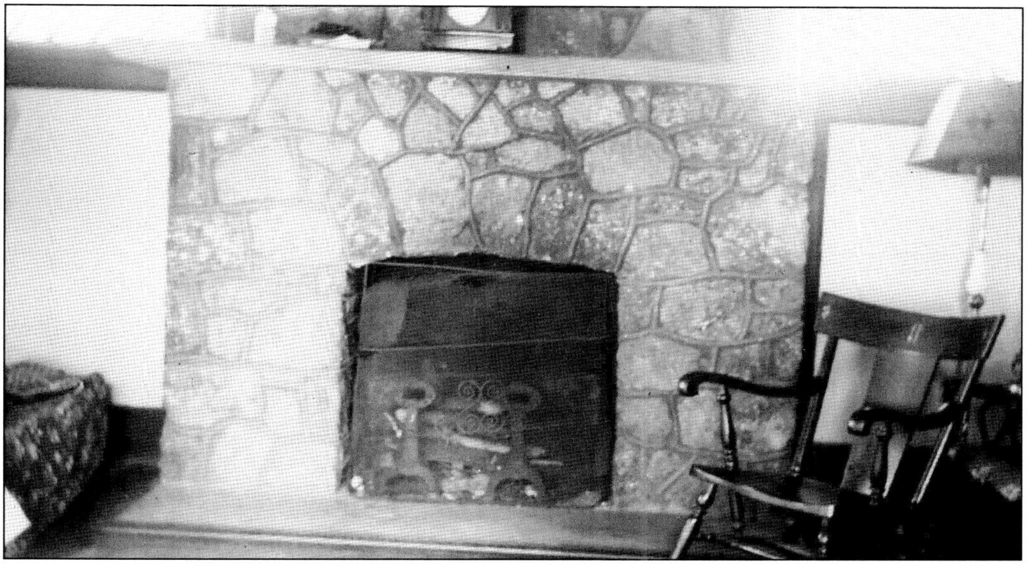

Peanut stone was found in large quantity in the Leonardo-Atlantic Highlands area, and much of it is still visible in gateposts and fences. It also went into less visible fireplaces. The Navy had earlier used the house to quarter personnel but later demolished the home in the early 1960s.

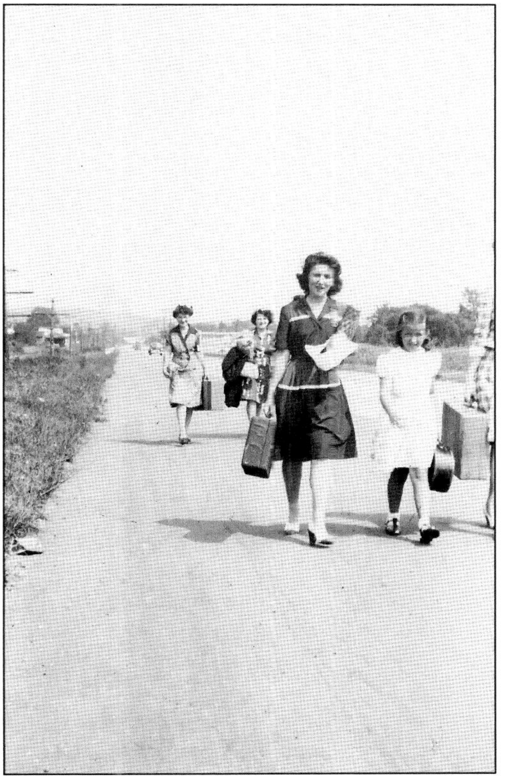

The Navy had begun acquisition proceedings, and the family knew the summer of 1943 would be their last in their fine home. The place was in proximity to the Leonardo railroad station. This August image shows Mary Jane "Peggy" Corballis (wearing a dark dress), her cousins Geraldine (to the right) and Eleanor (partially visible), and Aunts Anna (behind on left) and Nellie walking along Highway 36 to the house.

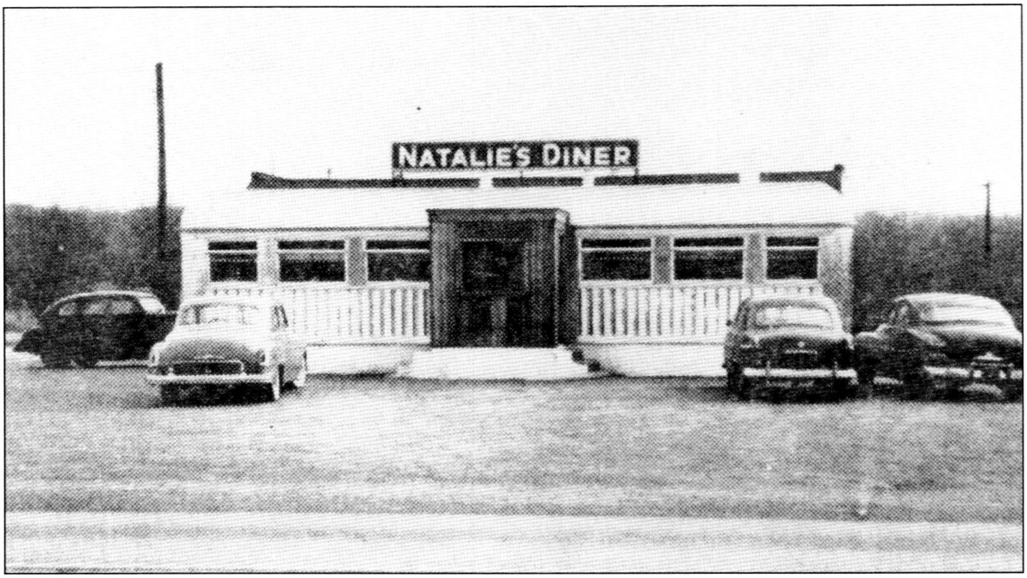

Diners are the quintessential New Jersey eatery, their standing tied to our dense development and extensive road network. Tony Natale, owner of the White Crystal Diner in Atlantic Highlands, told the inside story of this Highway 36 diner's original name, seen here in an early 1950s postcard. Tony's father ordered a sign after opening the restaurant *c.* 1950. The sign maker misspelled his name, but agreed to a $75 discount in exchange for Natale's keeping the flawed product. Thus, it was "Natalie's."

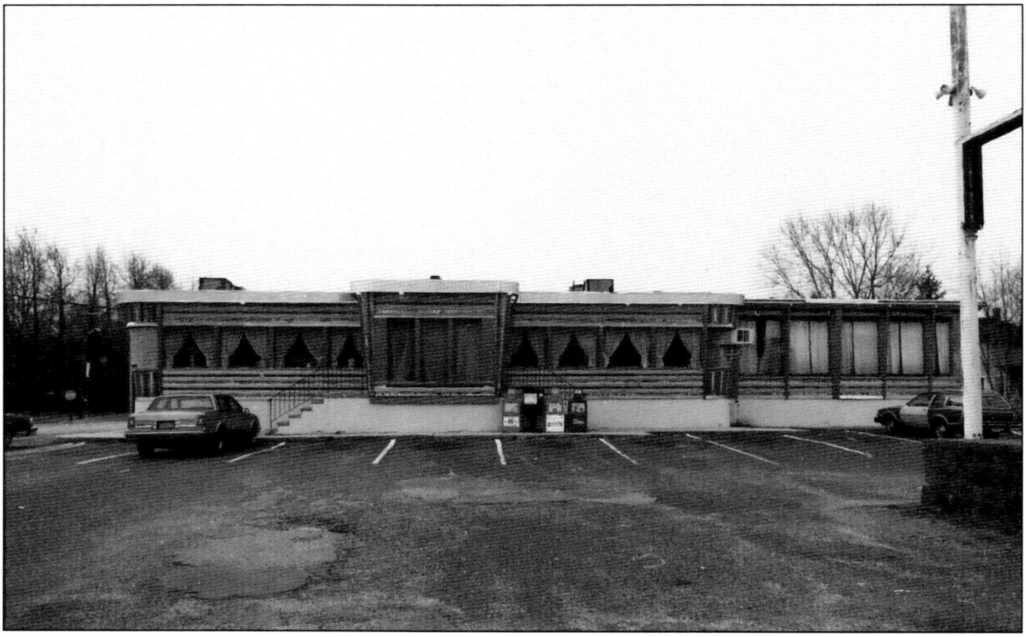

A wing was added on the west, while the entire structure was streamlined, in time becoming known as the Sandy Hook Diner. It fell victim to changing roadside eating preferences in the late 1980s. The site, east of Avenue D, is easy to spot. Just look for the golden arches.

Four

The Riverfront

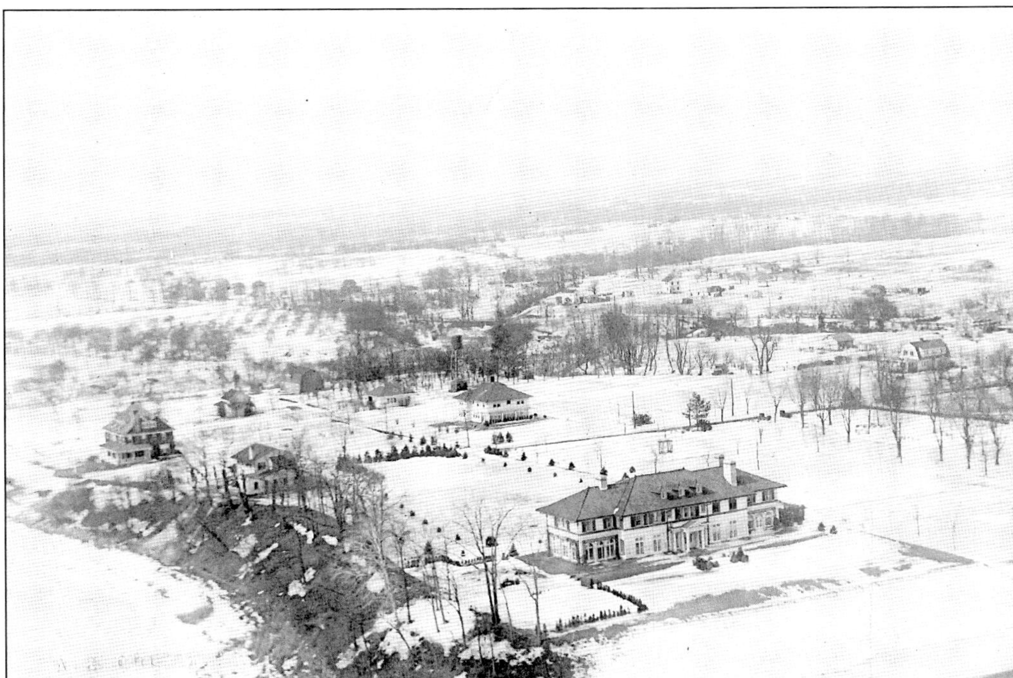

Blossom Cove, the name of the Everett L. Brown house and the cove on the north bank of the Navesink River which the home faces, was built in 1915. Its tile-roofed, stucco-clad Italian Renaissance Revival style was used often by Red Bank architect Ernest Arend in that period, notably in the design of a house nearby on Navesink River Road, in that of another on the Red Bank shore of the Navesink, and in his own house on Broad Street in Red Bank. The photograph, perhaps c. 1920, is by noted Red Bank photographer Andrew Coleman. The street runs parallel to the house, behind the garage near the shore in the rear of the lot.

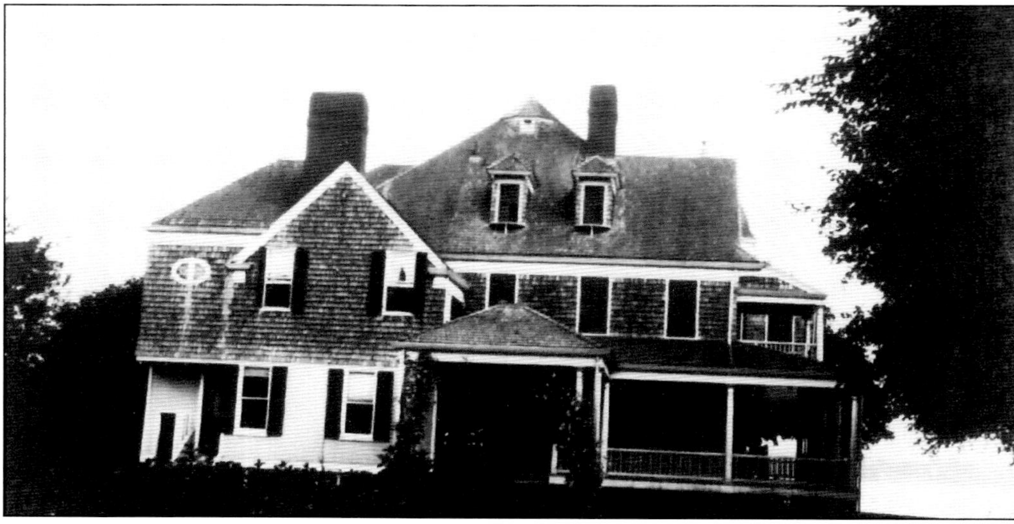

The north elevation of the J. Christian Hupfel house at 458 Navesink River Road, belonging to one of the township's finest Queen Anne style houses, is seen in a c. 1920s view (the south elevation is on p. 50 of Vol. I). It was designed by Fair Haven architect Robert D. Chandler and completed in 1894. The house is faithfully preserved. Hupfel was a New York brewer whose brewery and townhouse were both on East 38th Street. The Hupfels enjoyed the sporting life, and evidence of this is provided by photographs, including that on the cover of Volume I, and the presence of tennis courts and docking facilities.

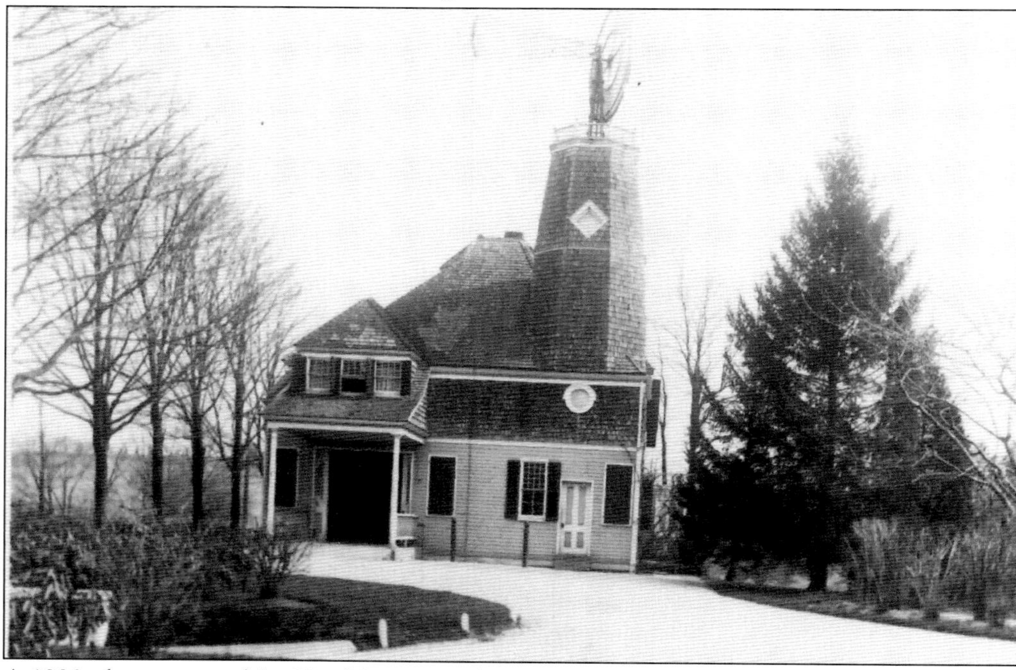

A 1920s description of the Hupfel garage indicated room for nine or more cars, two horse stalls, a four-room caretaker's apartment, and three extra rooms for other help. A water tank was in the tower with an electric pump servicing an artesian well, while a gasoline-powered motor pumped surface water. The garage deteriorated and has been rebuilt over many years.

John H. Patterson, born 1834 in Middletown, spent three years of early manhood in California where he began his political activism. He married Margaret Pringle in 1860, while maintaining an oyster business in Middletown. Patterson failed in an electoral bid for Congress but did serve in the House of Representatives as sergeant at arms and doorkeeper. Prior to those positions, he had been Monmouth County sheriff, and after them, he was warden of the State Prison at Trenton. Sheriff Patterson's other businesses included farming and shipping. He died at the old family homestead (Vol. I, p. 51) in 1909 and is pictured here *c.* 1890s.

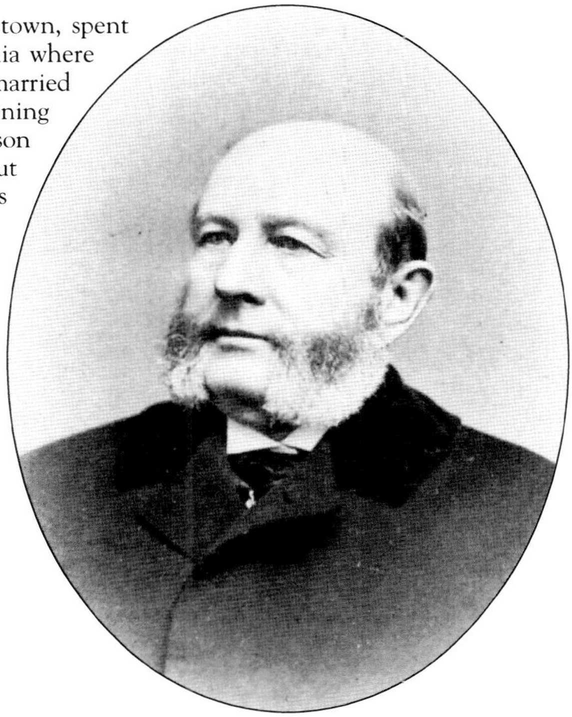

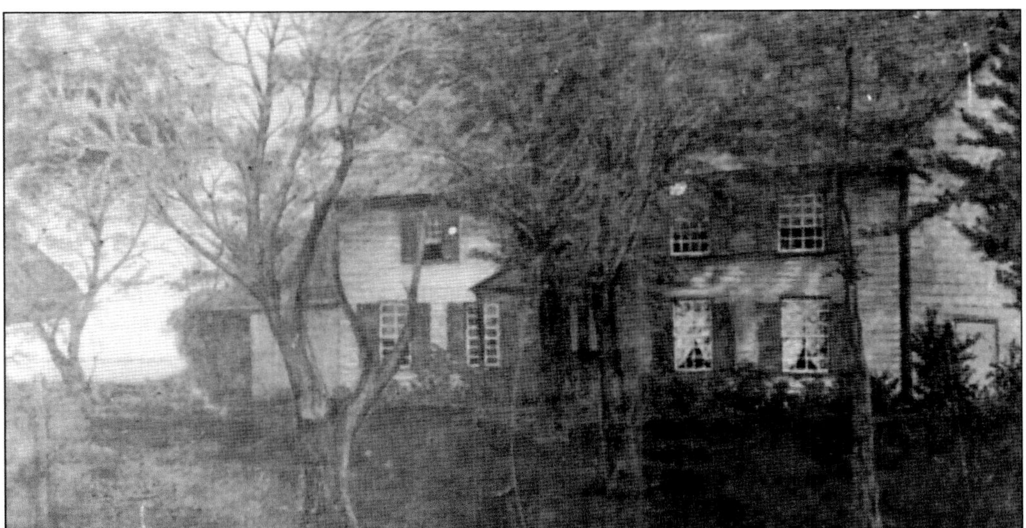

The original photograph at Rutgers labels this as the "John B. Patterson House," from a painting by R. Shaw. The Pattersons owned hundreds of acres of property bordering the Navesink River near Blossom Cove and extending north well inland. Some of their houses were illustrated in Volume I on pp. 51–52, with the entire group meriting a comprehensive study. This one, apparently near the river, was built in two sections; the part at right with the twelve over eight windows was probably a typical area eighteenth-century Georgian side hall plan house. (Special Collections and Archives, Rutgers University Libraries.)

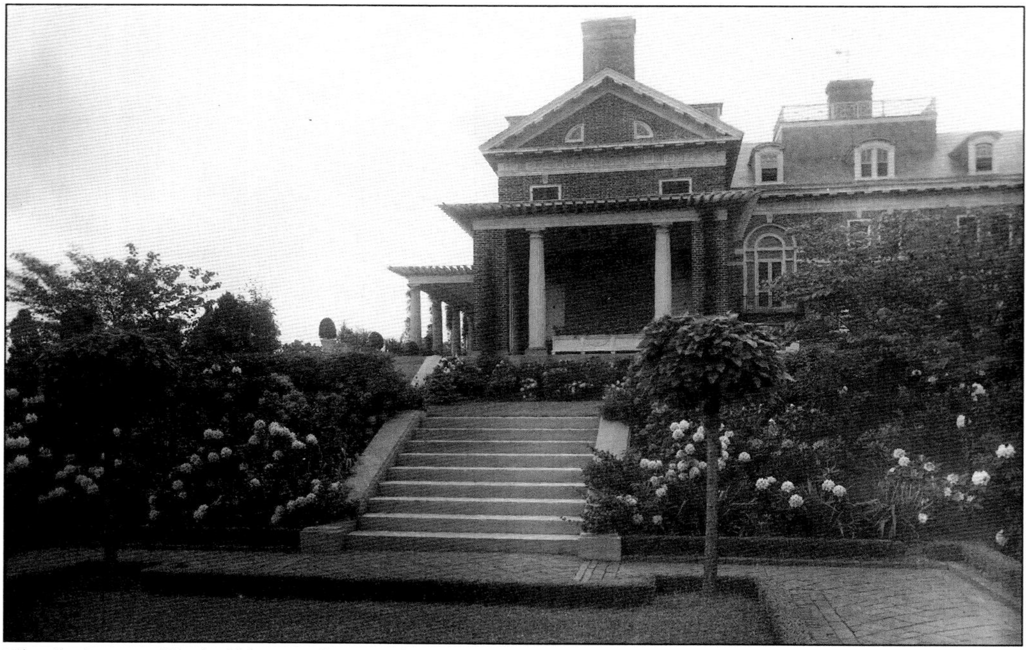

The J. Amory Haskell house (see Vol. I, p. 122) was designed in the Georgian Revival style by New York architects York and Sawyer, later better known for their banks and hospitals, and was built in 1910–11. This *c.* 1920 view of the side reflects an alteration to the original structure, with a pergola remodeled into a porch. The house descended to a pool and surrounding garden (Vol. I, p. 123). It was destroyed by fire in July 1966.

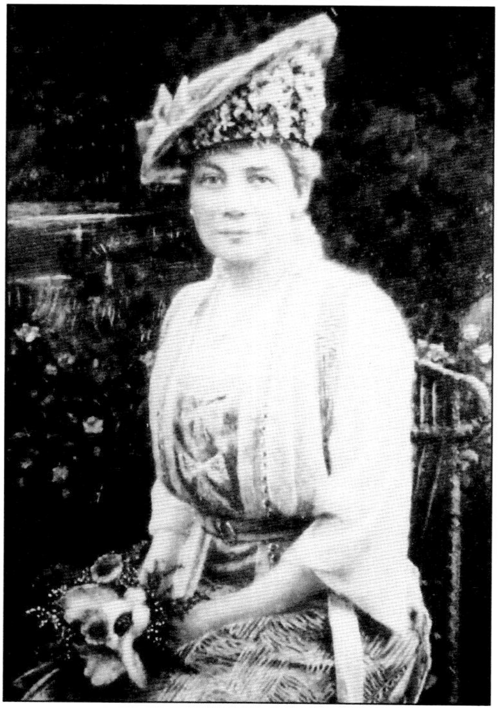

Margaret Moore Riker Haskell was born 1864 at Oak Hill, the Newtown, Queens, New York home of her maternal grandparents (Vol. I, p. 123). She married Jonathan Amory Haskell in 1891, and their early domiciles were in Pennsylvania and Wilmington, Delaware. They bought a Sea Bright house in 1895 and 240 acres of farmland in 1907, soon building the house above. The Haskells had one son and two daughters. Margaret Haskell was interested in music and local history, later buying Marlpit Hall (p. 28) and giving it to the Monmouth County Historical Association. Her consuming interest, the collecting of American antiques, earned her stature as one of the leading collectors of her generation. She died in 1942.

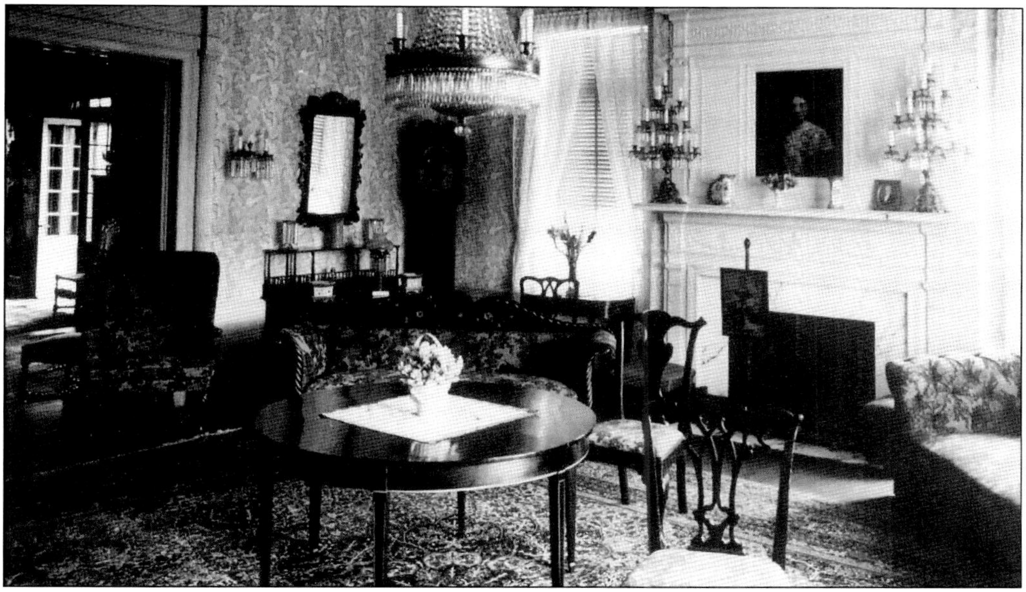

The living room of what the family called Brick House at Oak Hill Farm is shown here in a view from perhaps *c.* 1912. In time, it would become crowded with antique furniture, as would all of Mrs. Haskell's living space. Her specialty was Pennsylvania and New Jersey furniture from the 1730–1830 period. The Parke-Bernet sale of her collection was one of the greatest ever. The introduction to their catalog noted, "it includes the largest and most complete collection ever assembled of the seat furniture of the Philadelphia cabinetmakers . . . some of the best piecrust and card tables of the same period . . . representative shell-covered highboys and lowboys . . . claw-and -ball foot desks and bureaus."

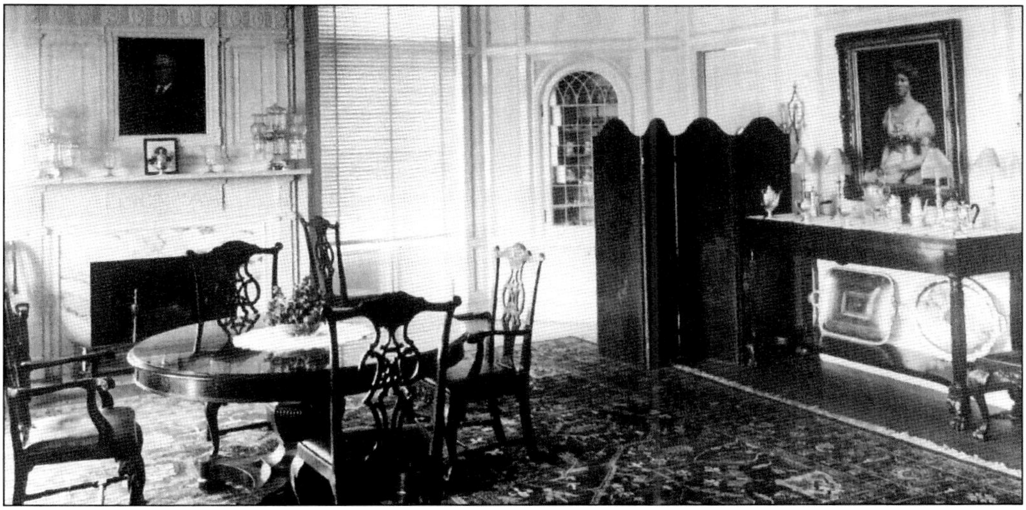

The Brick House dining room appears here *c.* 1912. The Haskell silver collection would attain astounding breadth and depth, including the work of the major silversmiths of her focus period and other crafters. She lent generously, with noted exhibitions of parts of her holdings being mounted at the Metropolitan Museum of Art, the Brooklyn Museum, and the Monmouth County Historical Association, among others. The latter celebrated Margaret Haskell as a legendary collector with a 1996 commemorative exhibition.

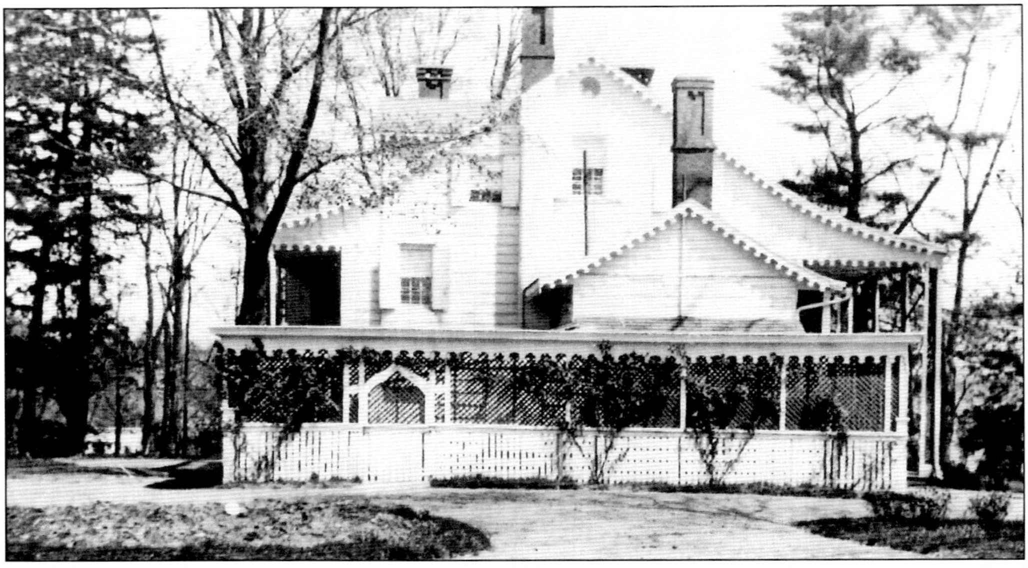

The riverfront house at 786 Navesink River Road was seen in a recent view on p. 119 of Volume II. The core of this often-expanded house dates from the eighteenth century when the property was owned by the Johnston family, with this house likely occupied by Henry Johnston, a Continental Army soldier. The earlier view and this one are both looking east, with the wing in this foreground likely added by noted nineteenth-century owner Hermanus B. Duryea. This image likely dates to c. 1920, following the 1917 purchase of the house by Peter Turnbull.

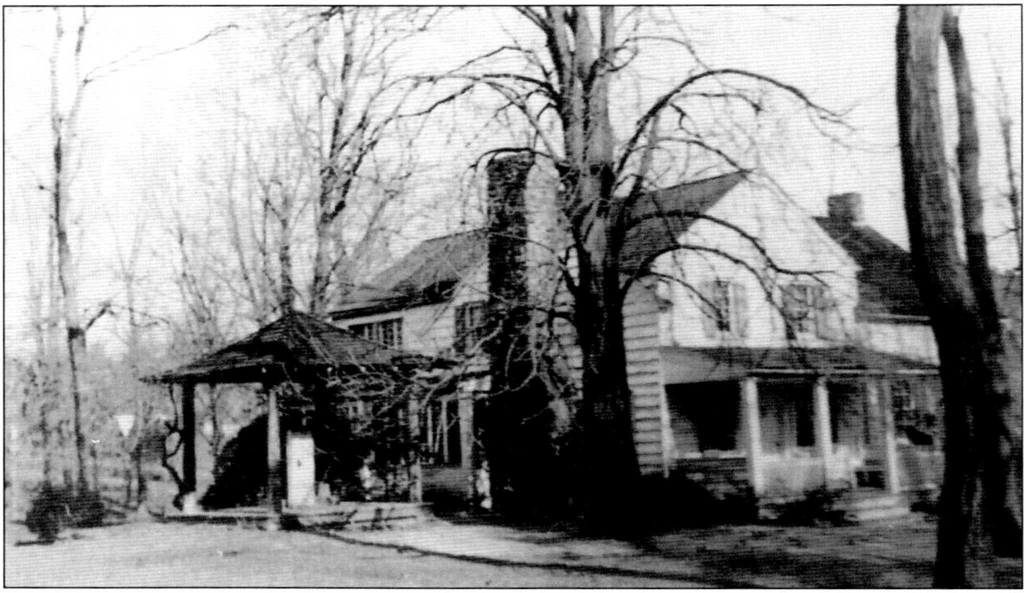

The Lambert Johnston house is located closer to Navesink River Road on property once part of the same parcel as the house above. Lambert and Mattias Johnston are enumerated on the 1798 Middletown Tax List, the best guide to late-nineteenth-century Middletown property ownership. This house is associated in legend with a founding father who, if legend is to be believed, slept nearly everywhere in the colonies; however, absence of confirmation precludes mention of his name. (Collection of the Monmouth County Historical Association.)

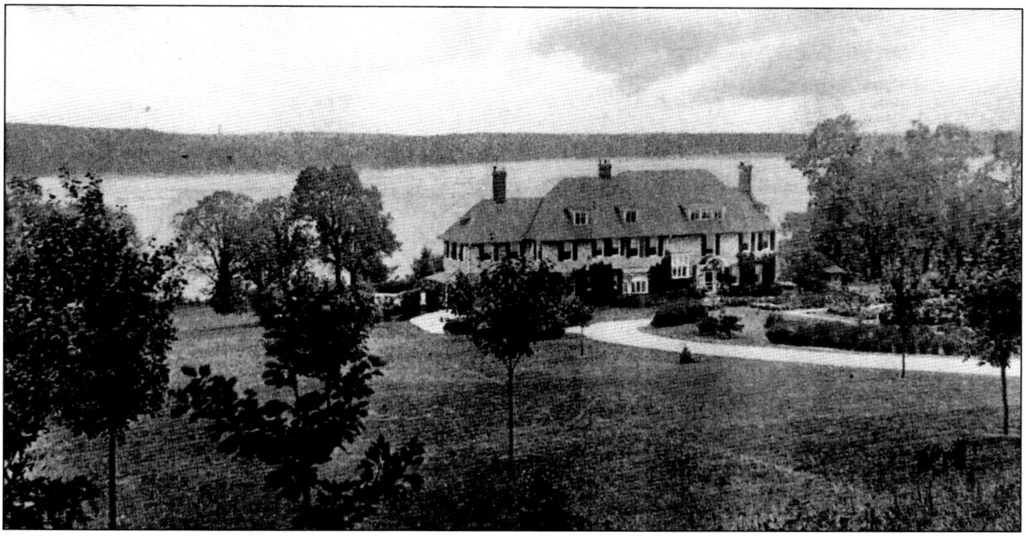

James May Duane hired Nehemiah Brower to build his Colonial Revival house at 810 Navesink River Road on the former Norman A. Brown farm, but the architect of the structure is unknown. The house's south elevation was seen in Volume I on p. 46 in an aerial view. The north, seen here in a c. 1910 postcard, has been rendered unrecognizable by the 1980s erection of an inappropriate round tower. The estate, named Kilronan, was sold by the Duane family in 1947. (Collection of John Rhody.)

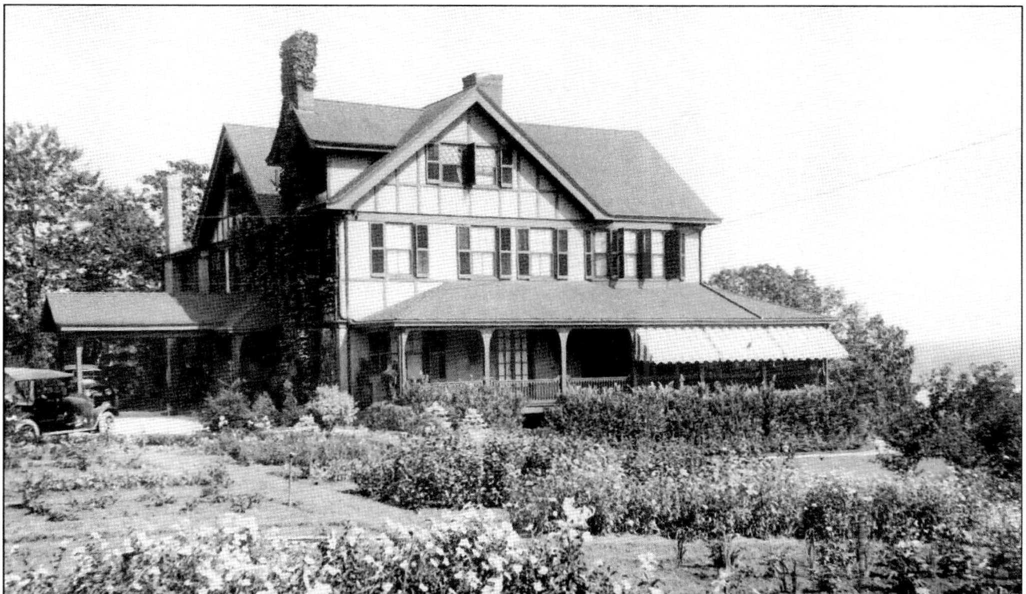

This c. 1920s image of Four Views, the Vincent Lamarche house at 884 Navesink River Road, is older than the recent image in Volume I on p. 44, but it still shows the stucco cladding the author attributes to a remodeling by 1918 buyer Maurice Kozminski. The house was built in 1898 by an unknown architect and is located on the easternmost lot of the tract divided for the seven children of Belgian importer Hyacinthe Lamarche.

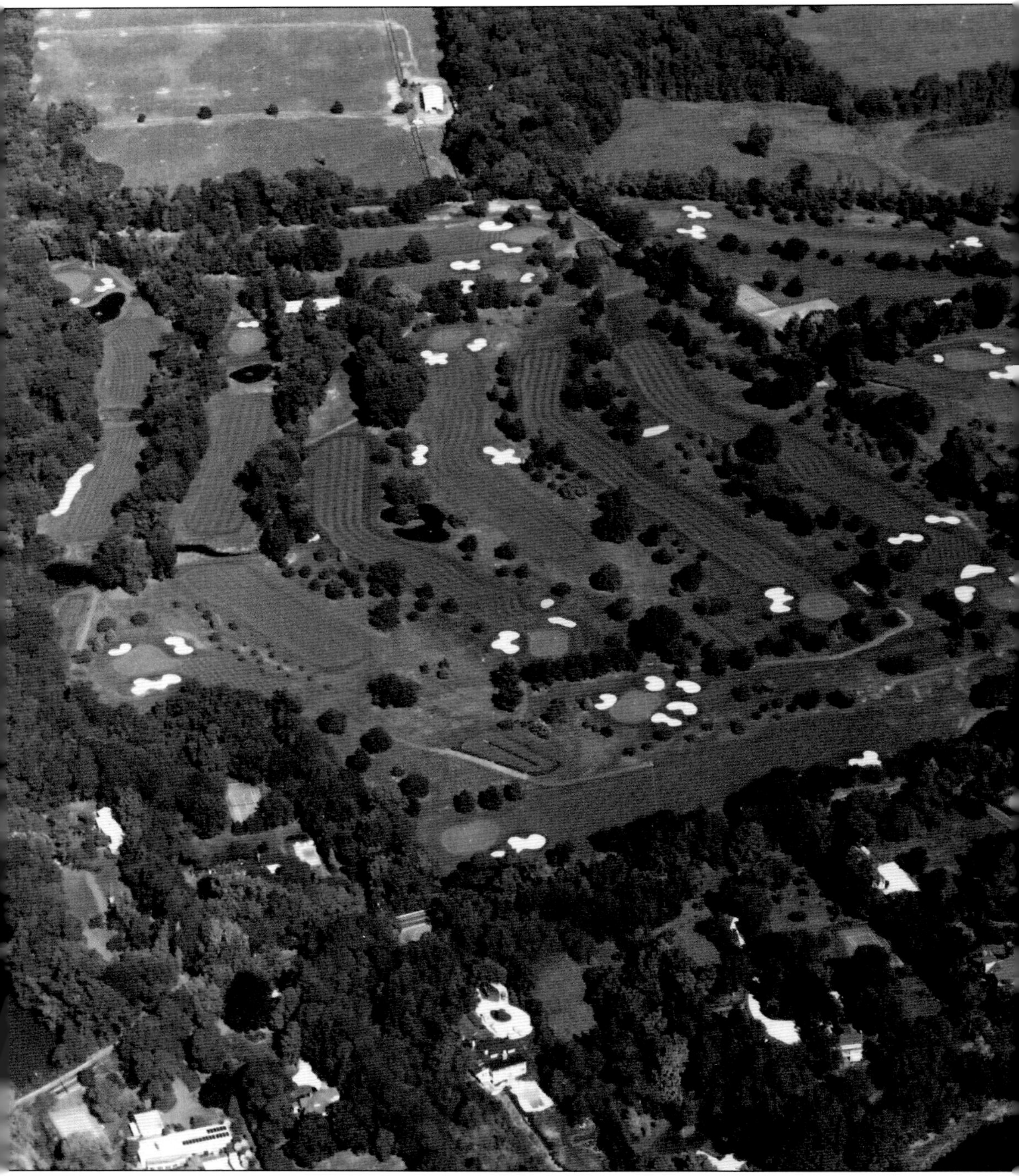

Photographer Chuck Patulak and pilot Walter Kaslow of P. & K. Aerial Photography in Perth Amboy have photographed many of Middletown's riverfront houses and others in nearby estate areas. This recent view captures the Navesink Country Club. The clubhouse, right of the page fold, above center, was seen in Volume I on p. 49 as the Samuel Riker house. This image runs on the shore from the pond at 444 Navesink River Road, at left, to the Frank Hurd house at 578

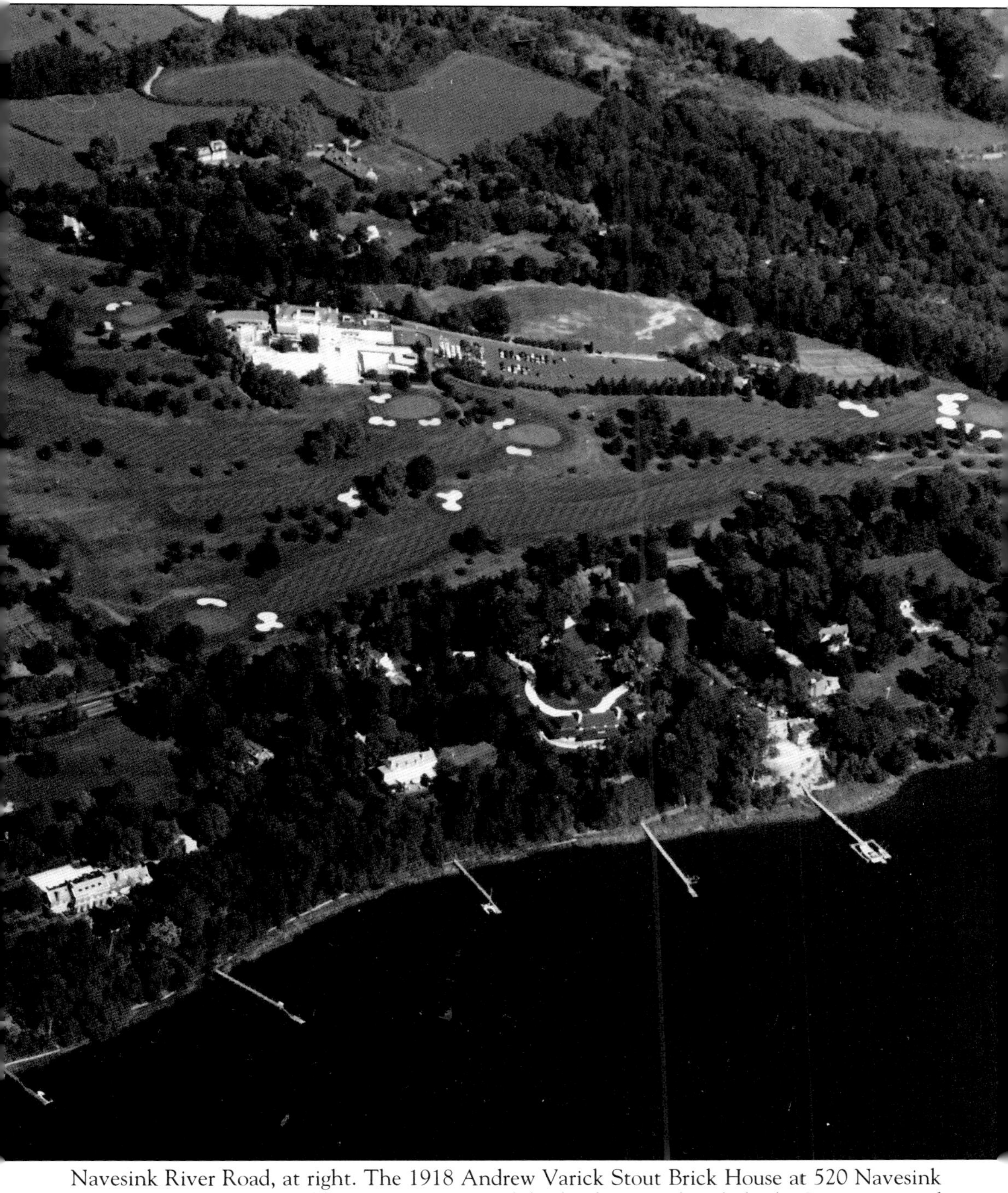

Navesink River Road, at right. The 1918 Andrew Varick Stout Brick House at 520 Navesink River Road is near the fold. Historic owners of the land pictured include the Pattersons and McClanes. Lufburrow Lane, the street bisecting the golf course, was named for the ancient farm-owning family. Cooper Road is at top, with the Haskell estate north of it.

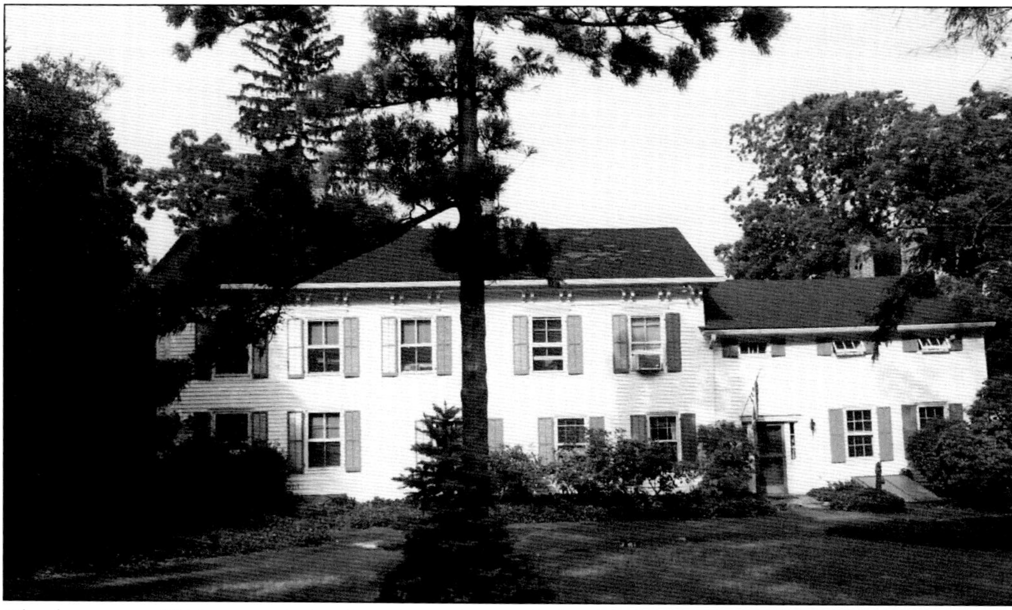

The house at 501 Locust Point Road on the south bank of Clay Pit Creek, west of the bridge, was associated with the Mount family for much of the nineteenth and part of the twentieth centuries. The low section at right is a twentieth-century kitchen addition; to its west is the oldest section of the house. A second half of the nineteenth-century expansion is at left.

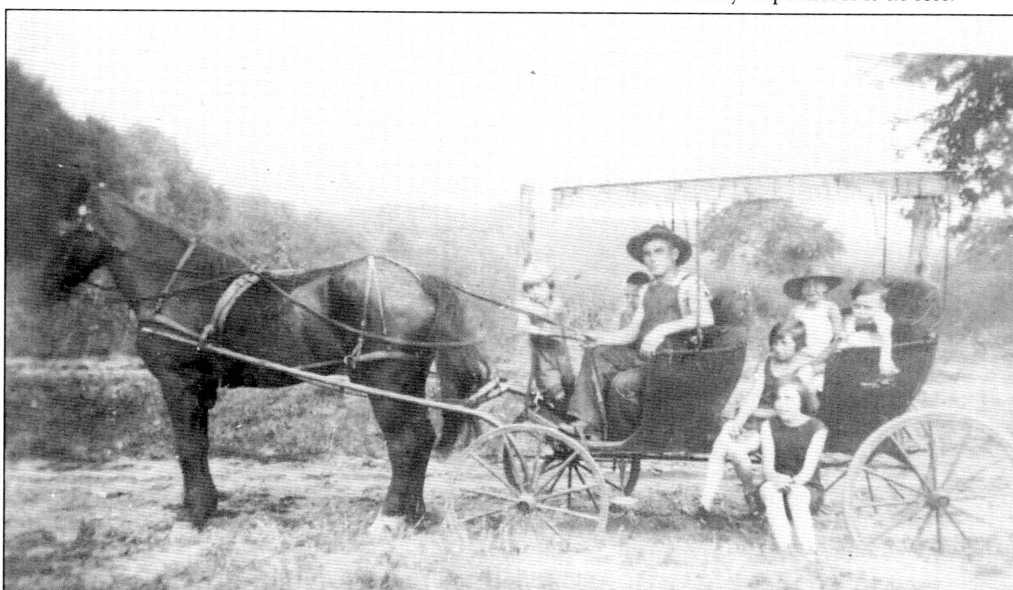

Ferdinand Heidel, his horse, carriage, and family are seen on Locust Point Road in 1925. Sons Bill and Dick are to his right. His daughter Catherine is seated on the side, and her Holland cousins (children of her mother's sister): Ida (seated), Jack (with hat), and Robert. Catherine, now Kay Groves and also the lender of the picture, recalls driving her father, an iron molder in Newark, to the Atlantic Highlands railroad station with this horse while she was still a youth.

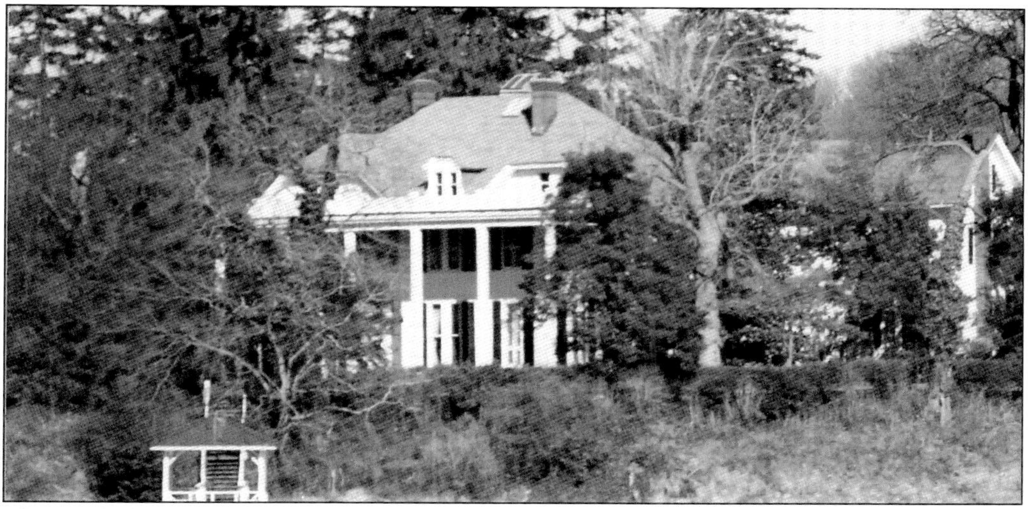

The south facade of the house on the north shore of Clay Pit Creek just east of the bridge, seen in a 1990 view, is dominated by a two-story portico, a likely Colonial Revival addition. It was long the summer home of an eccentric, Albert H. Randell. He had a number of local disputes over property borders. He refused to accept mail with his name misspelled Randall (a variant accepted by other family members), a position in contrast with that of the author, who accepts any misspelling of either name that his bank accepts. A.H. Randell also refused to accept postcards, messages lacking the dignity of an envelope enclosure. See his *Register* obituary on November 7, 1900.

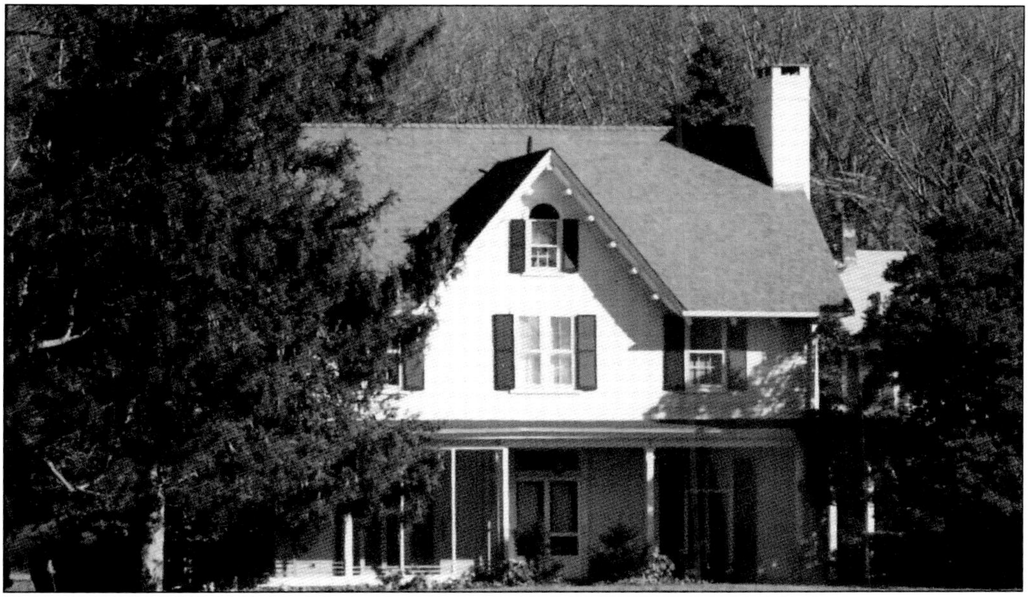

The second house east of the Clay Pit Creek bridge and Locust Avenue belonged to the Washington family, whose most well-known member was rock scientist Henry Washington (1867–1934), who remodeled a smokehouse into a laboratory. His mother was a Stephens, a member of the Newark family that settled the area *c.* 1820. Also see Volume I on p. 106. This house appears to have been built in the mid-nineteenth century, but lack of access to the north shore hinders historical analysis of both properties on this page.

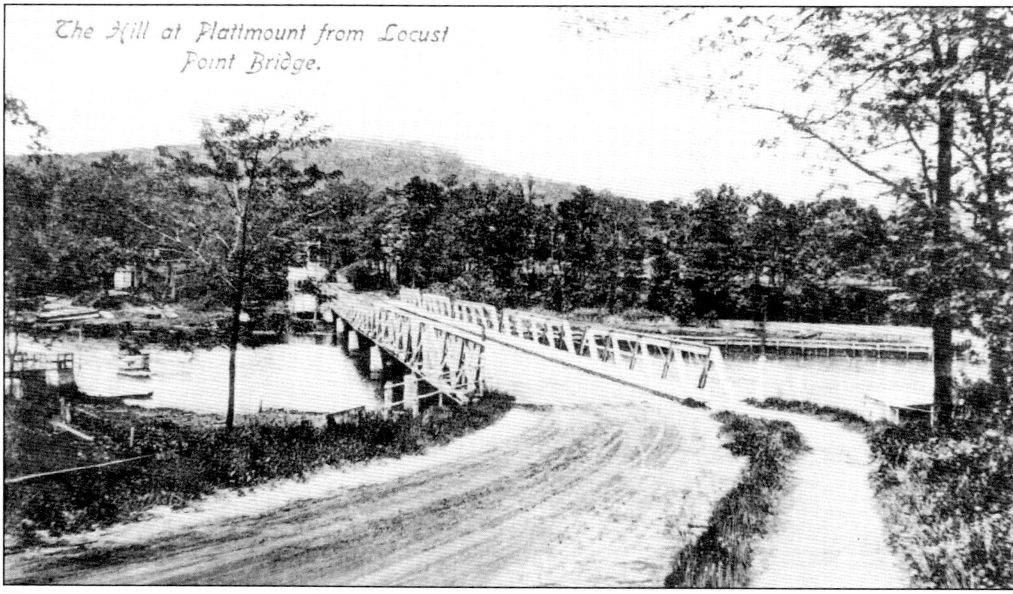

Plattmount was an 1897 real estate development embracing the ancient Mount farm, with at least part of it descending through the heirs of Lydia Jane Platt, a daughter of Andrew Mount. The tract's southeast corner was the north bank of Clay Pit Creek at Locust Avenue, shown here c. 1910 from a postcard published by Frank A Morehouse illustrating the famous Clay Pit Creek bridge. The tract extended to the hilly land north of Navesink Avenue.

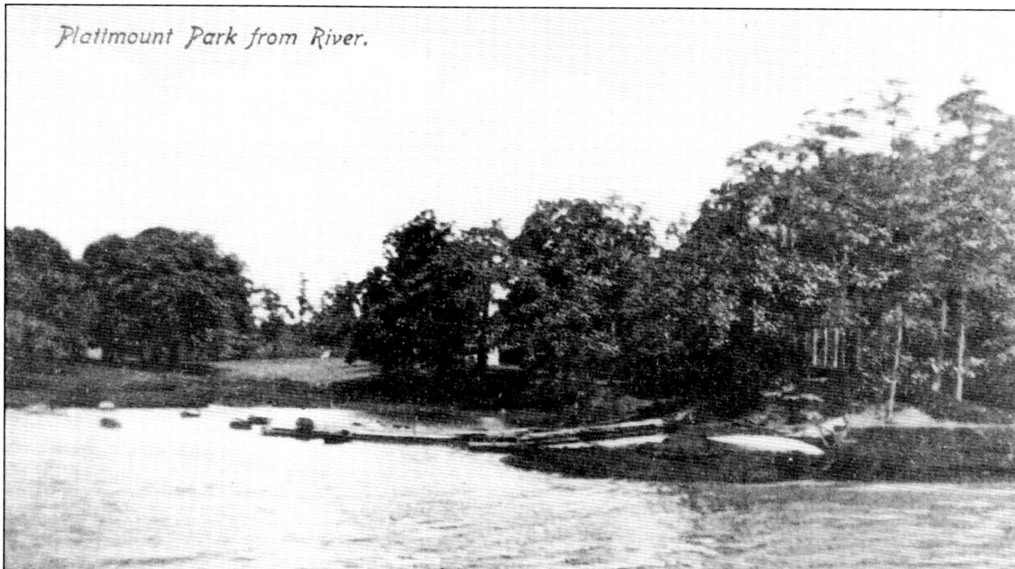

Plattmount Park, set aside for the exclusive use of Plattmount property holders, was located from the bank of the creek to the south side of Linden Avenue. A boarding house was opposite on the north side of Linden. Although the park was not extensively built up, in 1907 a bowling alley was opened and new walks were laid out. The property had come under the control of the First National Bank of Plattsburg; its development was slow. This tract retains its natural character today.

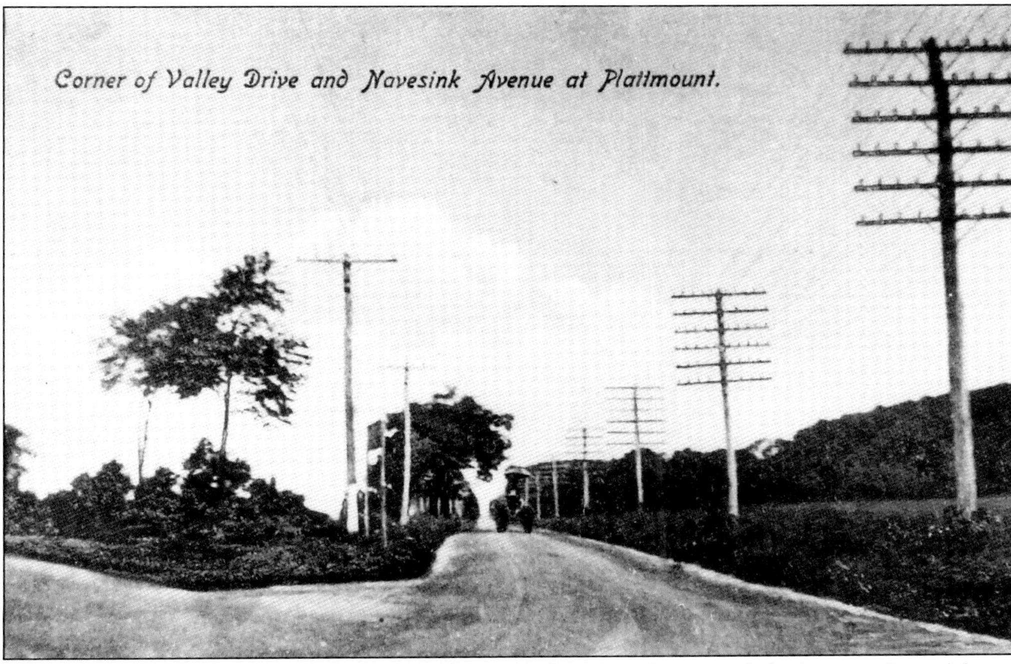

This, the third in a c. 1910 promotional postcard series, shows at left the pie-shaped lot at the captioned juncture, now the site of a Dutch Colonial Revival house at Valley Drive. Plattmount lots were sold at auction by 1909, when the deed restriction on minimum house cost was lowered to $1,000. Lot size was reduced to allow 25-foot frontages by 1910 and gradual development ensued.

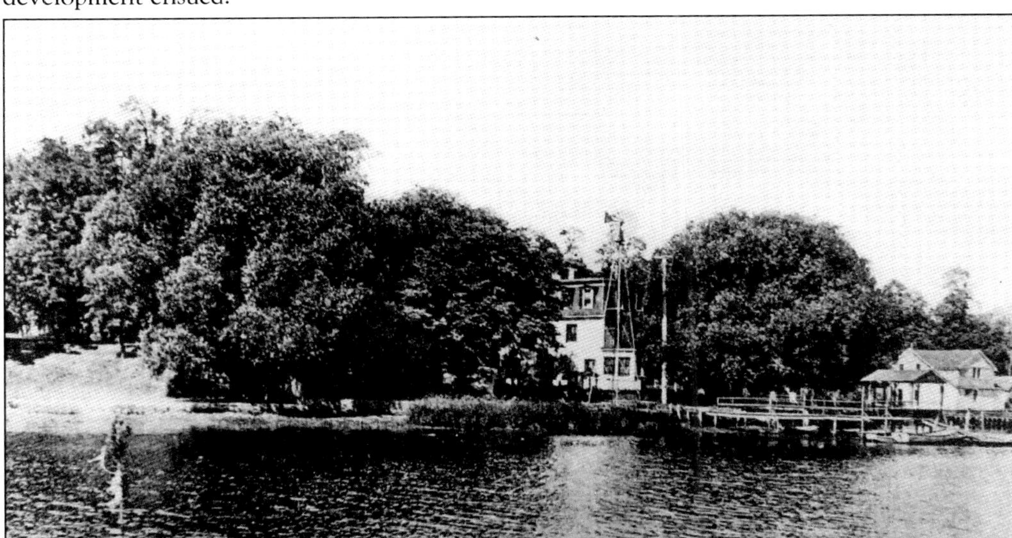

Clay Pit Creek was long a recreational waterway and hosted the mooring of houseboats. This is a c. 1910 postcard view of the south bank, east of the Clay Pit Creek bridge. The front of the New Amsterdam Hotel is seen in Volume I on p. 107. (Collection of John Rhody.)

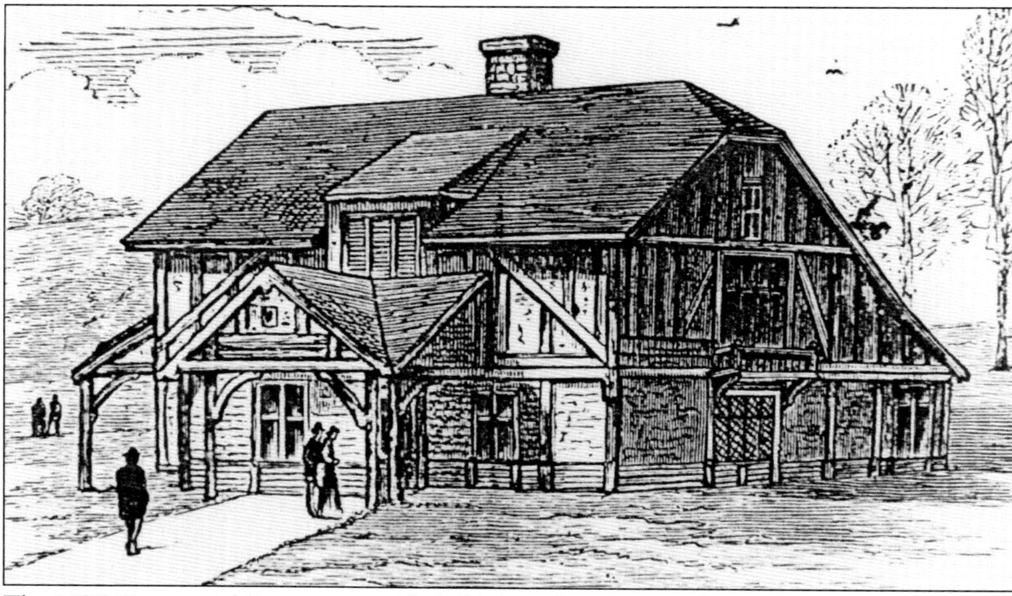

The 1876 Centennial Exposition in Philadelphia, the country's first major world's fair, may be best remembered for revealing the nation's growing industrial might. Many states had exhibition buildings. This is Connecticut's building, from a Frank Leslie publication on the exposition, designed in the Stick Style that had emerged as a major design influence on the Atlantic coast. This building and several others from the exposition were moved to shore communities, with most being remodeled as homes.

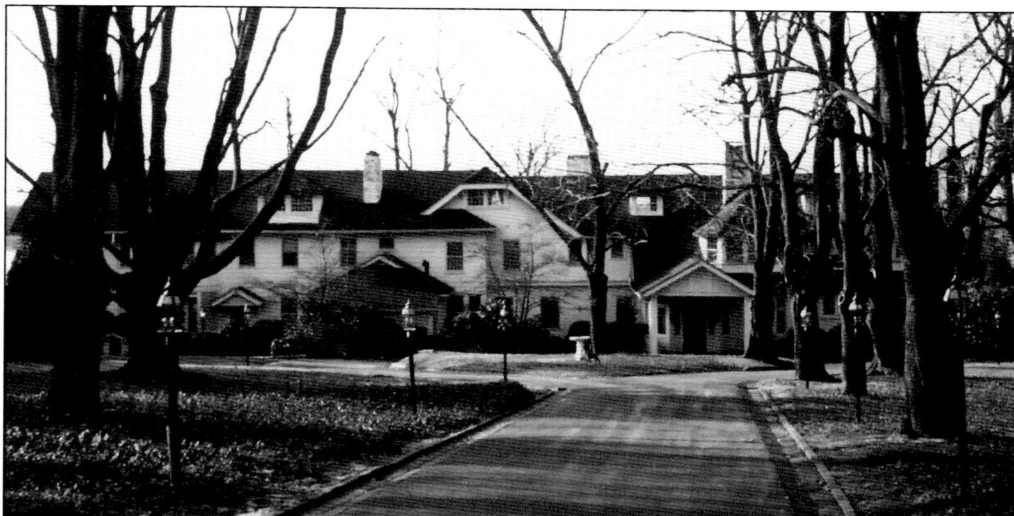

A Miss McCreedy had the Connecticut building moved in sections to Sea Bright. John A. Rutherford bought it in 1915 and had it moved on scows to his Navesink River Road property, number 700 today, on the east bank of McClees Creek. The house was expanded on several occasions; the center section of this 1990 image reveals the older building. Note the jerkinhead peak of the center gable, the slope of its roof, and the belt course over the first floor. The house was later owned by George Bodman. Does any reader have a picture of the house being moved? One was reportedly taken by a local postcard publisher.

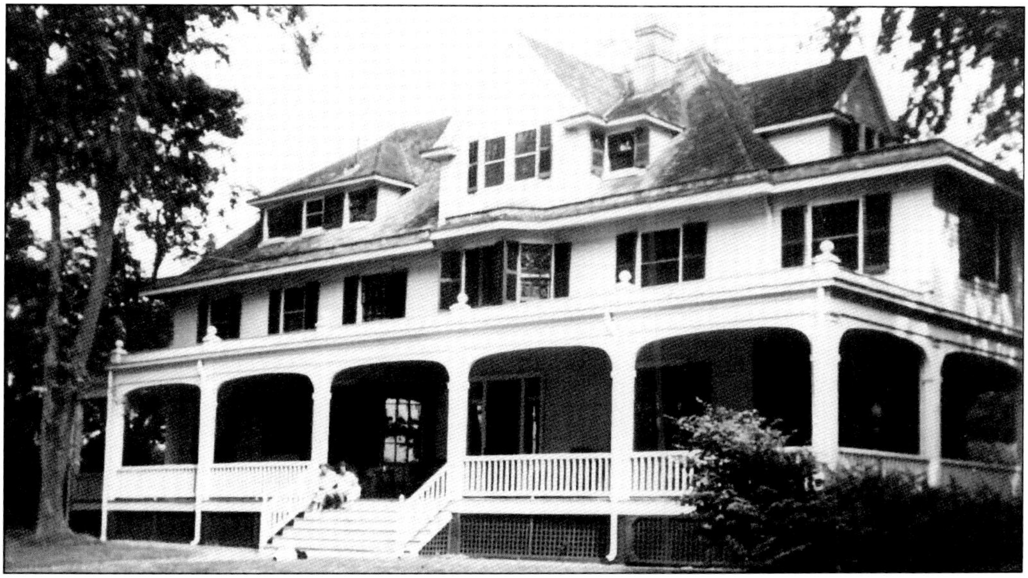

Louis H. Amey built the large Colonial Revival house at 928 Navesink River Road in 1901, having sold an older house on the site that was moved nearby. His builder was his neighbor, Nehemiah Brower. The property, situated high over the river, includes a number of outbuildings. This view of the south facade from *c.* 1950 is faithfully preserved, as recent changes are subtle. These alterations include the erection of an observation tower with stairs from the ground at left, replacement of the porch stairs with stone, the addition of second- and third-story balustrades, and a new color of pale olive.

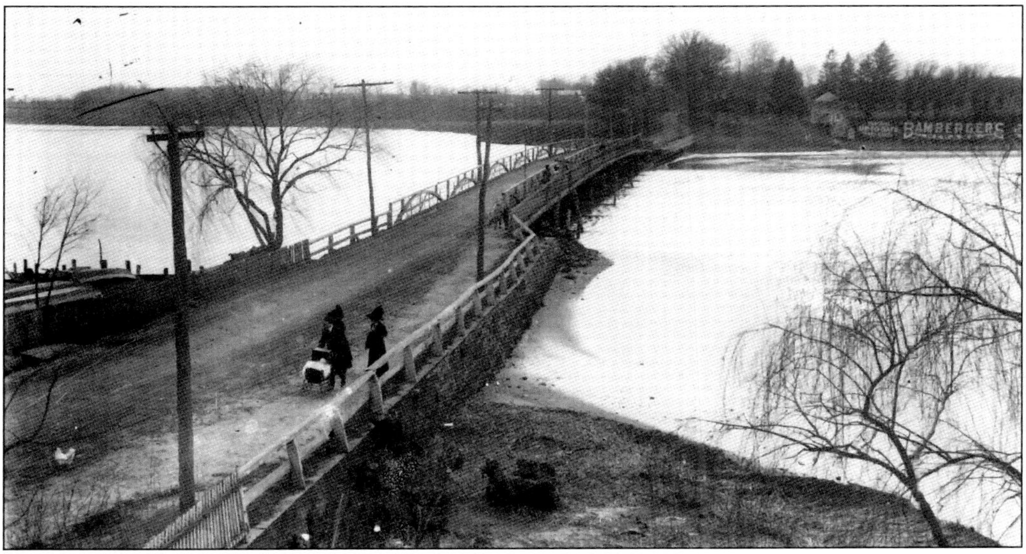

Hubbards Bridge, the West Front Street crossing of the Navesink River between Red Bank and Middletown, a rush-hour bottleneck today, was a quiet pedestrian path *c.* 1900. A truck broke through the roadway in 1915, precipitating the *c.* 1921 replacement of a span that had seemed inadequate for some time. Why is the chicken at left crossing the road? Remember, this image was taken long before the free-range bird began searching for the meaning of life. (The Dorn's Collection.)

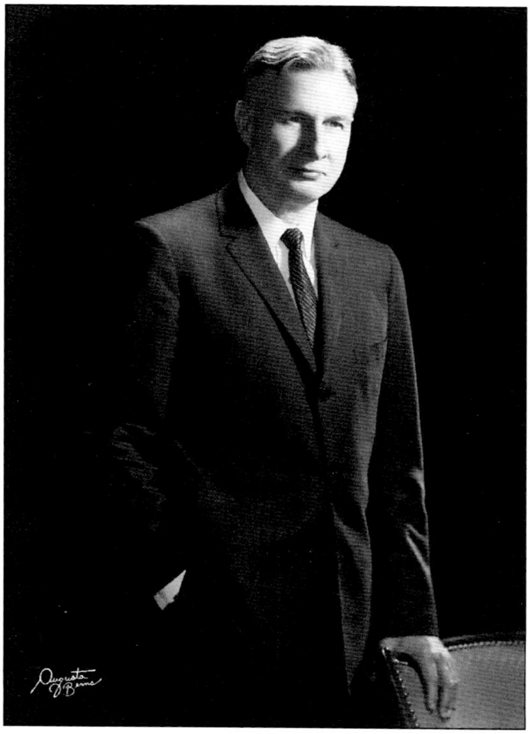

The Honorable Lawrence A. Carton Jr., valedictorian at Leonardo High School, magna cum laude graduate of Notre Dame, and scholarship winner at Harvard Law School, has a distinguished record as a lawyer, on the bench, and in the Army Quartermaster Corps during World War II. He served as Middletown's school board attorney for thirty-five years (for many years earning a mere $300), attaining local prominence during the Redcay case in the late 1930s. When asked which accomplishment he took most pride in, Judge Carton cited being mayor of Middletown. He was the township's first (earlier executives chaired the township committee) and noted that the office was a wonderful challenge and opportunity for a caring person to help people in an era of a genuinely appreciative public. Judge Carton preserved Portland, the Hartshorne waterfront estate (see Vol. I, pp. 118–121), while developing Hartshorne Woods.

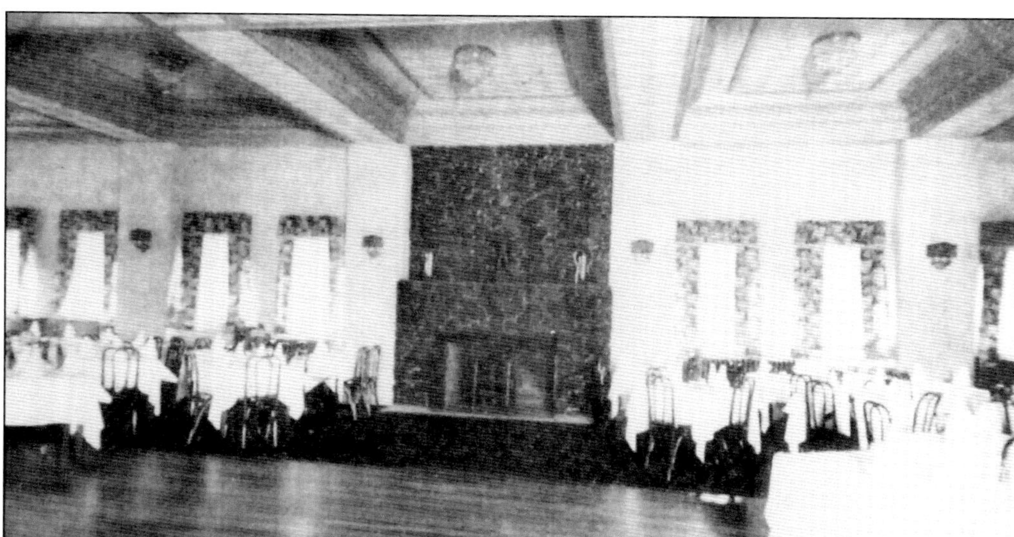

The Shrewsbury River Country Club was a short-lived 1920s golf and social club south of Highway 35 and west of the Navesink River. The land became more valuable for real estate, with the Shrewsbury River Holding Company developing it in the late 1920s. It organized a club for land-owning members; part of the clubhouse still stands on Lake Shore Drive, remodeled as a residence. This view of the dining hall is from a c. 1920s postcard. (Collection of Michael Steinhorn.)

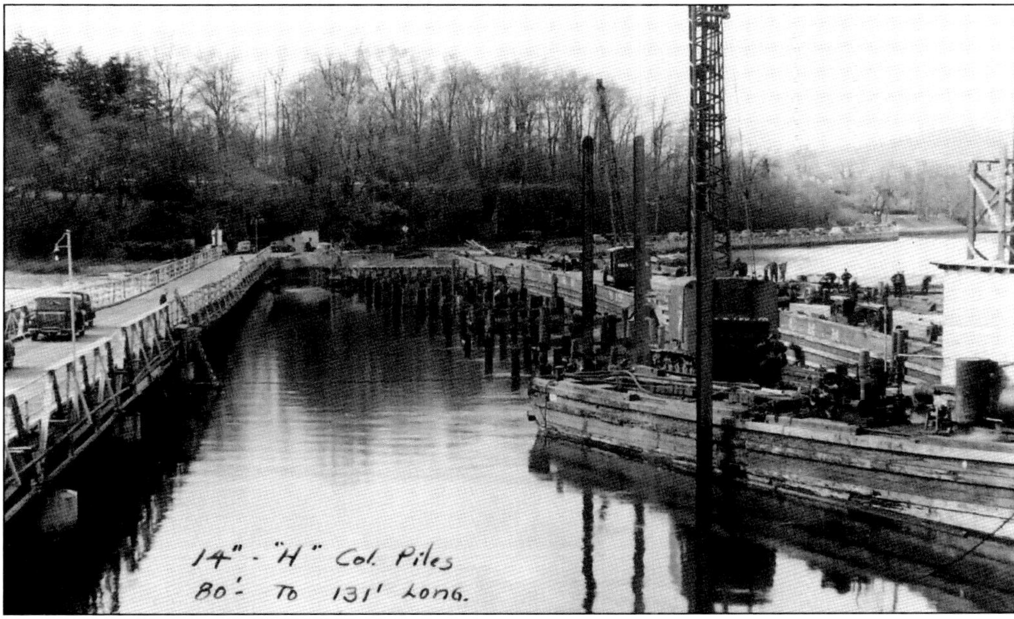

The old Oceanic Bridge was in poor condition in the 1930s, with a ten mile-per-hour speed limit imposed in 1937 to reduce the risk of its collapse. A new bridge was built in 1939–40, opening on March 16th. The Rumson entrance was relocated east one block to Bingham Avenue. Fred T. Ley & Company of New York was awarded the contract with a low bid of $997,298 as part of a projected cost of around $1,150,000, for which the Public Works Administration granted $513, 000. (Collection of John Rhody.)

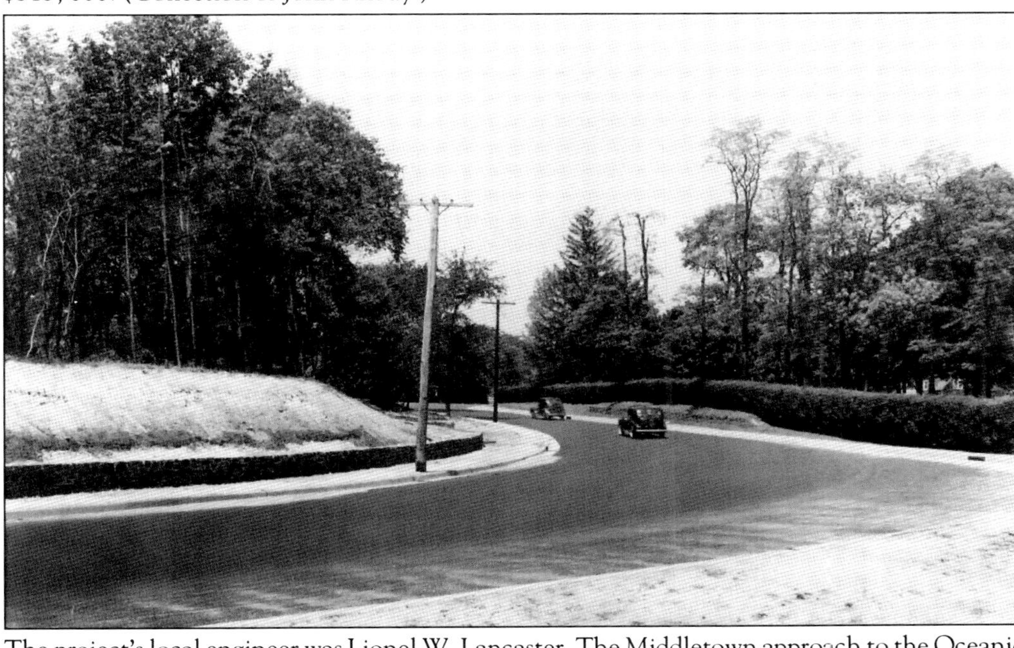

The project's local engineer was Lionel W. Lancaster. The Middletown approach to the Oceanic Bridge is little changed since the 1940 opening of the present span. The road is wider, and the curb on the west side was rebuilt and enhanced in 1996. (Collection of John Rhody.)

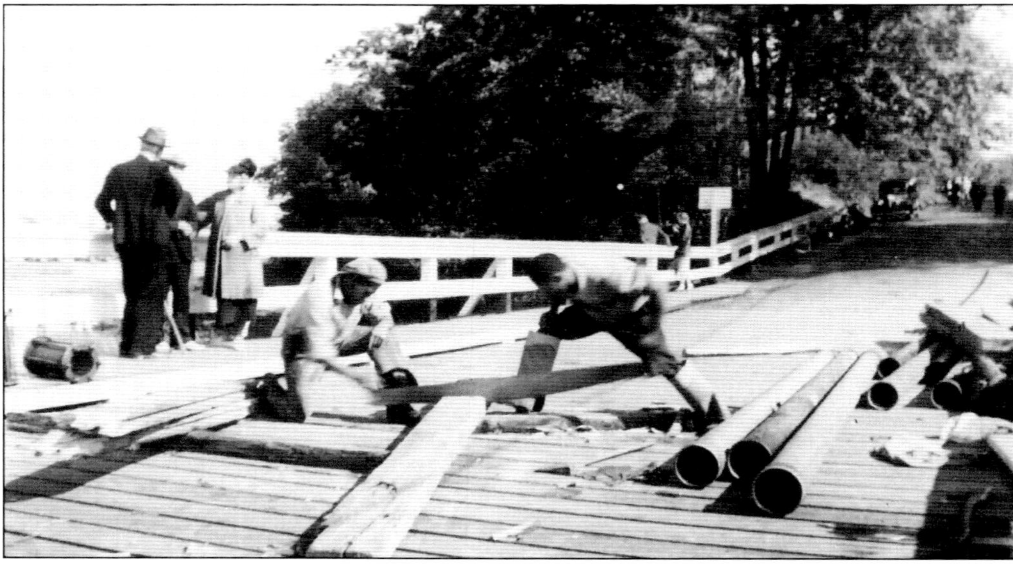

Repairs are being made to the Quigleys Creek bridge (Vol. I, p. 111) after the washout of the 1938 storm. The view is south, looking towards Front Street.

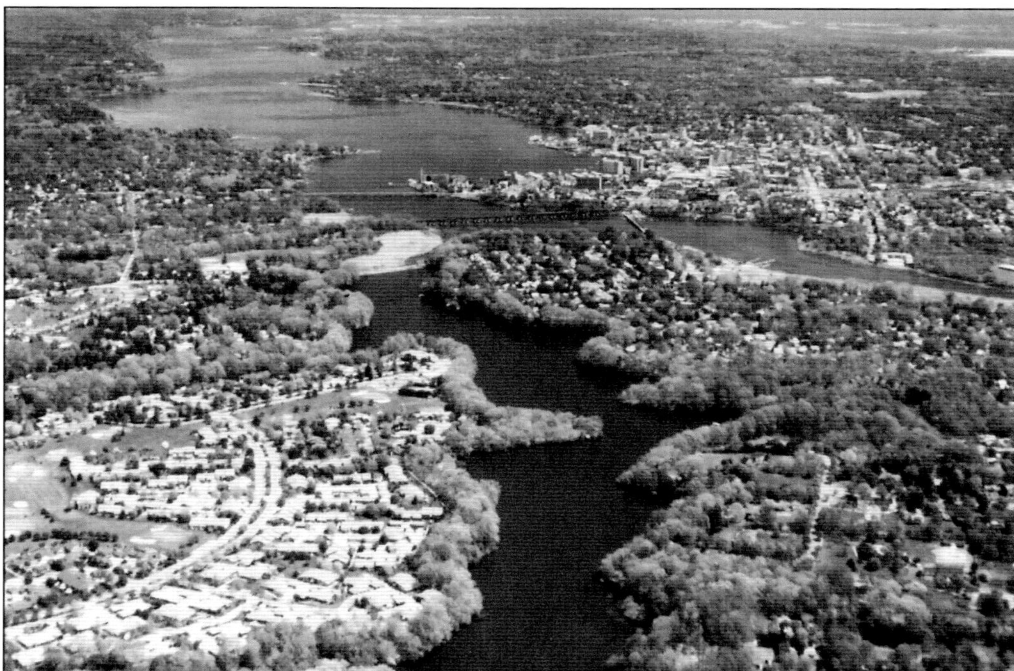

Photography Unlimited by Dorn's has had an aerial operation from its 1937 beginnings, with founder Daniel W. Dorn Sr. taking time out to serve for the Navy in World War II. Current operations include a variety of commercial and individual assignments, including taking shots of wedding groups! Shadow Lake Village is on the left, with that man-made lake formed from a creek running down the center; Swimming River is at left. Both are tributaries of the Navesink River. (The Dorn's Collection.)